Transitional Ministry Today

Transitional Ministry Today

Successful Strategies for Churches and Pastors

Edited by Norman B. Bendroth

An Alban Institute Book

ROWMAN & LITTLEFIELD
Lanham • Boulder • New York • London

Published by Rowman & Littlefield
A wholly owned subsidary of The Rowman & Littlefield Publishing Group, Inc.
4501 Forbes Boulevard, Suite 200, Lanham, Maryland 20706
www.rowman.com

Unit A, Whitacre Mews, 26-34 Stannery Street, London SE11 4AB

British Library Cataloguing in Publication Information Available

Library of Congress Cataloging-in-Publication Data
Transitional ministry today : successful strategies for churches and pastors / edited by Norman B.
Bendroth.
pages cm
"An Alban Institute book."
Includes bibliographical references and index.
ISBN 978-1-56699-766-9 (cloth : alk. paper) -- ISBN 978-1-56699-750-8 (pbk. : alk. paper) -- ISBN
978-1-56699-751-5 (electronic)
1. Interim clergy. 2. Change--Religious aspects--Christianity. I. Bendroth, Norman B., editor.
BV676.3.I58 2014
253--dc23
2014033957

∞™ The paper used in this publication meets the minimum requirements of American
National Standard for Information Sciences Permanence of Paper for Printed Library
Materials, ANSI/NISO Z39.48-1992.

Printed in the United States of America

For David,
Dear brother, wonderful friend, lover of the Church,

and

Peggy,
My polestar, delight, and fellow traveler

Contents

Acknowledgments

There is an old New England saying that if you ever see a turtle on a stump, he didn't get there by himself. Like most major ventures, we never do them completely on our own. I would first of all like to thank the Louisville Institute for providing me with a Pastoral Study Project Program grant to undertake this project. The funds allowed me to spend a more leisurely summer doing research, writing, and continuing education. A grant from the Carpenter Foundation was also a boon to this project. Its funding provided opportunities to gather authors and transitional ministry practitioners together for conversations in Indianapolis, Cleveland, and Boston.

I am particularly grateful to John Mokossion, executive director, and Dayl Hufford, clinical director, of the New England Pastoral Institute, where I am the coordinator of Church and Clergy Resources. Their faith in me and the project is deeply appreciated, and our hope is that this book may open up more ministry opportunities for this wonderful and creative agency.

Early conversation partners when this venture began included Nancy Ammerman, professor of sociology of religion at Boston University; Terry Foland, founding member of the Interim Ministry Network and active in the Association of Disciples Intentional Interim Ministers (ADIIM); Jim Lewis, former director of the Louisville Institute; Ken McFayden, professor of ministry and leadership development at Union Presbyterian Seminary in Richmond, Virginia; Bill McKinney, sociologist of religion and former president of the Pacific School of Religion; Susan Nienaber, former consultant with the Alban Institute, now with the Congregational Consulting Group; Karen Olson, missioner for ministry for the Episcopal Church of Minnestoa; Larry Ousley, director of the United Methodist Center for Intentional Growth; and Harris Schultz and Paul Svingen, active with the National Association of Lutheran Interim Pastors (NALIP).

I'd also like to thank my colleagues from the Interim Ministry Network, particularly Margaret Bain, Lynn Carman Bodden, Leigh Earley, Cynthia Hueey, John Keydel, Bob Livingston, Ineke Mitchell, Bill Peterson, Michael Remson, and Molly Dale Smith for their thoughts and contributions. The cohort of interim ministers from a variety of denominations and judicatory officials in the United Church of Christ within New England who gathered for conversation on a number of occasions were great sources of wisdom, kvetching, and shared practices. I especially want to thank Leslie Ann Chatfield, Susie Craig, Barbara Libby, Don Remick, Charlotte Wright, and Laura Westby.

For the past five years a gang we call the "Theologues" has gathered on most Friday nights for good food, drink, and conversation. At first we would pick a current event or theological topic to discuss. Now it's just a good excuse to eat and drink too much and unwind at the end of the week (and to theologize). Many thanks to Kate, Don, Mary, Anne, Nancy, Tony, Karen, and Peggy for their ongoing encouragement and huzzahs.

I would be remiss if I didn't give a big shout out to my editor, Beth Gaede. She saved me from many a faux pas by asking, "What's the antecedent?" "Huh?" "Is this what you really mean?" and much more. Thanks to her careful eye and comments on every chapter, this is a much better volume than it might have been.

My chief cheerleader, critic, and editor has been my wife of thirty-six years, Margaret Lamberts Bendroth. As a professional historian and director of the American Congregational Association she has been a wonderful conversation partner about the state of the Church past, present, and forecasting into the future. She, along with my two adult children, Nathan and Anna, and our menagerie of pets, is an inestimable source of joy and zaniness.

I

Transitional Ministry Today

Successful Strategies for Churches and Pastors

Chapter One

Whither Transitional Ministry?

Norman B. Bendroth

"The irony is that some specialists in transitional ministry are having a hard time making a transition," says Ken McFayden, professor of ministry and leadership development at Union Presbyterian Seminary in Richmond, Virginia. He is not alone in saying that it is time to rethink how denominations, churches, and intentional interim ministers do transitional ministry within twenty-first-century realities.

This project began during the summer of 2011 when I was between interim ministry positions. I had written a piece for *The Christian Century* on interim ministry, and they turned it down because it didn't tell of anything new going on within the practice. Also at that time, a number of articles came out that were critical of interim ministry. Several were by colleagues I respected.[1] While some of criticisms were based on misinformation and bad experiences with some interim ministers, there was enough restlessness about the current model to demand attention.

I began my research by calling judicatory officials across denominations who oversaw transitional ministry, interim ministry specialists, leaders of denominational interim ministry organizations (and there are a lot of them), and observers of American church life. They in turn referred me to churches, judicatories, practitioners, and pastors who were doing creative work or experimenting with different models. This led to an article, "Rethinking Transitional Ministry," published in *Congregations* (an Alban Institute magazine), and a workshop at the Interim Ministry Network annual conference, which eventually blossomed into this book.

EARLY BEGINNINGS

The intellectual roots of interim ministry were planted in the late 1960s and early 1970s with research conducted by Loren Mead, Celia Hahn, and Bill Yon, all affiliates of the Alban Institute. Their study, "Project Test Pattern," which took place from 1969 to 1974, resulted in a paper presented by Loren Mead at the Association of Religion and Applied Behavioral Sciences titled "The Interim Pastor: A Neglected Role in Parish Development."[2] In his research among churches in transition, Mead found that the "in between time" was one of the most fertile times for congregational development. The prior model, if there was one, was to hire a seasoned retired pastor during the search process to "hold hands" and "water the plants." Instead of doing that, Mead argued, pastors should take advantage of the opportunities present.

The next two years brought a number of publications following up Mead's insights, including Celia Hahn's "The Minister Is Leaving." Alban began to assemble a team to study the question further. The result was a model of change revolving around a series of "developmental tasks" of interim ministry: "coming to terms with history," "discovering a new identity," negotiating "shifts of power and leadership changes," "rethinking denominational linkages," and "commitment to new leadership and a new future."[3]

With this foundational work established, a fledgling organization called the Interim Ministry Network (IMN) was spun off from Alban in 1981, dedicated to training and credentialing those who would be intentional interim ministers. What began as a group of denominational executives and ministers has today grown to be a professional organization with a membership of over 1,300 Christian and Jewish clergy from twenty-five to thirty denominations across the nation. Today, IMN provides training, referrals, standards, a Professional Transition Specialist designation, publications, and consulting.

Founders of the movement drew upon the work of psychologist Erik Erikson in formulating the person's psychosocial developmental tasks. Erikson postulated eight psychosocial development stages through which human beings should travel throughout their life spans to become healthy, well-adjusted persons. These were sequential steps moving from infancy to late adulthood. In each stage the ego develops as it successfully resolves crises or challenges that are introduced by outside social forces. Each stage builds on the successful completion of earlier stages. If a challenge is not successfully completed, character deficits may appear in the future.[4]

Robert J. Havighurst, a pioneer in the field of experimental education in the 1940s and 1950s, applied Erikson's insights to educational theory. The crown jewel of his research was on the "developmental task." The core of his thesis was that the process of living, from birth to death, consists of people working their way through from one stage of development to another, by solving their problems in each stage. . . . If the individual completes the task successfully, it leads him to happiness and success with future tasks. [5]

Havighurst's insights informed the development of interim ministry training and of the work needed in a congregation.

This language of "developmental tasks" applied to a congregation worked well when Christendom was alive and well in North America. Although Erikson's and Havighurst's theories applied to individuals, the initiators of interim ministry applied it to *churches*, which was appropriate at the time. Developmental task theory described an unfolding, sequential, continuous progress toward a specified objective. Change in local congregations echoed that as well. Change or development was continuous in that it advanced out of what had proceeded from the past and therefore could be anticipated and managed in the future.

The question raised by practitioners in transitional ministry today is whether the developmental tasks model is still viable. While the theory is helpful in understanding human development, today it is less useful in understanding congregational life. First, some argue, we live in an age of irregular, disjointed, sporadic change. Discontinuous change is unsettling and unanticipated; it creates situations that challenge our assumptions. The skills we have used in the past are not always helpful for this kind of change. Second, the tasks of transitional ministry are not sequential. They are interactive and dynamic. While the developmental tasks may need attention during the course of the interim time, the need to understand the context of each congregation and the systems that impact it, both within and without, is paramount. Third, there is a sense in which the tasks are never "completed successfully," or "finished," but are areas of congregational life that should be continually evaluated, revised, and adapted in light of current realities. [6] New understandings of the role and usefulness of developmental tasks will be explored in this book.

A LOOK BACK

Interim ministry has matured greatly in the past thirty-plus years, adapting to the insights of social sciences, theological reflection, and curriculum review. Looking back Loren Mead reflected upon the legacy of this ministry in an interview with Tony Robinson in a *Congregations* article. He observed that there is "a whole constituency among the clergy who found this style of ministry really fit them and was more challenging to them than 'ordinary' pastorates." The best of transitional ministers have gifts for analyzing congregations and their communities. They like having one foot in the congregation as pastor and teacher and one outside as observer and consultant. They like to think systemically and pose the right questions.

Mead still finds interim ministry to be a powerful tool in congregations ready to do the work, but he notes that too many judicatories can be ham-handed in its use thinking it can fit indiscriminately in most settings. Not every congregation needs an interim minister, nor does one size fit all situations.

Moreover, Mead observes, judicatory officials assign to interim positions clergy who have a history of incompetence or other difficulties, the attitude too often being, "People who screw up in one place can at least hold down an interim spot." He calls this view "stupid." An ethical issue he acknowledges is that some clergy use an interim position to "hi-jack a long-term job," or to drag out the length of a position, which discredits the whole profession. In spite of these shortcomings, Mead still sees "the interim pastorate as a really important, valuable resource to the churches."[7]

OUR CURRENT CONTEXT

While interim ministry has served the church well since its inception, much has changed in the culture, the church, and its mission since Mead and his colleagues conceived of the ministry and IMN was launched. Since then the decline of mainline churches has proceeded at an alarming rate. Sharp divisions in our politics and public discourse have heightened incivility in our public life and this has spilled into churches. The rise of world religions in the United States is a new and growing phenomenon. Denominational loyalty is not much of a factor for people choosing a church. A new category of religious practice, "None," is in ascendancy, and increasingly people say they are "spiritual but not religious." Events, programs, banners, mailings, posters—tools used in the old "attractional" model of church growth—no longer bring in new members as they once did. Long past are the days when all churches had to do was open their doors and people would wander in. Christendom has passed.[8]

These changes impact not only transitional ministry, but all ministry, making all clergy, in a sense, transitional ministers. In short, the whole context of doing ministry of any kind has undergone a sea change. Many of our churches are already becoming condominiums, art galleries, or brewpubs, because they have been unwilling or unable to adapt to these changes. Unless congregations and pastors understand and take these phenomena seriously, the trend will continue.

While many clergy are aware of these trends, people of the pew are not. They are reeling from the changes they have seen in their congregation since its halcyon days and wonder what has happened. What follows is a primer that tracks factors that have contributed to decline and how social theorists and observers of American church life interpret it. Knowing the causes of our situation will offer insight and understanding into the challenges and opportunities before us that will help us rethink what transitional ministry might look like in the years ahead.

A number of years ago General Motors tried to market Oldsmobile to a younger generation to boost its sagging sales and to overcome the perception that an Olds was an old man's car. After showing off the sporty new model, the background voice pronounced, "It's not your father's Oldsmobile." Unfortunately, the strategy didn't work, and the once stolid Oldsmobile was dropped from GM's line. The same is true of the mainline church today. Stalwart members can't understand why people don't want to come to their church anymore. They need to realize, "It's not your parents' church anymore."

I, for instance, was born in 1953, and my parents bought their first home in 1955. It was a little Cape Cod–style house on a cul-de-sac in a brand-new, postwar, baby boom neighborhood. New families and kids were in abundant supply. I walked to the nearby elementary school, and we all worshipped at the local United Methodist Church. It was a shiny new facility served by a handsome young minister with a wife and 2.5 kids. The place was packed with two Sunday morning services, Sunday school classes for all, and a huge youth group. Today the congregation is barely hanging on by its fingernails.

American Civil Religion

What happened? The postwar boom of mainline churches was actually an anomaly. The end of the war, a flourishing economy and rising middle class, the threat of godless communism, and a set of shared values that weren't necessarily Christian fueled the ascendency of church. Social theorists call the melding of Christian and American values "American civil religion." The term "civil religion" was coined by sociologist Robert Bellah to describe the set of rituals, doctrines, and beliefs that develop around nations, which become the sacred myth that binds citizens in common allegiance.[9] Daniel Marsh of Boston University has pointed out the similarities between biblical history and American history.[10] America's book of Genesis is the Mayflower Compact. Its exodus is the Declaration of Independence. The book of the law is the Constitution and the Bill of Rights. Its psalms include the "Star Spangled Banner" and "God Bless America." Lincoln's Second Inaugural address is its prophetic denouncement.

Rituals include saying the pledge of allegiance in our schools, singing "The Star Spangled Banner" at sporting events, having parades and ceremonies honoring the war dead, and invoking the blessing of some higher power at political events. The virtues of democracy, individual liberty, the right to private property, family, free enterprise, and a commitment to faith are part of its doctrines. Faith in this system of thought is vague and undefined. It is best exemplified in President Eisenhower's statement, "This country was founded on faith and I don't care in what."

Civil religion and Christian religion can look deceptively similar, especially in the era I've described, so much so that it is easy to merge the two into one, like many American churches do on patriotic holidays. Many of us in ministry encountered this pressure to have the church be more patriotic in spades in the years after 9/11. Civil religion is not a state religion, but rather a set of practices and beliefs that makes sacred national values, national heroes, national history, and national ideals. It is not necessarily a bad thing; it is often the glue that holds societies together. However, to equate the kingdom of God with the United States of America is not only a pale comparison, it is bad theology. The commonwealth of God is a global community that transcends all nation-states and embraces all peoples. Rather than endorsing any national agenda, the Gospel calls all such pretensions to power into question. Churches today need to be distinctive from the dominant culture and to offer an alternative to its values.[11]

From Homogeneous to Heterogeneous

Today the United States is a much more ethnically and religiously diverse society than it was in the era of thriving churches. In 1955 Will Herberg could write a sociology of religion describing America called *Protestant – Catholic – Jew.*[12] Forty-six years later Diana Eck of Harvard would write a book titled *A New Religious America: How a "Christian Country" Has Become the World's Most Religiously Diverse Nation.*[13] This demographic shift was due largely to the Immigration and Naturalization Act of 1965, which followed in the wake of the civil rights movement, opening up the United States to a wave of new immigrants who were much more diverse than the European immigrants of past movements. After the Vietnam War many families from Southeast Asia arrived, bringing Hinduism, Buddhism, and animist religions with them.

As the twenty-first century begins, we are just starting to grasp the implications of these realities. My daughter, who is Amerasian, graduated from a large urban high school where thirty-two different language groups were represented. There are more practicing Muslims in the United States today than there are Episcopalians and United Church of Christ members combined. More people of African descent live in America than in any country except Nigeria, and more Cubans live in Miami than in Havana.

In the face of this religious diversity, American civil religion was and is ill equipped to help Christians answer a new set of questions, such as What do we believe? What is distinctive about our faith? What is the meaning behind our rituals and traditions? How are we to participate in the public square? While wanting to be open and accepting of other faiths, what is the content of our own? Addressing these new questions is a task that churches in transition must take up.

Shifting Sources of Authority

Historians observe that the 1960s and 1970s were years of unprecedented tumult that shook us to our roots. The Vietnam War divided the nation as none before had. Partly as a consequence of the war, a new drug culture emerged. Three popular civic leaders—President Kennedy, Martin Luther King, Jr., and Bobby Kennedy—were assassinated. Watergate brought down a president and scandalized the nation. The divorce rate began rising to 50 percent. Contraceptives gave women unprecedented control of their lives, and abortion became more available. The civil rights movement and the women's movement challenged social arrangements that had been in place for generations. All of the institutions that had given us stability were coming unraveled, and a new generation jettisoned once shared moral norms. These shifts spilled into our churches, and there was divisive conflict over the war in Vietnam, the role of women, divorce, and the civil rights movement. There was a head-on battle between the values of civil religion and Christian faith.

Phyllis Tickle, founding editor of the religion department at *Publishers Weekly* and keen observer of Emergence Christianity, argues that whenever there is tumult in history, there is a concomitant questioning of authority. As an example, she notes that Luther's principle of *sola scriptura, scriptura sola* has eroded over time with the discovery that the world is not flat, that the universe is heliocentric, slavery is immoral, women have rights equal to those of men, and homosexuality is not a choice. In every one of these examples, truth that was thought to be unshakeable was shaken. While some reread their Bible through historical and cultural lenses, others reasserted biblical inerrancy as a dike against the rising tide of new awareness. [14]

American civil religion was not prepared to deal with these traumas. Since social institutions and trust had broken down and the traditional reliable authority of the family, church, and state seemed suddenly undependable, people were at sea and the church was not providing answers.

Shifting Beliefs

In addition, what Americans believe today is vastly different than what they believed in the 1950s through the 1970s. Surveys of religious belief in America in the 1960s consistently found that approximately 95 percent of Americans were certain that God existed. In 2008 the Pew Research Center conducted a substantial and comprehensive study called the Religious Landscape Survey (there has not been a subsequent study of this magnitude since then). The survey asked participants, "Do you believe in God or a universal spirit?" (The 1960 survey did not include "universal spirit.") This time around 71 percent said they were "certain" God or a universal spirit existed; 17 percent expressed doubts; 4 percent claimed a lot of doubts; 5 percent were sure no God existed; and 3 percent didn't know. What is noteworthy is a 26 percent drop in the certainty that God exists in twenty-eight years.[15]

One of the more fascinating phenomena of shifting beliefs is the rise of those researchers call "Nones." In 1960 this group barely registered on the polls. By 2008, those self-identified as "nones" or "unaffiliated" rose to 16 percent.[16] These are individuals, largely in their twenties and thirties, who say they have no religious affiliation. Five years later that number increased from just over 15 percent to just under 20 percent of all U.S. adults. Their ranks now include more than 13 million self-described atheists and agnostics (nearly 6 percent of the U.S. public), as well as nearly 33 million people who say they have no particular religious affiliation (14 percent).[17]

There have also been great shifts in whether Americans call themselves "religious" or "spiritual." In 1999, a Gallup Poll asking whether respondents understood themselves as spiritual or religious, 30 percent said spiritual only; 54 percent, religious only; 6 percent, both spiritual and religious; and 9 percent, neither spiritual nor religious. Ten years later, Princeton Survey Research asked the same question and found these results: spiritual only, 30 percent; religious only, 9 percent; both spiritual and religious, 48 percent; and neither spiritual nor religious, 9 percent. Another survey by the Pew Research Center's Forum on Religion & Public Life, conducted jointly with the PBS television program *Religion & Ethics Newsweekly*, found that 68 percent of the forty-six million adults who describe themselves as "unaffiliated" say they believe in God, 58 percent say they often feel a profound connection with nature, 37 percent classify themselves as "spiritual" but not "religious," and 21 percent say they pray every day.[18]

Their numbers include those raised as Catholic, mainline Christians, and evangelicals as well as those not raised in any particular religious tradition. Many "Nones" are repelled by popular depictions of the Christian faith as politically right wing, anti-science, homophobic, judgmental, insensitive, exclusive, and dull.[19] Young adults appear to want a spirituality that grounds them and connects them to the transcendent but find traditional or organized religion unable or unwilling to meet that need.[20]

A New World View

Since the heyday of mainline churches, there has been a global shift in how our culture makes sense of and interprets reality. We have moved from modernity to postmodernity. Modernity is the intellectual and cultural heritage of the Enlightenment project, namely the rejection of traditional and religious sources of authority in favor of reason and knowledge as the road to human emancipation. The benchmarks of modernity, which mainliners embraced, included a trust in reason, progress, technology, individualism, personal autonomy, and tolerance. Postmodernity challenges the notion that there is anything such as universal truth or one story (called a "metanarrative")[21] that can speak for all of humanity. While there may be "ultimate" or "universal truth," it is very hard to grasp. No one has a "God's eye" view of the world.[22] Our geography, social class, gender, sexual orientation, race, nationality, and so on radically shape how we perceive and understand the world. Hence, women's studies, African American studies, and gay studies have become academic disciplines. We have feminist Christians, ecumenical Christians, liberationist Christians, evangelical Christians, progressive Christians, Asian Christians, and African Christians.

Modernity operated under the assumption that the world was essentially linear. It functioned on the belief that human beings have the ability to plan, achieve progress, and solve problems using science and technology. If there was an effect, there must be a cause. If there is a problem, you find the cause and fix it. The world works mechanistically, like a machine with moving parts and predictable behavior. If a part is broken, you replace it. Postmodernity has a loss of faith in science and rationality as the only source of knowledge and truth, a loss of belief in progress, and increased skepticism about any theories that claim to be able to produce a better future. Postmodernity sees the world systemically with an interconnection of many pieces, influences, and forces. This is why the Internet is called the World Wide Web.

Postmodernity is the worldview that "Gen Xers," "Gen Yers," and "Millenialists," those born after 1964, grew up in. They have no binding story, as did previous generations. They lack confidence in the institutions that sustained previous generations and are suspicious of trite answers. The world of laptops, iPhones, Facebook, and reality TV informs their worldview, providing overwhelming choices and an exposure to a mountain of information. This creates a world that is in perpetual motion with no center of gravity. Sociologist Peter Berger calls this "the vertigo of relativity."[23]

Mainline Decline

Not only has the culture changed in the past four decades; so have our churches. Mainline Protestant churches have been hurtling downhill for at least four decades. David T. Olson, director of the American Church Research Project, did a comprehensive study based on a national database of over two-hundred-thousand churches. The evidence shows that the overall United States population is growing exponentially faster than the church and that evangelical, mainline Protestant, and Roman Catholic churches are all in decline. To keep up with population growth, Olsen submits, 2,900 more churches would need to be started every year.[24]

Statistically, every Sunday, somewhere in the United States seventy-one churches will celebrate their last Sunday service. Annually, some 3,700 churches end up closing their doors.[25] Researcher George Barna says that churches lose an estimated 2,765,000 attendees each year,[26] but others say these figures are difficult to claim with certainty.[27] The latest figures from the Association of Religion Data Archives (ARDA)[28] shows the average loss for seven mainline churches (American Baptist Churches; Episcopal Church; Evangelical Lutheran Church in America; Presbyterian Church, USA; Reformed Church in America; United Church of Christ; and the United Methodist Church) between 1980 and 2010 was 26.3 percent.

Sociologists of religion and observers of American church life have offered a host of reasons for the decline of mainline churches over the decades. In most instances decline is measured in loss of membership and worship attendance. Others speak of decline in terms of loss of influence.

In 1976, Dean Kelly asserted that conservative churches were growing in numbers because they had higher expectations and stricter standards of behavior and doctrine for their members. Mainline denominations lost members, he said, because they did not provide clear-cut, convincing answers to questions concerning the meaning of life, motivate commitment in their members for shared mission, require a strict code of conduct, and discipline their members for failure to live up to it.[29]

Late sociologist and Catholic priest Andrew Greeley argued shrinking attendance and membership was due to the drop in births among mainliners with the advent of the birth control pill.[30] The next generation was not filling the pews because there were not as many of them.

Sociologists Rodney Stark and Roger Finke asserted that historic churches lost their market share in the colonial era and never recovered because they did not provide sufficient motivation to remain faithful. They called this occurrence "stigma and sacrifice." The stigma came from not adhering to group practice (no drinking or smoking) and belief (creedal affirmation or speaking in tongues). By meeting these expectations of the group, members gain acceptance and affirmation of the group and distinguish themselves from surrounding society. Sacrifice consists of the investments required to gain and retain membership in the group. The high cost of commitment screens out members whose dedication and participation would be much less.[31] This is really a newer version of Kelly, arguing that the decline of mainline churches is their own fault, as opposed to secularization theory, which sees decline as almost inevitable.

The secularization thesis is that as societies modernize, they become less religious. This process is both external (a gradual fading of the influence of religion from the public square) and internal (a gradual accommodation of

Also, people aren't joiners like they used to be
scouts   Masons
Elks .

religion to the culture). As society considers science and rational thinking as the primary sources of truth, so religion loses its authority. A key component of the theory is that secularization and modernization go hand in hand. As societies modernize, religion will necessarily fade. Back in the 1980s a host of sociologists who adhered to this theory predicted that the rising tide of secularization would eventually displace religion in America. That has not proven to be the case.

José Casanova, a sociologist of religion at Georgetown University, sees secularization manifested in three ways: the decline of religious beliefs and practices in modern societies; the privatization of religion and, hence, its diminishing influence in the public sphere; and the differentiation of the secular spheres (state, economy, science) from religion. [32]

Proponents of secularization theory cite as evidence the widespread decline in worship attendance, the contraction of denominations, and the increasing absence of religion in the public square. Scholars such as Rodney Stark and Peter Berger have argued that levels of religiosity are not declining, while other scholars such as Mark Chaves [33] have countered by introducing the idea of neo-secularization, which broadens the definition of secularization to include the decline of religious authority and its ability to influence society, even if religious activity may not be declining in the United States.

There is truth in all of these theories. When churches have high expectations and raise the bar for membership, joining the community acquires more value and requires more commitment. Birthrates are declining among more affluent and educated couples, who tend to populate mainline churches. The previous generation is not being replaced. The growth of the economy and technology and the knowledge explosion have greatly impacted how people understand and experience religion. So, regardless of which theory is true, we still have a big challenge in front of us that will require a great deal of wisdom and energy to meet.

The Whole Story?

Do these stories and stark statistics tell the whole story of the demise of mainline Christianity? Is our current state just a bleak picture of mainline fecklessness or the inevitable decline of religion? Several significant historians of American religion think there is much of our heritage to be proud of and to recover that may contribute to how we rethink transitional ministry.

David Hollinger, an intellectual historian at Berkeley, wrote a significant essay called "After Cloven Tongues of Fire: Ecumenical Protestantism and the Modern American Encounter with Diversity." [34] His thesis is that those who lament the demise of mainline Protestantism (he calls them "survivalists") have an incomplete picture about the impact their tradition has had on American culture. Hollinger prefers "ecumenical" to "mainline," "liberal," or other labels to describe historic, old-line churches. "Mainline," he explains, "is too general and can cover most anything." "Liberal" can apply to culture and politics and not just to theology. "Ecumenical," he says, is a "commodious religious expanse." He contrasts "ecumenicals" with "evangelicals" and argues that the former have always had an activist, reforming bent, while the latter emphasized personal salvation.[35] Until the 1970s, ecumenicals were the public face of Christianity.

But that all changed in the decades after World War II. During the 1940s, 1950s, and 1960s, mainline Protestant leaders, says Hollinger, were "giving themselves hell."[36] They recognized the complicity of their institutions and churches in the ethnocentrism and sectarianism of the United States. Whereas evangelicals resisted diversity and embraced the notion of a "Christian America," ecumenicals actively promoted a multicultural Christianity and questioned whether American values and Christian values were consonant with one another.

The 1960s proved to be a watershed moment as ecumenical leaders, heavily involved in the civil rights movement, feminism, changing sexual mores, and the Vietnam War, received severe pushback from pew-sitters back home, many of whom embraced the "God and Country" values of most middle-class Americans. Those in leadership were not prepared for this revolt. Mainline churches prospered most when they were closely aligned to other major American institutions, such as government and business, but lost numbers when their leaders took positions that distanced them from popular notions of the "American way of life." Evangelicals gladly espoused the values of American civil religion, which eventually led to their ascendancy as the dominant religious voice in the public square, but mainline churchgoers did not flock to those churches, if at all.

Ecumenical leaders were thoroughly countercultural and rooted their convictions in scripture and theology but failed in communicating these persuasions to local churches in a convincing way. Relative to evangelicals and much of middle-class America, Hollinger says, ecumenists have been "more accepting of religious diversity, more sympathetic to anti-racist legislation and judicial rulings, more skeptical of American foreign policy, more supportive of abortion rights, more concerned with civil liberties issues, more tolerant of non-marital cohabitation, and more accepting of same-sex relationships."[37] These values, which many Americans now embrace as normative, are in no small part due to ecumenical leaders' efforts to engage local congregations, expose them to ideas they might have otherwise missed, and enable communities of faith to be a halfway house between conservative Christianity and outright secularism.[38] As sociologist N. J. Demarath III has argued, ecumenical leaders may have lost American Protestantism, but they won the United States.[39]

The demise of Protestant establishment churches occurred, Hollinger contends, because the children raised in that tradition, where they had learned the values of acceptance of diversity and tolerance of difference, did not see the indispensable need for communities of faith or theology to sustain and advance those values. Christianity was only one of many useful vehicles to promote the ideals they learned there. Religion became a personal choice instead of a vital necessity.[40]

What this suggests is that instead of being "Chicken Littles" about the death throes of mainline religion in America, we need to take pride in the accomplishments of our forebears. The tradition has much more depth and resiliency than we might think. Mainline Protestants need to continue in the tradition that takes both theology *and* social action seriously; that appreciates the social sciences, the critical study of scripture, *and* practicing the presence of God made known in Jesus Christ; that appreciates tradition (not to be confused with convention) *and* new ways of expressing the faith; that values the gifts of culture *and* remains countercultural and distinctively Christian.[41]

Navigating the New Landscape

The previous pages tell the story of many mainline churches. Once mainline Protestant churches were the custodians of the dominant American culture; now we are sidelined. Once theologians like Reinhold Niebuhr and Paul Tillich graced the covers of *Time* and *Life* magazines; now Rick Warren, Bill Hybels, and Tony Perkins, leaders of evangelical megachurches and ministries, are featured. Once we were the only show in town; now we have to share the public square with many religions and worldviews. Quaker theologian Elton Trueblood called the faith of the postwar years "cut flower Christianity"; it had all the foliage and flowers of Christian faith, but no roots.

What are some broad principles that we can glean from the foregoing observations to help us navigate these choppy waters? First, transitional ministers need to educate congregations about these new realities. Having leaders or the congregation read one of the books cited in this chapter would be eye opening. Keeping the contrasts between "now" and "then" in the pulpit, newsletter, and board meetings is a way to help folks reframe their current context. With one foot in the life of the congregation as the pastor and the other outside as a consultant and coach, the transitional minister can offer a bird's-eye view of congregational norms and habits. For instance, "I notice that you spend your publicity budget on ads in the religion section in local newspapers. Did you know that no one under forty would ever look at a newspaper to find a church?" Or, "I observe that you only spend 17 percent of your budget on programs. The largest portion is spent on salaries, the building, and utilities. If we want to minister to the hurts and hopes outside of our four walls, what might have to change?"

Second, transitional ministers need to be adaptive leaders. Leadership is not about problem solving, but about bringing about a change in perspective. Ron Heifetz, leadership guru at Harvard Business School, has made the shrewd observation that all human organizations, including churches, have to adapt or die.[42] We witness the same pattern in the biological world: when the environment changes, species need to learn to adapt or they go extinct. Most institutions are used to solving technical problems, that is, when you see a problem, you brainstorm about solutions, and you apply them to the problem. So, for instance, if you have a sinus infection, you go to a doctor, she asks your symptoms and prescribes an antibiotic, and within a week to ten days the infection is gone.

An adaptive problem is one that requires us to change our values, attitudes, or habits of behavior. When you have a rare form of cancer for which there is no known cure, you try different treatments and protocols, which are often trial and error. You might combine that with homeopathic therapy, diet, exercise, and meditation. You're kind of making it up as you go along. This is where many of our churches find themselves.

For a local church a technical problem is "Where do we find another room for our sixth grade Sunday school class?" An adaptive problem is "Given the competition we have with athletics, the crazy schedules of families, and the cyberworld, what might a ministry that reaches and forms middle school students look like?"

Adaptive leaders help congregations answer three questions: "What are your values?" "What is your purpose?" and "What is the process?" Or, in other words, "Do you behave as you say you believe?" Adaptive leadership helps congregations move through change that enables the capacity to thrive.

Third, transitional ministers need to be harbingers of hope and not prophets of doom. To be sure, many congregations might be overwhelmed and extremely discouraged when they hear the news of what they're up against. But one of the jobs of the transitional minister is to move congregations beyond the "survivalist" mode to a "possibilities" mode. They should not give into the narrative of their own demise. Transitional ministers can also educate congregations about the powerful legacy they stand within.

In a *New York Times* op-ed column on the decline of mainline churches, conservative columnist Ross Douthat hopes "that liberal Christianity recovers a religious reason for its own existence," citing the significant and continuing impact the tradition has had on American society.[43] He quotes Gary Dorrien, Reinhold Niebuhr professor of Christian Ethics at Union Seminary, who reminds us that the Christianity that animated causes such as the Social Gospel and the civil rights movement was much more orthodox than present-day liberal faith. Its leaders had a "deep grounding in Bible study, family devotions, personal prayer and worship." They argued for progressive reform in the context of "a personal transcendent God . . . the divinity of Christ, the need of personal redemption and the importance of Christian missions."[44]

The "takeaway" in Douthat's article is that the mainline church thrived when it had a deep grounding in theology and Christian practice, coupled with social service and action. Consequently, the faith we share and communicate must be *transformational.* The Christian faith does not offer good advice, but good news. Our lives and our world can be transformed by the grace, mercy, and power of the Living God. Evangelicals often call this transformation conversion, imploring us to be "born again." What ecumenical Christians advocate is a different sort of transformation—that we must be "born again and again and again." Christianity is an expedition with many turning points, peak experiences, and corrections.

Today when people are hungry for meaning or an experience of the divine and explore becoming part of a religious community, they do so not out of a sense of duty, but out of an internal yearning, a crisis in their life, or a relationship with a church member. Churches in the ecumenical tradition are at their best when they help people find and make meaning of their lives, relationships, and world events in the light of the Christian story told in preaching and implanted within by providing opportunities for scripture study, Christian formation, and practicing the classical spiritual disciplines.

This is the challenge and the goal of all churches today, to be the church of Jesus Christ that engages culture and feeds human hearts and minds with the Gospel. It is my contention that all churches are in transition, whether they have a settled pastor or an interim pastor, whether they are small or tall-steeple churches. The powerful changes that I have outlined above impact us and set the context for this book. The chapters that follow address in practical terms how we might travel this new landscape before us.

REFLECTING AND DOING

The authors of the chapters ahead are drawn from a wide range of experiences, from different denominations, from all around the country. Some, like myself, have been practitioners of transitional ministry for many years. Others have served on seminary faculties and have actively promoted interim ministry and written on it. Still others are seasoned pastors who now coach, consult, or have specialized ministries. Some are big believers in interim ministry and others are skeptics. We don't necessarily speak with one voice in these pages.

The book is divided into two sections: "Transitional Ministry for a New Day," focusing on theory, and "New Models and Methods," dealing with practice. The first section offers fresh thinking about a theology of transitional ministry. Drawing upon wisdom literature, David Sawyer, a Presbyterian minister and former director of the Doctor of Ministry degree in Interim Ministry program at Louisville Seminary, argues that today's transitional ministers need to be like the "sages" of Israel. Cameron Trimble, UCC church renewal authority and codirector of the Center for Progressive Renewal, provides an overview of our changing religious landscape and how we might practice ministry. John Keydel, seasoned interim pastor and judicatory staff for ministry transitions in the Episcopal Church, presents the new curriculum of the Interim Ministry Network. The new approach emphasizes focus points and the need for flexibility and adaptive strategies that focus on imagining a different future rather than focus on problems. Beverly and George Thompson, co-interim Presbyterian pastors and specialists, write about the capacities needed for effective leadership during transitional times using the contrasting images of a "cornfield maze" and a "labyrinth." Bianca Duemling, former assistant director of Intercultural Ministries for the Emmanuel Gospel Center in Boston and now the director of the Berlin (Germany) Institute for Urban Transformation, has done groundbreaking work and research on how minority churches respond to and manage transitions.

Part II looks at new models and methods that have been tried and tested or proposed for laboratory use. Several authors explore specialty areas of transitional time or unique situations that churches encounter. For example, veteran UCC pastor and church consultant Tony Robinson makes the case for a "succession model" of pastoral transition for tall-steeple churches. The leadership dynamics are different from small or midsized churches, and these churches can lose momentum during the interim time. Michael Piazza, experienced UCC pastor, coach, consultant, and codirector of the Center for Progressive Renewal, is impatient when churches turn inward during "in between" times, arguing that this is the key time to focus on revitalization, renewal, and redevelopment. Therapist and Episcopal priest Rob Voyle finds the insights and use of appreciative inquiry for doing interim work to be superior to those based upon Bowen and Friedman family systems theory and forcefully argues so. Deborah Pope-Lance writes about ministry after a trauma or clergy betrayal out of her experience as a therapist and a Unitarian Universalist Association (UUA) interim minister. With the large number of churches in decline or that will close in the next two decades, UCC interim minister Gretchen Switzer lays out a process of hospice care for churches that are in serious decline or closing born of her experience doing so. In the final chapter I observe the shared themes that the authors have articulated and a variety of models that are being developed by denominations and local judicatories.

The purpose of this collection is to present some fresh thinking and propose some new practices and directions for transitional ministry, but more especially to start a conversation. Many of the authors and those actively engaged in interim ministry have started those conversations in national settings, in regions and states, and among cohorts of churches across denominations. The questions have focused on the definition of excellence in interim ministry and the kinds of capacities and skills needed by clergy. How do we measure outcomes and how do we define success? And, most pressing, how do we do transitional ministry in the current sea change of North American culture?

I invite you to become part of the conversation.

REFLECTION QUESTIONS

1. In your experience, how has the practice of ministry and interim ministry changed in the past three decades? How has the changing culture impacted that?
2. Do you think the decline in mainline churches is an occasion for lament or hope? Why or why not?
3. David Hollinger asserts that the mainline church had a significant impact on society and culture in the 1950s and 1960s. Leaders supported civil and women's rights, advanced racial and multicultural diversity, and opposed the war in Vietnam. The church did not, however, pass on the biblical and theological underpinnings that supported these values to the next generation. Consequently, younger generations did not see the need to participate in a local church, even as they held these values. Do you agree or disagree with Hollinger? What lessons might we learn as we pass along the faith to the next generation?
4. What qualities and skills do you think transitional ministers must have to be effective today?

Chapter Two

Rethinking Theological Reflection on Transitional Ministry

David R. Sawyer

I was talking with another interim ministry educator about how to improve the curriculum for educating interim pastors when it occurred to me that the theory behind interim ministry education of the past did not take into account the rapid pace of change in congregational life. Much of what has been taught in classes preparing pastors for transitional ministry is based on organizational development (OD) change theory from the 1940s. The OD model of organizational change charted the progress of change in three stages: unfreeze the organization's sense of stability, change what needs to be changed, and then refreeze the system in a new and healthier way. When interim ministry was in its early stages of development in the 1980s, much of the literature assumed that congregations experienced change predominately when a pastor left, and that was the crucial time of unfreezing. The role of the transitional/interim pastor was to help the congregation address that big change in their lives, encourage them to unfreeze and change any aspects of their life together to prepare for the next pastor, and then step aside to allow the congregation to resume its stable continuity when its new pastor arrived.

Church leaders in the twenty-first century are much more aware of the challenge of constant change both within the church and in the culture around it. Evidence of cultural change can be seen in the following areas:

- Advances in scientific knowledge, from Newtonian physics to quantum physics; MRI studies of the brain; and genetic manipulation
- Growing concerns about the environment, with losses of farmland and wilderness, increasing dependence on nonrenewable fuels, and increases of awareness of needs for conservation

21

- New modes of communication, as seen in digitalization of the world, the twenty-four-hour news cycle, smartphones, and social media
- Crises in economics, with an increasing gap between rich and poor, increasing dependence on global markets with considerable interdependence of the economies of the nations
- Shifts in the demographic makeup of America, as Europeans and Christians are becoming minorities in America
- Evolving customs of family, with shifts in marriage forms, gender roles, and identities
- Enhanced awareness of security issues, with terrorism, ethnic strife, shifting dangers of violence at home and war abroad
- Changed role of religion in the world, as major religions are less able to hold societies together, and as more people are moving away from traditional beliefs and practices

Change is also becoming the norm inside congregations as well. Several mainline or old-line denominations are shaken by controversies that not only impact the whole denomination but also set off turbulence in their congregations. And every congregation experiences the more familiar life changes of births, deaths, marriages, divorces, illness, job transfers, and the aging of its current membership. For example, when I worked with the leaders of the Justinsburg church (not its real name) in a time of transition, they had to face the reality that when that particular group had become active in the church, they had all had young children. As they looked around the room, the fact that almost all of them were empty nesters was a clear reminder of the change in their lives and in their church.

The persistent effect of external and internal change on congregations requires transitional leaders to get beyond organizational change efforts and address the challenges of change through theological reflection. Leaders need to help congregations see where God is in the change and ask what God is calling them to do in response. The Christian church has shifted theological stances in every culture and every era to fit into and to translate itself for the ears and hearts of people of each time and place. Our theological thinking about the practice of ministry needs to shift as well.

I recall from my years on faculties of interim education events with the Interim Ministry Network and with Presbyterians that the hardest part of the curriculum for pastors to master was thinking theologically about the challenges of their congregations, and I also know that many experienced pastors have a hard time with case study methods that ask them to apply their understanding of how God works in the world to the specific situation. The object of this chapter is to offer a practice for thinking theologically about how God is at work in our congregations that can be put to use by wise pastoral leaders.

WISDOM LITERATURE — A SOURCE FOR THEOLOGICAL REFLECTION

While rich material for understanding twenty-first-century Christianity appears throughout the Bible, I find my best theological and practical inspiration in the wisdom writings. The Hebrew Bible has five wisdom books, including the canons of the Roman and Orthodox traditions—Proverbs, Ecclesiastes (Qoheleth), Job, the Wisdom of Solomon, and Sirach. Some of the psalms also take wisdom forms as well. In the Christian scriptures, the Sermon on the Mount and James are commonly considered to be wisdom writings. Perhaps because these books and passages do not fit neatly into traditional Christian theology they don't get as much attention as other forms of literature in the Bible. But I believe effective theological reflection for the practices of leadership is about helping the people of God learn wisdom. By wisdom, I mean knowing "who one is and how one should live."[1]

The distinctive practice of the sages can be seen by comparing them to the traditional leadership roles in the Hebrew scriptures.

- Prophets—called in crisis to see and proclaim where the people have gone astray
- Priests—authorized to mediate the presence and forgiveness of God in worship
- Monarchs or rulers, kings in the traditional language—anointed to godly governance
- Rabbis, those who emerged after the exile and destruction of the temple—trained to teach the Torah, to interpret the laws of God to the lives of the people

The sages, who emerged in the postexilic community, are usually left off that traditional list. In the twenty-first-century church, leaders will continue to play roles from the traditional list, but transitional leaders can learn a lot from the sages who were gifted with wise theological reflection to guide families and communities in dreaming and interpreting dreams. Sages in the Hebrew communities have been called by Walter Brueggemann the practical theologians of the Bible.[2] They drew their understanding from knowledge of the way the world works; they recognized the enigmas and daily-ness of life; and they knew God through their experience of piety and deep study of the scriptures. Transitional pastors can learn much about doing theological reflection for today's church from the way the sages integrated secular understandings of the nature of the world into their deep faith in the Torah, the first five books of the Bible. Like the sages, wise transitional ministers can make their practice of ministry a creative mix of tradition and experience. The wise leader will integrate theology with the way the world works as a connected and evolving ecosystem, and will listen carefully to the wisdom of the people they lead to be sure they frame their inspirational leadership in ways that fit the context.

Leading like a sage fits the twentieth century's theological shift from revelation-based to experience-based theology. In response to the neo-orthodox insistence that Christians' understanding of "God" could be informed only by divine revelation, the process and liberation theologians adapted the experience and insights of twentieth-century science, such as evolutionary biology, relativity and quantum physics, field theory, contemporary mathematics, and depth psychology, and constructed fresh and relevant ways to articulate their faith.[3] The theological innovations of the past century recall the practice of the sages and offer us a good grounding for doing theology in the twenty-first century.

At its best, theological reflection on the practice of ministry in a rapidly changing, postmodern world is a three-way conversation among the situations in which we find ourselves, our best knowledge about the world and human nature, and inspiration from the long and evolving traditions of faith through the ages.

QUALITIES OF WISE THEOLOGICAL REFLECTION

The three-way conversations of the sages can be seen in the wisdom of the Epistle of James. Although Martin Luther referred to James as an "epistle of straw" because of the absence of overt references to the gospel of Jesus and to grace, it offers wise guidance for the Christian life, drawing on wisdom literature and practical theology. I would respectfully argue with Luther that we need real and practical materials like straw to make the bricks of a faithful life.

I have found particular inspiration for theological reflection for transitional ministry in the Epistle of James. Three nuggets of a wisdom approach to theological reflection from the first chapter of James are the reality of challenge and change, the need to remember our connection with God and the Earth, and importance of listening to the context of ministry in the church and in the world. These three areas match my own sense of the current challenges to church leadership, and they point us toward three qualities of theological reflection that respond to the basic questions of this chapter: What's going on here? How can we use the best human knowledge of our time to make sense of it? And what does God have to do with it?

LET YOUR THEOLOGY BE CREATIVE

> Consider it a sheer gift, friends, when tests and challenges come at you from
> all sides. . . . Let it do its work so you become mature and well developed.
> (James 1:2, 4)[4]

In an era of rapid change, when "tests and challenges" compete with stability
in human life, it's good to be reminded that theology is also dynamic and
changing. Any good review of the history of theology reveals that the style
and content of theological thinking has shifted and grown in response to
changing geographies, worldviews, and social concerns. Early church struggles with dualistic worldviews, such as Gnosticism, pushed leaders to adopt
both Hebrew and Christian writings into the canon of the Bible to emphasize
that the creator of the world was the same God as the world's redeemer. In
the middle ages, the dramatic divide between the life of faith and the deep
sufferings of humanity prompted new theological thinking about how to
articulate the faith that used the best logic of philosophy and also took into
account the limits of reason to fully grasp the mystery of God. The expansion
of scientific thinking and global exploration during the Renaissance
prompted the Reformers to blaze new trails of theology regarding God's
relationship with the world—as the ultimate planner and controller in Calvin's thinking—while also rebelling against old authoritarian forms of religious institutional control. In the early twentieth century, both progressive and
fundamentalist theologies emerged to answer the questions raised by contemporary science. In each age and every situation, theology has changed to
meet the tests of the times. It can be said to be continually maturing in
response to its challenges.

The practice of the sages had a quality of creativity by holding onto the
best thinking of their traditions while fully embracing the challenges and
tests of their time. The creative task of theology in our time is the "sheer gift"
of the tests and challenges of change. Transitional leaders are in a critical
position to encourage congregations to see that God is active in change, that
truth is not static, and that new words and metaphors can inform and enliven
traditional expressions of faith.

Naming the Presence of God in Our Situation

The assumption behind creative theological reflection is that God is actively
and creatively present in all aspects of creation. Instead of entertaining de-
bates about particular beliefs about God, the creative practitioner expects to
find meaning, mystery, and hope in ordinary experience and is ready to make
sense of them by claiming a place for the holy within and among them. As an
alternative to assuming that revelation ceased when the Biblical canon was

closed early in the first millennium of the Common Era, the creative theologian is open to new and hopeful ways of talking about God and the hope of
God's transforming presence.

No doubt you have your own stories of where you have seen God's spirit
at work in a moment of change, innovation, or transformation. Sometimes in
a meeting an idea seems to come out of nowhere and takes the group on a
track none of them had imagined before.

That's what happened when the Lilac Lane Church, the fictional name of
a real inner-ring suburban congregation that had enjoyed high visibility on its
heavily traveled highway, received the news that Lilac Lane was going to be
reconfigured into a limited access expressway. Even more discouraging was
the plan to construct sound walls in front of the church building, hiding it
from passing traffic. Members and leaders worried that without easy access
and visibility they might experience a rapid decline in membership. They
wondered if the congregation would have to relocate and possibly lose the
sense of solidarity with their current neighborhood. A planning committee,
already in place when the news came, reflected the despair of the whole
congregation in feeling helpless in the face of changes over which they had
no control. As the committee considered their narrowing options, someone
had the inspired idea that they could simply ask the highway department to
lower a section of the sound barriers directly in front of the church. Suddenly
the group saw a possibility they had not imagined before. They identified it
as a sign that God was moving in the situation to bring about a creative
solution. They began to see God not only in the new possibility, but in the
opportunities presented by the crisis of change itself. The news from the
highway department prompted them to be imaginative about their identity as
"Lilac Lane Church" and what God was calling them to be in the next
chapter of their life together. Sometimes the movement of God's spirit can
only be seen in hindsight, but it is always a good thing to nudge our creativity
to ask ourselves where God might be in the changes we're facing.

Finding Truth in the Creative Moment

As the church changes and its theology shifts, ways of establishing the truth
claims of theology also change. "Anyone who sets himself up as 'religious'
by talking a good game is self-deceived," says the Epistle of James. But truth
could be found when the community would "reach out to the homeless and
loveless in their plight" (James 1:26–27). For James, and for a creative theological reflection, truth is not a static affirmation/confession. It is a process of
sifting through our "intuitions, our passions, our bodily experiences, and our
relations"[5] to find a path that is faithful to our true selves and to our best
understanding of who God is. For the Lilac Lane congregation their new
sense of mission rang absolutely true to them, to their sense of God's claim

on their life together, to the way they had carried out their congregation's life in the past, and as a compassionate way to be themselves and contribute meaningfully to their neighborhood.

This way of finding truth is no more or no less subjective than the older tradition that claimed truth was in the specific revelation in the past. Past beliefs about who God is and what God does were themselves human constructions that made sense of the faith experience at the time. A new time and a new set of experiences of faith and the challenges to that faith prompt the church and its leaders to create new expressions of that faith. The truth of these expressions is validated by the faith community of the time.

Constructing New Ways to Express Faith for Action Now

Recognizing God's activity in change and accepting the community's sense of truth frees the transitional leader to engage in a constructive exercise of creating new symbols and meanings for the moment. To be constructive, a leader can open the way to a new synthesis of the great traditions and the best current knowledge of what's happening in the world right now. Without abandoning an ongoing study of traditional doctrines and rules, the transitional leader seeks innovative ways of expressing them. One vignette from this history of doctrine illustrates how theology as we have received it grew and developed through the years in response to human needs and decisions. History shows that the doctrine of original sin is not original to primitive Christianity. It was constructed in the fifth century by Augustine in reaction to the theology of the Celtic theologian, Pelagius, who held that all humans had in them the spark of God and could choose between good and evil. A long and heated debate between competing views surrounded the issue, and largely due to the politics of the time, the decision rendered favored Augustine's views. As a result Rome made a decision that closed the door on other possibilities. In that moment, J. Philip Newell argues, Christianity chose original sin and total depravity as the winning metaphor.[6] Newell's point is that now is the time to reconsider the issue in the light of current understandings of the human creature. If, according to that view of the history, the doctrine of original sin was a human construction of the faith that was deemed orthodox at the time, then it makes sense to creatively reinterpret Christian views of the relative goodness of human beings in the present time.

Creative theological reflection makes use of new metaphors for understanding both God and humanity in the twenty-first century. For example, in the gospels Jesus frequently insisted that his followers become like children. If, as the traditional original sin metaphor suggests, children are inherently bad, becoming like children would seem like a bad idea. But we could interpret Jesus's directive more hopefully if we understand from our experience that children, while sometimes selfish and cruel, are also inherently curious, adventurous, and artistic, willing to learn and grow and change. Defining the salvation story in terms of human possibilities rather than human depravity could open theological reflection to focus on how humans are saved from the evils and traps of life by being transformed by real present possibilities. In this way creative thinking brings actual human experience into dialogue with traditional doctrine to understand the way of God for today.

Such constructive creativity in theological reflection is not totally new. Even the Torah, often referred to as the "Five Books of the Law" in the Hebrew scriptures, is considered to be as much a document of wisdom instruction as it is a set of laws, in the sense of rules and commands. The people of God were to hear and study the instructions for living in the world (Deuteronomy 31:13). They were not called primarily to become an obedient people; they were called to be a people of simple wisdom. Old Testament scholar Johanna W. H. van Wijk-Bos makes a strong case that the Torah was created to transform the nation of Israel into a wise people who could continually interpret the scriptures to respond faithfully to their changing circumstances.[7] Similarly, the transitional leader engaged in creative theological reflection to teach the people of the church the ways of wisdom.

Just as a good preacher selects fresh and pertinent images and stories to illustrate a sermon, so the transitional leader selects metaphors and story lines to encourage helpful and theological reflection of a congregation's members and leaders of a church. Following the metaphor of becoming like a child, it is constructive to ask what kinds of leadership work best in the challenges and tests of a changing world. What type of leadership is best suited to curious, adventurous, creative people? New theological thinking could prompt leaders to be inviting, encouraging, and empowering, encouraging congregations to learn and grow and become something more than they are right now. It's more about acting like a sage than a judge.

I interpret James's words that "every desirable and beneficial gift comes down from heaven" as a description of the way creativity works in church leadership. The creative spirit of God flows in and through leaders in times of change to give gifts of new perspectives on God's presence in each situation, gifts of validation of the deeper truth of their theological reflections, and gifts of new interpretations and metaphors to inform the shape of ministry in the present.

LET YOUR THEOLOGY BE CONNECTED

In simple humility let our gardener, God, landscape you with the Word, making a salvation-garden of your life. (James 1:21)

In theological reflection transitional leaders need to get the big picture. A theology that is holistic recognizes how everything is interconnected. In verse 21 of the first chapter, James picks up a biblical theme that has been underutilized in the theologies of the past few centuries—that of the garden, an ecological paradise. Tradition set creation stories in a lush garden landscape. Much of the history of the Bible took place in preindustrial, agricultural cultures. Even the closing image in the last book of the Bible evokes an urban garden of many fabled beauty. As the world became industrialized, the church's theology moved away from the garden metaphor and replaced it with the machine. At one point in the history of thought God was imagined as a clockmaker who set the universe in motion and stepped away to observe as humans discovered the wonders of its design. While there are elements of the world and of community life that can be understood from a technical view, an organic, holistic perspective reveals mysteries we have not been able to discern previously.

I've been teaching church leaders to think systemically about the church for over a quarter of a century. To help people understand connectivity, I've used metaphors of a family, a spiderweb, a circle versus a straight line, the hologram, and the ecology of a river watershed. I don't know why I had not thought of the garden before, but when I read Eric Liu and Nick Hanauer's book, *The Gardens of Democracy*,[8] I adopted it enthusiastically. In that book they distinguish between thinking of human community, or a democracy in their focus, as a machine and as a garden. A machine has multiple, replaceable parts. When a machine fails to work, it can be fixed. Some part can be taken out and replaced with another part. By contrast, a garden can't be turned on and off, and it cannot just be run until it breaks and then be fixed. It requires ongoing care and tending. Liu and Hanauer describe the distinction this way:

> Gardenbrain presupposes instability and unpredictability, and thus expects a continuous need for seeding, feeding, and weeding, ever-changing systems. To be a gardener is not to let nature take its course; it is to *tend*. It is to accept responsibility for nurturing the good growth and killing the bad.[9]

Thinking theologically, the words "to tend" reflect the language of the creation stories in Genesis. In the second story, the human being is directed to "till it and to keep it." Even the language often interpreted as domination and ownership in the first creation story has been translated by some scholars as "to protect and defend." The image of God as the gardener suggests a more careful and respectful interaction of God with creation. Instead of a controlling, micromanager of a machinelike universe, God is pictured as a thoughtful collaborator with the realities of creation, ordering and nurturing the earth, patiently allowing for the work of the soil and seasons to come to fruition while guarding the long-term sustainability of the whole, and encouraging the good and discouraging the destructive elements.

The metaphor of God as farmer and the ways we can imagine God relating to the interconnected creation is played out well in Wendell Berry's description of a farmer in the person of Athey Keith in the novel *Jayber Crow*, whose conserving principle of farming was seen

> in the balance between crops (including hay and pasture) and livestock. The farm would have no more livestock than it could carry without strain. No more land would be plowed for grain crops than could be fertilized with manure from the animals. No more grain would be grown than the animals could eat. Except in the case of unexpected surpluses or deficiencies, the farm did not sell or buy livestock feed. "I mean my grain and hay to leave my place *on foot*," Athey liked to say. [10] (p. 185)

The metaphor of the church as a garden and the image of God as a tender of the earth and its creatures can offer a new shape to the choices and strategies of transitional leaders. It shifts the role of leader away from a either a controller or a mechanic, and encourages a sense that the leader is a partner in the ongoing life of a congregation. Tending a garden is not necessarily easier than driving and maintaining a machine. A garden can be frustrating and confusing until one sees the patterns and connections among all of the elements that make it a healthy whole. Remembering God as the ultimate gardener, a church leader approaches the garden with a sense of respect and appreciation. The choices a leader makes can be guided by balancing a concern for the outcomes—the programs, the growth of members, the excellence of worship and fellowship and service—with a concern for sustainability. The leader will seek solutions to church problems that fit the natural and authentic identity of the congregation instead of imposing artificial remedies that may or may not address the actual source of the problems. And when the garden is disturbed by unhealthy influences, imbalances, or infestations, the transitional leader looks below the surface to find where God may be nudging the garden to adapt to new conditions and alternative possibilities.

The garden metaphor prompts the transitional leader to see how everything in the congregation is interconnected. Why, for example, is the chair of the education committee opposing anything the pastor proposes? Perhaps it's connected with the fact that the chair of the education committee is best friends with the secretary, who was just let go because of a time of personnel restructuring. Why are some members of the church afraid of the president of the women's guild? Why do they let her get away with mistreating anyone who contradicts her? It could be connected with the fact that her husband is the powerful police chief in this small town, and her mother is the administrative assistant to the mayor. When one sees the connections, one can understand that this kind of bullying happens all the time in the administration of the town, and so it also works in the congregation.

Seeing the church as an organic, interconnected whole, as an ecological system, gives a leader perspective. By looking beyond the individual performances and the isolated incidents in the situation the leader is able to see patterns of behavior. When a leader can step back from the confusion of a difficult situation, the underlying process can come into focus. The examples in the previous paragraph are instructive. Instead of taking a member's attacks personally, a pastor can see how the member is placing loyalty to a friend or family member above the best interests of the whole congregation. Other patterns that are seen in some congregations are unclear boundaries, fuzzy organizational structures, triangular relationships that leave some people as "odd one out," or emotional reactions that are out of proportion to the situation at hand. Members of congregations and ministers and staff members do not act as individuals in a vacuum. They are interconnected with every other part of the congregation in complex and fascinating ways. Looking for patterns is one way to step back from the confusion.

Similarly, it is easy to think that the theological meaning behind a particular situation is limited to the faith or morality of either the pastor or an individual member. While the responsibility and freedom of each individual is important, the influences of group, society, and culture as well as of nature are also worthy of notice. As the image of the Earth has grown smaller and more connected, and as science has unlocked even more mysterious and contradictory elements of the universe, we find it harder to assume that God is concerned only with the life of individual humans on an obscure satellite of a diminutive star. A faithful mind-set for the twenty-first century takes its cues from the best knowledge of the time and takes a larger perspective. I am recommending in this chapter that leaders for the church in the twenty-first century expand their horizons to see how God's creative love works in the world. This suggests a theology that sees abundant interconnections in every situation.

Let your theological reflection seek a larger, holistic perspective on your situation. Learn to see how things that appear on the surface to be isolated phenomena are really part of an overall organizing structure. Let your leadership take its cues from the balanced, respectful care of God the gardener so that your garden can flourish in the light of God's love.

LET YOUR THEOLOGY BE CONTEXTUAL

Post this at all the intersections, dear friends: Lead with your ears, follow up with your tongue, and let anger straggle along in the rear. (James 1:19–20).

For the transitional leader, theological reflection is not done in a vacuum. It has to answer the basic questions of "What's going on, what does God have to do with it, and what shall we do?" "What's going on" is going on in the real circumstances of the congregation. The Epistle of James suggests that a priority for the Christian community is listening. Often the first impulse of leaders is to enter a situation as an expert and to apply ready-made knowledge to whatever the situation happens to be. In contrast, a leader who admits to not knowing everything about the situation and approaches each problem with curiosity is leading with the ears.

Listening for the context brings to mind the first of the process tasks of the interim leader (See chapter 6 in the revised edition of Allan Gripe's *The Interim Pastor's Manual*[11]). The phrase "joining the system" came from the field of family therapy in which counselors recognized the need to gain an emotional foothold with a resistive family. The leader joins the system by connecting emotionally and physically with the ecology of a congregation. To do this kind of listening is to recognize that the transitional pastor does not stand outside the congregation to guide and correct, but works within the social patterns of the congregation. One can join the system by adopting some of the congregation's obvious patterns of speaking and behaving. The leader listens to speech patterns, formal or colloquial, and ways members address each other with first names or with family titles, such as mister/missus or brother/sister. The leader observes informal dress codes, noting whether the members attend meetings in their Sunday dress-up clothes or in casual or even work clothes, and whether they dress up or down to better fit in. I have found through the years that when I am alert and attentive, a congregation will live out in front of me its true identity. To join is to be present to the congregation as a whole. To join is to assume that the congregation is doing the best it can, from its own inner wisdom, and that even the most difficult people are operating out of their own best sense of what is right.

There is no universal, one-size-fits-all theology. The creative spirit of God relates to each person, each situation, and each congregation uniquely in each moment. Let your theology be specifically tailored to the people, place, and time as much as humanly possible by listening and living within the confines of the context. To do theological reflection contextually is to bring into the foreground the people, place, culture, politics, and history of a situation. Listening to and learning from the context provides the agenda for the theological task. The contextual questions determine whether the leader employs a theology of mission or a theology of compassion, a theology of hope or a theology of comfort, a theology of reconciliation, or a theology of judgment. The church I served in Ohio in the 1970s was located in a nearly all European–American municipality, which bordered two predominantly African American communities. Many urban experts predicted that housing integration would be the next big transition for that community. Several of the Protestant and Catholic pastors of the area discussed together ways to understand and address the expected fear and flight among our congregations. The prophetic theology of the 1960s was still buzzing among us, and it was tempting to preach a theology of judgment on the unspoken racism in the community's soul. But we also realized that condemnation seldom leads to a change of heart or mind. As a group, we turned to thinking about the situation from the perspectives of reconciliation—"God was in Christ reconciling the world to God's self"—and equipping—"for the building up of the Body of Christ." Reading the context from those points of view led the ministerial group to offer programs of education and familiarization that included arranging joint worship services and shared meals with neighboring African American churches. Members of my congregation enjoyed sharing among themselves how surprised they were that they shared similar worship styles but very different food styles with their black neighbors. In that time of transition, thoughtful theological reflection on the place, the time, the people, and the actual possibilities of the situation shaped the leadership agenda.

Contextual theological reflection also determines the language and style of leadership. One way to read the context for ministry is by listening for the underlying worldview or story type. Hopewell's classic work, *Congregation*,[12] uses four types of narrative to assess the basic outlook of a congregation. The four types are tragic, comic, ironic, and romantic. In my Ohio congregation mentioned in the previous paragraph, the members lived with a deep comic sense that everything is likely to turn out all right in the end. The congregation would not have recognized themselves as deeply racist, as might have been the case if they had held a more tragic worldview. They preferred to think of themselves as mostly baffled by new experiences, and believed that God was working to make it all come together. That's why responding to the imminent crisis of housing integration succeeded by bringing different people together instead of by railing against tragic flaws.

Listening to the context also includes hearing what can be openly discussed and what cannot in the situation. As an example, an interim pastor discovered that an extensive, unacknowledged history of previous pastors' sexual boundary violations burdened the congregation. Believing that an honest airing of burdensome secrets can be redemptive, the interim tried several different ways to engage conversations on the subject. Each was met with either silence or hostility. Reworking his theological reflection around the notion that healthy practices of the Christian community could also lead to redemption, the interim pastor refocused his leadership interventions on strengthening the organizational structures of the congregation. He worked to clarify the roles of staff members and taught the personnel committee how to do thorough and appreciative staff evaluations. As he worked with the church board he helped them find ways to play a more assertive role in setting the

rules and activities of the congregation, and he taught officers and members
to assert their rightful leadership authority. While these did not seem like
enough to address a serious concern, they were the only possibilities he could
manage at the time. A couple of years later, when the next pastor stepped
across sexual boundaries, the congregation's lay leaders were ready to assume appropriate leadership, name the offense for what it was, and ask for
help from denominational officers. These examples demonstrate how the
context shapes the theology and the strategy of the transitional leader.

The contextual quality of theological reflection is the most sensual of the
three. It is about listening, as James insists. It is about attachment to the
sights and feels of a congregation, and it feels a bit like a potter shaping clay
for a lovely pot by molding the words and action of leadership to the form
and character of the congregation.

DOING THEOLOGICAL REFLECTION FOR TRANSITIONAL MINISTRY

Transitional church leaders are no longer the promoters or managers of
change in their congregations. Change is already and always happening in
and around the congregation. The unique task of the theologically trained
interim leader is to guide the congregation in asking the questions, What is
going on here, what does God have to do with it, and what do we do now?
While this chapter does not offer a step-by-step method for theological reflection, it encourages three particular qualities of theological thinking that
help leaders connect with the world in the twenty-first century while remain-
ing true to faith traditions. Leaders who attempt to embody those qualities
will be better able to keep their minds flexible and open to addressing issues
and problems the church has never faced before. That kind of flexibility was
seen in the sages of the Bible, who rethought their faith tradition by integrating their own lived experience with the best thinking about how the world
worked from their own and their neighbors' cultures. When our theological
reflection is creative, connected, and contextual, we recognize that our world
is changing more rapidly and more radically than ever before. We can put to
good use our most creative imagination to find fresh ways to construct the
messages of hope and transformation to fit a changing situation. We gain a
sense of a big-picture perspective when we see how each congregation is an
ecological organism set in its own environment. We can settle into our context by taking cues from the stories of the place and time and people where
we are. When we can see how our thinking is characterized by these qualities, our actions will be more likely to be seen as wise.

REFLECTION QUESTIONS

1. What difference might it make in your thinking and your leadership if you used the wisdom literature as the biblical basis of your theological reflection as compared with using the Pentateuch, the prophets, the Gospels, or the Pauline literature?
2. To what extent has your theological thinking changed in the past decade and in what ways has it changed? What prompted it to change?
3. In what ways would an ecological or garden metaphor affect your perceptions and your theological understanding of your congregation in comparison with more linear machine metaphors?
4. Name some examples of how your use of religious language, theological concepts, and ministry strategies change when you are working in different congregational contexts?

Chapter Three

The Changing Landscape of the American Church

Cameron Trimble

If you ever take the train from the Delancey Street–Essex Street station on the Lower East Side of Manhattan, New York, you are likely to see something increasingly rare: people helping one another. Since New York City issued service cuts in 2010, this station has fallen victim to a pesky quirk. The uptown F and M lines are physically segregated.

For much of Manhattan, the two lines stop at the same stations and platforms; riders simply hop on the first arriving train. At Delancey Street, however, the F train is downstairs, a short walk from the M but out of view from the other train's platform. There are no station announcements telling riders when the trains are arriving. Passengers have taken matters into their own hands, however, forming a line from one platform to the other to relay the announcement of the arriving trains, like an old-fashioned game of "telephone." Even those who speak other languages are getting in on the game. They know to stand in the middle of the line, raising their chances of finding someone to help them translate. In the end, *everyone* gets on the train.

Perhaps this is an apt parable of our times as Christian leaders in the church. Because the decline in church participation has forced seismic changes in our denominational and local church structures, we now are riding on two seemingly separate trains: the I train of institutional church and the E train of the emerging church.[1] We are standing on the stairs between two platforms, listening carefully to learn which train will arrive first in the churches we are serving. Some of us are longing to ride both.

The key to discerning our best track is in the listening. By most accounts, it is too soon to know why, how, and in what ways the church is changing. We can see trends emerging in theology, worship styles, church size, and leadership roles that give us some clues about the near future. At this point, however, no one is prepared to say when the next train or, more likely, trains of widely adopted Christian theology and practice will arrive, where they will take us, or even what they will be called. We simply know we need to listen and watch in hopeful anticipation. We stand on the platforms together with our questions: Will denominations survive, or are they a relic of the past? Will local churches still hire full-time clergy, or are bivocational pastors the leaders of the future? Will churches need privately owned buildings, or will we use shared, common space? What will our future as the body of Christ hold?

The challenge for those of us leading churches today is that we still are actively serving congregations across the world that look to us for answers to these questions. Members ask us about vision, strategy, theology, and structure, looking for some sense of confidence that, while everything is changing at a rapid pace, we are faithfully being "church." We are just not sure what that is. For those of us serving within denominational structures, we are locked into organizations that merit numeric growth, financial solvency, and institutional support. These are the measure of success and perhaps should remain a strong indicator of health in the future. Somewhere deep within, however, we feel increasingly emphatic nudges to serve the more fragile communities of the homeless, the voiceless, the nontraditionalists, and the mystics among us, knowing that these dear saints have never been particularly valued by institutions that ultimately need to pay their bills.

Pastors and lay participants alike are living in liminal space. Thomas Brackett, the Episcopal Church Center's Missioner for Church Planting, Ministry Redevelopment and Fresh Expressions of Church, uses a wonderful image to talk about this journey of living "in between." He says that the call of the church today is to move from being the hospice ward to being the birthing center. He writes:

> Many of our church leaders are realizing that, for most of their careers, they have been offering a kind of hospice ministry to their congregations and diocese. It is not just the flagging attendance and the graying of our denomination's membership that push them to acknowledge the ennui of our beloved institutions. It is also the noted absence of fresh visions and dreams that would normally bubble up from our younger members. There seems to be a fresh hunger for the Spirit's promise to give above and beyond anything we can ask or imagine. (Ephesians 3:20–21)[2]

While so much about the changing landscape of ministry remains unclear, what we can say with certainty is that the church as we knew it in most of our lifetimes no longer exists. As science fiction writer William Gibson notes, "The future is already here—it is just unevenly distributed." The question is, how now shall we live?

To be fair, not only church is changing at a radical pace. The December 2010 issue of *Time* magazine highlighted the failure of a number of major American institutions in the previous ten years. We saw the failure of our political system in the botched 2000 presidential election, the failure of our military mission in Iraq, the failure of our economic mediating and distribution systems with the emergence of Napster and other peer-sharing platforms that threatened major industries built on controlled distribution of products and information, the failure of our global economic position as China passed America in gross domestic product, and the failure of our economic system in the crash of 2008 to 2010, to name a few.[3] Everything is changing. The church is simply caught in the wave.

Yet here we are. How now shall we live? Perhaps the more productive questions we might ask today are not questions of institutional survival but rather questions of spiritual awakening. The essential question remains: What does the changing landscape of ministry mean for those serving in interim ministry?

Interim ministry historically has served an important role in church life, as churches transition from one settled pastor to another. Developed in the 1980s as a strategy for helping congregations navigate transitions, the "intentional" interim minister was trained in essential skills, including family systems theory, conflict resolution, and change management. The creators of the concept and the training made key assumptions about the churches that these leaders would be serving, and these assumptions became the guideposts by which an entire ecosystem of curriculum, training, and coaching came into being. They believed that most churches served by interims:

- Are disconnected from their history,
- Have not developed an identity that fits their current circumstances,
- Have a need for some shifts in church leadership,
- Have weak links to their denomination, and/or
- Have not made a commitment to a new future or redefined purpose.

In other words, they believed that many congregations in the United States were weak in at least one of these five areas and needed intentional intervention before they could move forward to a fruitful future. That was likely true then—I suspect it would be worse today—and taking a systematic and programmatic approach to pastoral transitions initially produced positive results in many congregations. Alas, those results were not to last. During the past few years, many church leaders have begun to question the assumptions guiding interim ministry, as well as the need for this vocation. Placed within the larger conversation of how church is changing, questions about the impact, role, and goals of interim ministry point to larger adaptive challenges pushing against organized religion in the world. As one of my colleagues said, "We can talk about fixing interim ministry, but until we address the larger questions of the emerging church, 'fixing' interim ministry is like putting lipstick on a pig." It is a memorable image.

GETTING OUT OUR CRYSTAL BALL

I am invited to speak at dozens of events each year throughout the United States, Canada, and the United Kingdom about one primary topic: What is the future of the church? I sense that people hope I will pull out my crystal ball, set it in the middle of a stage, wave my hands over it, and dramatically predict the changes that are coming. I have considered trying it. I suspect I could be as accurate as our local meteorologists!

In lieu of that, I suggest we look at four forces in our culture and, therefore, within the church (as church always reflects its context and culture) that give us clues to our future: resources, technology, demographics, and governance. Looking at them closely, we can begin to glimpse our future. Having vision for future congregational life matters a great deal: while these forces are always at work, their outcomes are not predetermined. We have a choice about the kind of church we are today and will create in the future.

Resources

Resources are the raw materials we use to shape our physical reality. Human progress has been propelled by a simple formula:

Advances in technology + new resources + imagination = innovation

If the first Christians who gathered in the catacombs could witness our present and see, and understand, the resources we now take for granted, I suspect they would faint from shock. We are the beneficiaries of thousands of years of liturgy (spiritual resources), millions of fellow sojourners who claimed the Christian story as their own (human resources), and billions (if not trillions) of dollars in assets to "spread the Good News" (financial resources). We have a lot to work with. How we use these resources going forward will be most telling.

Today, local churches and denominations are unsure how to claim, celebrate, and use their resources. The resources that have historically supported the mission of the church seem to be declining at a breathtaking pace. Liturgies that once transported our souls to a divine encounter with the living Christ have become stale; younger generations are leaving the church, if they were ever in church to begin with; and local church and denominational budgets are tanking. Our dominant collective narrative for the past forty years has been the story of failure, decline, abandonment, and despair. It is no wonder that the strong focus of transitional ministry work has been around processing grief.

Let me say again that we have a choice about the kind of church we are today and will create in the future. Reversing our "decline-oriented" thinking, let me suggest that we actually have more resources than ever before for shaping and strengthening the church in North America. We are seeing a number of exciting "resource repurposing" experiments. Creative and innovative women and men are wrestling with the bigger questions of faith, liturgy, worship, and theology, giving us profoundly transformational Spirit experiences. These leaders have discovered the liberating truth that we no longer need denominational systems to create life-giving ministry; we no longer need three- or four-year degrees to call ourselves pastors; we no longer need privately owned buildings for our sanctuaries; and we no longer need full-time staff to organize our ministries. The resources for the emerging church remain focused on spiritual, human, and financial assets, but how and why they are used is changing dramatically.

Today we are the beneficiaries of new possibilities. Among the most interesting laboratories of innovation is the Fresh Expressions movement that began in England in 2004 with two convergent events. The first event came from the work of a committee under the leadership of Bishop Graham Cray when the group published *Mission-Shaped Church: Church Planting and Fresh Expressions of Church in a Changing Context*. This book sparked a flurry of excitement within the Church of England and became a seed that sprouted a new day of church planting. The second event happened almost simultaneously when Archbishop Rowan Williams read Brian McLaren's book *A Generous Orthodoxy* on a plane ride. McLaren's work so deeply affected him that, when he got home, he immediately got to work creating the Office of Fresh Expressions. He asked Bishop Cray to lead this new office, observing that "the Spirit is doing a new thing among us." He assigned this new office the task of creating a new

> form of church for our changing culture, established primarily for the benefit of people who are not yet members of any church [that] will come into being through principles of listening, service, incarnational mission and making disciples [and] will have the potential to become a mature expression of church shaped by the gospel and the enduring marks of the church and for its cultural context.[4]

Fresh Expression churches are missional (serving people outside church); contextual (listening to people and entering their culture); educational (making discipleship a priority); and ecclesial (interested in new forms of worship and doing ministry).[5] Fresh Expressions now has made its way to North America through the Episcopal Church and has strongly influenced other movements like the Emergent Church movement. The Spirit is breaking us open for new possibilities.

Emergence Christianity also deserves some mention here, and it is best explained in Phyllis Tickle's book *Emergence Christianity: What It Is, Where It Is Going, and Why It Matters.* Emergence Christianity may seem like a new idea to many of us within the mainline church, but as Tickle teaches us, it in fact has been brewing for a couple hundred years. While it remains somewhat hard to explain, those in the emergence "conversation" mostly agree that they are disillusioned with the institutional church and support the deconstruction of modern Christian worship, modern evangelism, and modern Christian community.[6] Emergent church communities and leaders are looking for ways to reimagine liturgies, reform rituals, and reclaim ancient Christian praxis. The most well-known of these churches include Solomon's Porch in Minneapolis, House for All Sinners and Saints in Denver, St. Gregory's in San Francisco, Buffalo Community of the Holy Spirit, and Christ the Savior in Washington, DC. These communities are radically different in shape, structure, and demographics, but all of them can teach us a great deal about being a Christian community in a postmodern world.

A close cousin of the Emergence Christianity conversation is a new concept called Convergence Christianity. First articulated by Eric Elnes, pastor of Countryside United Church of Christ and host of Darkwood Brew, Convergence Christianity points to a growing reality that past theological and social boundaries that separated people are falling away. Looking at people gathering in a field in North Carolina for the Wild Goose Music Festival, we see a powerful example of the most unlikely friendships born out of common longings. Evangelicals who are tired of hating gay people are connecting with mainline people who miss emotionally moving worship experiences. Roman Catholics who believe that women should be priests are connecting with progressive Pentecostals who yearn for organizational structures to further their ministry. People are finding one another at points of deep theological need driven by a longing to somehow, someway live at peace with themselves, each other, and the Earth. Their common human longings—their convergence—pull them toward one another and minimize theological and political differences that once would have driven them apart.

Two other communities must be named because of their growing impact on North American Christian practice. The Taizé Community is an ecumenical monastic order in Burgundy, France. Founded in 1940 by Brother Roger Schutz, it is composed of more than a hundred brothers, from Protestant and Catholic traditions, who originate from approximately thirty countries across the world.[7] This community has given Christian churches around the world some of the most extraordinary music of our time. Around the same time, the Iona Community began in Glasgow, Scotland, as a project led by Church of Scotland minister George MacLeod to close the gap he perceived between the church and working people.[8] The Iona Community has reinvigorated the need for social justice within contemplative life.

Innovation in our "resources" is not limited to these movements or communities. Local churches within mainline denominations—the contextualized incubators of the Spirit's work in the world—also are claiming more creative license in how they minister to those in their neighborhoods. Congregations find themselves needing to question everything, from the shape of their sanctuaries to the role of their clergy, as they reinvent their ministries in this new age. As philosopher Jean Houston notes, people today are experiencing ten to one hundred times the life experiences of their ancestors a few generations previous.[9] Change is the new constant, making it prudent for every pastor to consider her work "transitional." To successfully navigate these new winds of the Spirit with their congregations, pastors need new maps and guides. Like the ancient way finders who navigated the pacific seas by studying the waves, we must develop the eyes and ears to hear the still, small voice of the Spirit showing us a new way.

Looking further ahead, we see hints of larger cultural shifts, though I would not yet substantiate them beyond a mere observation:

1. We are searching for new funding models for ministry (which are different from new funding models for church). Crowd funding, defined as the collective effort of people who network and then pool their money to support efforts initiated by other people or organizations, is allowing more individuals to access smaller donations in larger quantities, which, over time, can add up to major funding. Kickstartministry.com is one example of how we might fund the churches of the future.

2. New churches will continue the trend of sharing space with a variety of partners rather than owning their own buildings. This will not be universally true, of course, but new churches are likely to be more transient, have shorter life spans, and hold environmental stewardship as a core value. Why build when we have so many empty buildings already?

3. The increase in the number of Hispanic people in North America, which I will touch on later, will provide a new pool of spiritual, human, and financial resources. Any denomination that ignores the impact and influence of this demographic shift in North America will do so to its own peril.

4. Amazing liturgies, songs, chants, rituals, and services are exploding in churches, not just in North America, but around the globe. Globalization may, in fact, be the savior of the church in North America. With the infusion of diversity in people, cultures, practices, and experiences, Christianity has never had more exciting expressions than today. For anyone who has endured a boring worship service, I say, "Thanks be to God."

Technology

We typically use the word "technology" to describe a new electronic gadget, but in its purest sense, technology is making and using tools, machines, techniques, and systems to solve problems or achieve a goal. It is the medium of invention. The problem we have today is that we are inventing at record pace! Every day we hear of an amazing advance in medicine, communication, commerce, manufacturing, education, or the arts. Why not the church?

The good news is that more and more churches use the Internet as a medium of mobilization. Leaders use church websites as announcement boards for community activity, and they are generally a hub for more participation-based technologies like blogs, Facebook groups, and Twitter accounts. Blogs are an especially popular means of communication within the church. Through them, members converse about theology, philosophy, art, culture, politics, and social justice, within and among their congregation and across the broader community.

What must also be noted is that because of our expediency in creating new technologies, we are poorly equipped to manage the rate of change we are experiencing in every other area of life, and with its resistance to change, the church is forty years behind the curve! Past theories of change assumed that cultures advanced through predictable periods of change followed by periods of stabilization. As periods of stabilization are shortening, we must now reconsider everything, from the effectiveness of strategic planning, to how we teach students, to how we understand the concept of leadership.

In the 2012 version of the "Did You Know" video, created by Karl Fisch, a Colorado high school's director of technology, to illustrate the rapidly changing world, Fisch noted that the jobs most in demand in 2010 did not exist in 2004.[10] That means that people are preparing for jobs that don't yet exist, using technologies that have not been invented, to solve problems that we don't yet know are problems. The U.S. Department of Labor is now estimating that a person today will have held ten to fourteen jobs by the age of thirty-eight.[11] The impact that so many people moving between jobs has on shifting demographics alone threatens to undermine our institutional foundations built on the assumption of lifetime membership and participation. We have moved beyond the age in which "working harder" is sufficient. The survival of the church will depend upon our capacity to use all of our technologies to innovate.

Some churches already are using the technology at their disposal. When Theryl Jones moved from Peoria, Illinois, to Atlanta, leaving behind her home church, she said it was comforting to know that her pastor in Peoria was just a few mouse clicks away. "I get daily devotionals from my pastor. I can download his sermons and the notes and be a part of small groups," said Jones. In an age in which people move every few years, attend different churches during the month, and do not need to carry cash for an offering, churches that don't embrace the twenty-first-century tools of technology are destined for extinction.

What technologies are changing church today? First, we must anticipate the need for wireless technology in worship. Congregants increasingly expect to have Internet access as they listen to sermons, to give their offering online, and to tell their friends about their church. Everything is going mobile, including worship. Second, electronic giving increasingly is replacing cash and checks, and churches that embrace electronic giving are seeing between 10 to 30 percent higher giving rates than those that do not.[12] In fact, many predict we will be a wallet-less country within the next twenty years. These shifts in what people give, how they give, and when they give will affect everything in congregational life, from day-to-day cash flow, to how and when a congregation might purchase a building, to how it structures compensation packages for its leadership. Finally, we cannot underestimate the importance of social media in our culture and its impact on our ministries. Evangelism in the twenty-first century is being carried out primarily online and primarily through personal endorsement.

With these technological advances churches have fewer excuses than ever to stay only within their four walls. With the birth of the Internet, we now have the capacity to build and sustain relationships anywhere in the world. Countryside Community Church in Omaha, Nebraska, was among the first to experiment with online church through their program "Darkwood Brew." Each week a group gathers in Omaha and broadcasts its service across the Internet for anyone in the world to join, exponentially expanding its congregation's capacity to connect with participants. Today, when you ask how many people participate in the faith life of Countryside Community Church, they would rightly say thousands. The services are interactive, allowing people off-site to chat with participants in the service. Perhaps the most intriguing blurring of the virtual and physical environments is when the pastor calls for communion. The gathered group in Omaha shares the bread and wine together while the remote viewers have bread and wine in their homes in front of their computer screens. It is an experiment in twenty-first-century church that we all should watch closely and from which we can learn. It could redefine how we understand church membership, faith formation, participation in the life of a church, and a church's participation in the life of an individual.

Demographics

"Demography is destiny," observed Auguste Comte, a French philosopher and sociologist who lived in the early nineteenth century, in the midst of the Industrial Revolution. Anyone looking at demographic trends within the church in North America fears the truth of Comte's statement. The church in North America is dying. In at least three mainline denominations, the average age of church participants is nearing sixty-five, yet global demographic trends are moving in the opposite direction, particularly in Middle Eastern countries, where more citizens are under the age of twenty-five than ever before in history. The result is that our churches are getting smaller, while wrestling with missing generations of people particularly between the ages of twenty-one and forty-five. When a demographic group this large is missing from the life of any organization, we can predict fewer people to support the ministries in time, talent, and money. With fewer people engaged and even fewer donating at the rates of previous generations, many congregations face tough decisions about the future of their ministries and the financial foundation of their future.

In his book *After the Baby Boomers: How Twenty- and Thirty- Somethings A re Shaping the Future of American Religion*, well-known sociologist of religion Robert Wuthnow highlights the growing generational crisis and sounds the alarm for leaders of the institutional church, saying that if we want to have a viable future, we must begin connecting with younger generations; they are the ones who can reimagine religious life in ways relevant for our current age. He writes:

> The single word that best describes young adults' approach to religion and spirituality—indeed life—is *tinkering*. A tinkerer puts together a life from whatever skills, ideas, and resources that are readily at hand. . . . Tinkerers are the most resourceful people in any era. If specialized skills are required, they have them. When they need help from experts, they seek it. But they do not rely on only one way of doing things. Their approach to life is practical. They get things done, and usually this happens by improvising, by piecing together an idea from here, a skill from there, and a contact from somewhere else. [13]

In a time when theology and ecclesiology need reinventing, a generation of "tinkerers" may be just what the church needs. Without them we may be destined to do the same thing and expect different results, which never worked well in the past but certainly will not lead to innovation today.

Generational categories are becoming increasingly complex as the pace of change in our culture continues to accelerate. When we run demographic reports, the companies tend to divide us into five categories: Silents, Boomers, Millennials, Gen-Xers, and Gen-Zers. These have provided us with useful labels to talk about different perspectives and experiences between the generations, but these artificial categories are increasingly unhelpful in accurately describing and distinguishing a person's worldview. People's cultural icons and experience with technology and the world events that have shaped their understanding of their context and themselves are radically different from year to year. In fact, there is simply no evidence that younger adults currently have been decisively shaped by a particular historical event in the same way that the baby boomers were by the Vietnam war or by their parents waiting until after World War II to marry and have children. [14]

To put the rate of change in our world into perspective, visit the Beloit College Mindset website (http://www.themindsetlist.com) and select a college graduation year for students born between 1980 and 1995. You will find some surprising, and perhaps shocking, facts about the young people to whom the list applies. For example, here are some of the things it has to say about the college class of 2016:

1. They have always lived in cyberspace and are addicted to "electronic narcotics."
2. Women have always piloted war planes and space shuttles.
3. White House security has never felt it necessary to wear rubber gloves when gay groups have visited.
4. They have come to political consciousness during a time of increasing doubts about America's future.
5. Genomes of living things have always been sequenced.

The way they see the world, the values they hold, and their understanding of history are dramatically different from those of most people in our pews. We are from different times and almost different worlds. Pastoring in this reality is presenting new challenges, especially for transitional ministers, who often seek to nurture better and stronger communication between church members, establishing those patterns in a fairly short time frame before moving to another church. Learning to integrate generations requires learning to see the world in a different way. Time and again, ministers and church leaders will run into the temptation of applying easy "fixes" to challenges rather than letting congregations wrestle with the generative questions of our time. It is a temptation we must avoid.

Let's complicate this conversation even more by looking at shifts in racial/ethnic groups. The "face" of North America is more diverse than ever before. Latinos are the largest and fastest growing minority group in North America, and most Latinos are Christian—either Catholic or Protestant. Hispanic membership is increasing in Christian congregations throughout the United States, posing major opportunities and challenges for the churches that serve them. Overall, the Hispanic community remains disproportionately affected by poverty, low education levels, poor health, and discrimination. [15] Churches connecting with Hispanic people are addressing these systemic challenges creatively and provide essential case studies for us to understand the dynamics of an increasingly multicultural world.

Likewise, Asian Americans are contributing to the diversity of the U.S. religious landscape. From less than 1 percent of the total U.S. population (including children) in 1965, Asian Americans have increased to 5.8 percent (or 18.2 million people in 2011, according to the U.S. Census).[16] In the process, they have been largely responsible for the growth of non-Abrahamic faiths in the United States, particularly Buddhism and Hinduism. Together, Buddhists and Hindus account for about the same share of the U.S. public as Jews (roughly 2 percent).[17] At the same time, however, most Asian Americans belong to the country's two largest religious groups: Christians and people who say they have no particular religious affiliation.[18] Taken together, the future of the mainline church looks far more diverse. Worship on Sunday morning is the most segregated hour of the week, and overcoming this is the monumental challenge for the future church.

Much more should be said about demographics, but I will list only one final observation. More and more people from the Northeast are moving to Southern cities. An analysis by demographer Wendell Cox of domestic migration for the nation's fifty-one largest metropolitan areas shows that the ten metropolises with the largest net gains from 2000 to 2009 are in the Sun Belt. The list is led by Phoenix and followed by Riverside–San Bernardino, California; Atlanta; Dallas-Ft. Worth; and Las Vegas. Increasingly, they also are moving into urban areas.[19] The challenge, of course, is that the vast majority of church buildings in North America were built when people lived in rural or suburban areas. We now face the challenge of having church buildings in places with declining populations and limited to no church presence in growing urban settings.

This is a moment of tremendous opportunity. Factoring in the reality that newer churches often opt for recycled space in storefronts, pubs, community centers, theaters, or established churches to host their faith communities; financial resources increasingly come from online "kickstarter" campaigns; technology allows us to connect with people regardless of geographic location; and an increasingly diverse secular population is transforming North America, the church now can "leapfrog" into new forms that meet new needs.

Governance

In his 1992 defeat of George H. W. Bush, Bill Clinton used the slogan, "It's the economy, stupid!" Although it was a memorable line, it was only partly true. What is more accurate is "It's the policies, stupid!" Government policies led the way to the economic recession that ultimately led Clinton to victory. If we wanted a new economy, we needed new policies. It was that simple. It is also true of the church.

The church we have today exists because of the policies we put in place to create it. Policies are the guide rails we use to govern ourselves and are the essential tools for accepting, integrating, and leading change. In other words, policies are how we shape our future *by design.* Church growth can be helped or hindered by the governing structure that a church has built. Today, far too many churches are dying under the weight of committee structures put in place during a bygone era. Perhaps the most important work of church leaders today is freeing churches from control-based management.

It is complicated working within an institutional frame. American statistician, professor, and author Edwards Deming rightly observed that systems produce what they are designed to produce.[20] Institutions are created for one main purpose: to preserve (or conserve) the resources gained by a previous generation. For the mainline church, this means, primarily, preserving and conserving the financial gains of previous generations, who created our endowments and built our buildings. Because of shifting resources, technology, and demographics, congregations are feeling increasing pressure to adapt to a world they were not designed to serve. Some are doing this better than others, of course, so let me offer a word of hope: it is in times of greatest desperation that we experience the greatest innovations.

The role of transitional ministers must be to rid congregations of needless administration, freeing them for permission-giving, innovative ministry. Dying churches seem to think that focusing on management, governance, and administration is the key to survival. Many have bylaws with more pages than the number of people in worship. It is clearly where their energy has gone and, probably, largely is still going. One wonders who or what they are trying to control. On the other hand, new, young, and thriving congregations often are guided by the principle, "If no one is going to die, then give it a try." Of course, their willingness to remain agile, responsive, and unregulated does get them into trouble at times, but rarely are the challenges they face fatal, while overregulated congregations inevitably are being strangled by their own efforts to control everything. Jesus described the Spirit as being like the wind: beyond our control. Too often the declining church's response to the uncontrollable has been to nail all of the windows tightly shut to keep the wind out.

Becoming a permission-giving church may require the death of a herd of sacred cows. Being unwilling to make that choice, though, will lead to all those cows dying of starvation. This imagery comes from church consultant Bill Easum's book *Sacred Cows Make Gourmet Burgers*, in which he talks about the dangers of churches addicted to control. He notes, "The Body of Christ is most effective when individuals are given permission to live out their God-given spiritual gifts on behalf of the Body rather than someone restraining what they can or cannot do."[21] Churches with healthy governance understand that their mission is making disciples, not making decisions.

PULLING IT ALL TOGETHER

This review of the shifts in our resources, technology, demographics, and governance does not predict our future, and certainly is not exhaustive, but it does highlight the choices that are before us and the kind of leadership that will be demanded of us. We can embrace the shifts in giving patterns and find ways to align our churches with them, or we can fail to evolve and miss an entire generation of people who no longer carry cash, value tithing, or attend worship every Sunday. We can continue to offer our worship services that lack flow, feeling, and inspiration while our church declines in attendance, or we can find new ways to use video, modern readings, and secular music to tell the Good News. We can review our governance structures and create permission-giving systems that promote our ministries, or we can cling to control-driven structures that preserve and conserve institutional power. We have a choice in the kind of church we are today and will create in the future.

Transitional pastors sit in the midst of these questions, helping navigate congregations through some of the most perilous storms of our time. Traditional, time-honored curriculums will not always work for this task. Instead, we would be wise to watch the wind and the waves with the discerning eye of the ancient way finders, learn from other sectors of our culture, and integrate our learning with an increasingly diverse, ever-changing world. Perhaps the most honest thing we can say about this moment is, none of us were trained for this.

In the film *Steel Magnolias*, just after Shelby's funeral, her mother M'Lynn, played by Sally Field, is walking through the cemetery, with her friends following behind. Her pain is raw, overwhelming her and us as we watch. Finally, in a moment of anger, she looks at her friends and says, "I just want to hit something. I want to hit it hard!" Her friends don't know what to do . . . until one of them grabs another, shoves her toward M'Lynn, and says, "Here. Hit this. Go ahead, M'Lynn. Slap her!" Suddenly, in the midst of terrible grief, they all are laughing at the deep, vulnerable absurdity of it all. In that moment, you cry and laugh at the same time. For many of us, this is what it feels like to lead in the "church" right now. We stand in the midst of deep loss while celebrating the friendships and faith that hold us together and hope that tomorrow brings new life.

For those of us passionate about the future of the church and believe that its best days are still ahead, our moment has come for a new kind of leader. The Christian church has lost its place of privilege and respect in our culture. People are no longer flocking to hear our sermons and fill our pews. We are increasingly finding ourselves on the margin, but there is wisdom to be gained. From that position of displacement, we begin to see that the Spirit is moving in new ways. There is a gift in ministering from the margin. We might finally look at ourselves without the power and the privilege that has defined us for so long and, in the end, gain the eyes to see and ears to hear a new way forward. Our best days are still ahead.

REFLECTION QUESTIONS

1. Trimble talks about four forces in our culture and churches that shape us today: resources, technology, demographics, and governance. How do you see these forces affecting your ministry and the congregations you serve?
2. How would the congregations you serve respond to these changes? Would they adapt or try innovation in the face of them?
3. How do you see churches in desperate situations trying new innovations?
4. Is survival the most realistic narrative for our churches today or do you think, as Trimble suggests, that our best days are still ahead?

Chapter Four

Focus Points and the Work of the Congregation

John Keydel

In the decades since the emergence of intentional interim ministry, the society and culture within which local faith communities express their timeless message has been transformed. New developments in technology and communications and media and entertainment, and globalization of trade and economics, medicine, manufacturing, and retailing have all created changes, the scope, scale, and pace of which are unprecedented.

Although not always recognized or appreciated, the same change dynamics have been reflected in the practice of interim ministry. During the past forty years, interim ministry has moved away from the language of diagnosis and pathology, with the characterization of the interim as an outside interventionist, embracing modern (even postmodern!) organizational development and strategic planning. Rather than using a problem-oriented approach, we have turned toward the basic affirmations that form the foundations of appreciative inquiry. We have encountered and even begun to embrace the challenges of complexity, emotional intelligence, and the viewpoint that the real work of an intentional interim minister is not so much to be the expert from out of town as much as it is to facilitate and support the work of the congregation as it moves through a time of transition.

During these decades, other approaches to the challenge of clergy transition and congregational development have also found a home under the broad rubric of interim or transitional ministry. These range from corporate-style succession planning, to hospice care, to the very broad range of congregational redevelopment options, to addressing congregationally specific situations such as building or capital campaigns, staffing realignment, or posttraumatic ministry, to name only a few. In the right situation, all of these can be important and worthwhile developments, and several of them are taken up elsewhere in this book.

In recent years, many of these shifts have been reflected in the training of new intentional interims, as well as in the educational content of annual Interim Ministry Network (IMN) conferences and many other continuing education events. The most recent of these shifts is the move from the original language of "five developmental tasks" to the perspective of focus points, adopted by the IMN board of directors in the spring of 2012, following the lead set by their strategic partners, the Center for Congregational Health.

There were a variety of reasons for this shift, but two in particular stand out. First was the widespread and deeply held notion that anything with a name like a "developmental task" at least implied the necessity of expert supervision and was thus probably the ultimate responsibility of the professional—the interim minister—rather than being the work of the members of a congregation. In the recently revised IMN curriculum, focus points are addressed in the component "Fundamentals of Transition Ministry—the Work of the Congregation," which clearly and repeatedly stresses that the real work of the intentional interim minister is to facilitate and coach, guide and support the members and leaders of the congregation as they engage the focus points. It is the ongoing work of the congregation and its leaders that ensures the long-term effectiveness of the transition work.

The second reason for the shift was to counter the persistent belief that the five developmental tasks were meant to be addressed and accomplished in sequence. A full understanding of the work on the focus points suggests the image of a spiral, expanding as it turns, each sweep offering an enhanced perspective and creating a cumulative understanding that is both deeper and broader than can be attained through the one-time accomplishment of a list of developmental tasks. Experience further indicates that, while the order of address is not necessarily linear, there is a natural flow to the cumulative process of working with the focus points, a flow that will provide the basis for this presentation.

Alice Mann and Gil Rendle ask three core questions in their invaluable guide to congregational planning, *Holy Conversations*: "Who are we?" "Who is God calling us to be?" and "Who is our neighbor?" As readers will see, the focus points—Heritage, Mission, Connections, Leadership, and Future—offer a way for congregations to reflect on those questions and prepare for a meaningful and productive future.

HERITAGE

The movement from the developmental task of "coming to terms with history" to the Heritage focus point is far more than a semantic shift. In place of the underlying sense of conflict, guilt, and remorse implied in the developmental task, Heritage begins with recognition and awareness, and moves to affirmation and embrace of the paths that have brought the congregation to the present. Work based on the developmental task often assumed that something terrible must have happened in the congregation's past and that the congregation was apparently unable to fully disclose those difficulties, resulting in repression, denial, or worse. This assumption has given way to the recognition that history is a dynamic and creative process, and the development of a vital sense of meaning and self-awareness is the result of an ongoing process of telling and retelling a congregation's defining stories.

How does the intentional interim guide a congregation as it updates and affirms its sense of heritage? The interim, by word and example, helps the congregation to create "safe spaces," opportunities at both the personal and corporate scale that encourage the members of a congregation to remember, recognize, and articulate the defining stories of their community. These stories do more than simply recount the events of the past. They also create a broader sense of identity, meaning, and purpose. The creation of the "safe space" and the elimination of shame and blame means that all of the events of the past can be safely and respectfully explored. The shared experience of participation in an ongoing heritage is an especially important part of the process of transmitting the traditions of a congregation to new members and thus, in growing congregations. Even in those few situations where there may have been misconduct, trauma, or conflict, those events can be safely, albeit perhaps painfully, acknowledged and grieved, even as habitual patterns of emotional response are recognized and acknowledged. Fortunately, most congregations don't have haunted closets, filled with the skeletons of past traumas. This reality reminds us that the purpose of the Heritage focus point is not therapeutic catharsis, but the articulation and affirmation of a shared past, its ongoing meaning, and the sense of purpose that it can provide.

The sharing of stories can be facilitated through a range of exercises, ranging from creating and reflecting on congregational time lines to telling the stories of our personal faith journeys, from writing a detailed congregational history to holding a full-scale appreciative inquiry summit. One-on-one structured conversations with an interim or consultant, based on a consistent set of simple questions, can also be an effective and confidential, yet transparent, way of allowing the members of a congregation to share difficult events and feelings, in some cases arising decades earlier. These apparently modest processes work with such power for two reasons: The first is that the creation of a safe space, within which even the "unspeakable" may safely be spoken, allows the member's experience to be voiced, heard, and acknowledged. As any pastor, counselor, or therapist knows, this experience of sharing and being heard can have a powerful positive effect.

The second is rooted in the fact that through the telling (and retelling) of important stories, humankind practices the critical work of sense making, creating and refining a community's structure of meaning. Through intensive shared reflection on the central stories, personal and congregational core values are uncovered and the meaning of symbols and the genesis of personal and corporate habits are recalled and reinterpreted, even when they have lain dormant for years, or even decades. As the congregation's interaction with the focus points continues to unfold, these processes of sense making are strengthened, even as the attention shifts from the past to a dynamic present.

MISSION

The developmental task corresponding to the Mission focus point was "discovering a new identity." A few congregations may indeed need to develop and communicate a whole new identity, but most congregations require not a new identity, but an affirmation and behavioral continuation of the sense of direction that arose through engagement with the Heritage focus point. Unless a congregation is truly at some kind of an impasse, a "new identity" is likely to be neither "discovered" nor an organic expression of the identity of the main body of the congregation. More likely, it will be imposed, either by a small group within or by a stakeholder from outside. As a result, such a "new identity" is not likely to get much traction when the time for action arrives.

When a congregation's heritage is understood as the path that the congregation has taken to arrive at the present, the Mission focus point invites the congregation to address the ways its core values and processes can be productively and naturally extended into the future. Mission brings the historical awareness of heritage into dialogue with the congregation's contemporary expressions of its identity and core values. Given space and support, this interaction naturally discussions about the congregation's sense of vocation and vision of the future: Who are we? Where are we going? Who and what are we called to be? How will we know that we have succeeded in that mission and vision? In many congregations, this sense of mission identity is a deep sense of abiding purpose that is gradually discerned by prayer, reflection, and careful listening by the members and leaders of a congregation.

As the congregation and its leaders engage in the primary work of this focus point—clarifying identity and core values, developing mission and vision statements, and perhaps even preparing short-term tactical plans—they should be alert to the temptation of the "easy answer." Especially in times of transition, congregations and their leaders can be drawn into the hope that the familiar. "We've always done it this way" can be seen as a way to avoid the anxiety and uncertainty of an emergent future.

The intentional interim minister can work to support and facilitate this developing mission identity through faithful preaching, regular congregational newsletter articles, and ongoing conversation about the process of discerning and discussing the future direction and mission of the congregation. To have a mission is to be sent out of the present situation into the future, and full engagement with this focus point allows a congregation to set out on that journey with faith, clarity, and confidence.

CONNECTIONS

The developmental task that was the precursor to Connections was "renewing denominational links." The Center for Congregational Health defines the Connections focus point as "discovering all the relationships a faith community builds outside of itself." This definition extends well beyond denominational linkages. Indeed, in a world of high-speed telecommunications and interconnected social media, the members of most congregations regularly participate in a number of communities. Consideration of this focus point provides a wonderful opportunity for a congregation to update its technology and communications processes, to build or refine web pages, and to explore various other social media and networking options. At the same time, congregational leaders need to be reminded that effective networks encompass far more than social media and telecommunications. Effectively engaging this focus point requires that a congregation be aware of the many and varied communities that the congregation and its members participate in, and by their active engagement, help shape.

In addition to encouraging congregations to address communications patterns and resources, Connections presents a prime opportunity to create or strengthen denominational, geographic, or ministry-focused groups. Participation in community-based networks (Habitat for Humanity, community gardens, feeding ministries, and the like) provides the opportunity for congregational members to grow in their awareness of the connections that many congregations actively support, to the benefit of both the congregation and the ministry network. These may include ecumenical and interfaith, special interest, and cross-cultural groups that may function at the local, regional, national, or international level. As *Holy Conversations* asks: "Who is our neighbor?"

A congregation that fully engages Connections will find that it possesses a deep wealth of community-based assets that can be combined with a renewed sense of heritage and mission as it prepares to move into a well-connected and supported future.

LEADERSHIP

The shift from the language of the developmental task "allowing needed leadership change" to simply Leadership is another example of the expansion of scope entailed in the shift from the developmental tasks to focus points. The interpretation and application of the developmental task frequently meant that someone (usually the expert interim, perhaps with congregational and denominational input) was expected to decide what changes in the leadership of the congregation were "needed" (usually a relic of close ties to the previous pastor or the result of objectionable practices), and then act to "allow" those changes to take place. The language implied the implementation of a preconceived plan, which occasionally bore a closer resemblance to a coup d'état than to the nurturing of emergent inquiry and the development of effective congregational ministry.

The Center for Congregational Health's definition of Leadership is "reviewing the membership needs and its ways of organizing and developing new and effective leadership." This language indicates a far more expansive perspective. Through attention to the focus points already discussed, the congregation and its leaders have the opportunity to discern the kinds of leadership required for the congregation and its members to move toward fulfillment of its Mission, in light of its unique Heritage and Connections. From a pastoral and political perspective, this approach can allow a congregation to honor those who have exercised leadership in the past, while recognizing that new ideas, approaches, and relationships may be necessary as the congregation moves into the future. Furthermore, and critically, this focus point applies to the abilities, passions, and experiences of all of the congregation's leaders—lay and ordained. Thus, it encourages planning and offering programs of gift identification and leadership development, as well as in articulating clear criteria for recruiting and selecting potential candidates for both lay and ordained positions. Because the processes of leadership discernment and development are firmly rooted in the Heritage, Mission, and Connections of the congregation, the leadership that emerges is much more likely to be aligned with the aspirations and passions of the congregation. Thus, it takes into account not only who leads, but how, identifying the skills, styles, and functions that align with the congregation's sense of mission, while recognizing the reality of ever-emerging and -changing contexts and connections, both internal and external. This approach is far better than simply hoping that new leaders will come and "tell us what to do."

FUTURE

Like the other focus points, the transition from the developmental task of "commitment to new direction" to Future represents a change of outlook that is less narrowly directive and more expansive. Many congregations simply do not require an entirely new direction. They may acknowledge that a faithful response to the call of mission and the reality of their connections may require them to be innovative, but they commit themselves to a future that is rooted in a deep understanding of their heritage. Thus, the mandate is not for change per se, but for an ongoing and future-oriented expression of the congregation's core values. Re-vision of the congregation's historic purpose, reinterpreted and updated in light of current realities and circumstances, probably results not in a wholly "new direction" so much as in a faithful response to a revitalized sense of mission.

When the focus points have been effectively engaged by a congregation and its leaders, the commitment that arises through this engagement is not simple acquiescence to some lowest common denominator—a sense of resigned or passive acceptance. Rather, it carries a degree of energy and investment that translates readily into active and engaged support. The result of this commitment and energy is an emergent future, rooted in the Heritage and Mission of the congregation, open to the new things that God may be calling them to participate in and ultimately to become. That future will certainly involve new clergy and ordained leaders, but their recruitment and selection will be congruent with the work that the congregation has done with the focus points, and the "fit" of abilities, passion, experience, character, and style will ensure that the future will be energetic and positive.

A few caveats must be kept in mind, however. First, this process takes time. Before the focus points can be effectively engaged, a period of several months is usually required for even a skilled and experienced intentional interim minister to cultivate the mutual trust and respect that form an essential foundation for congregational engagement with the focus points. Trust is ultimately a personal matter, and it must be earned by faithful and congruent speech and conduct—one must "walk the talk"—especially in a congregation that may have experienced conflict, trauma, or misconduct. While trust arises as people experience the interim pastor's personal integrity, respect arises from demonstrated professionalism, especially transparency, a willingness to be held accountable, and clear and open communication. Finally, both trust and respect must be mutual, experienced and expected by both congregation and interim minister. It is on this basis that an effective emergent model must proceed.

Second, there are no predetermined outcomes from this process. The process as described is not designed to ensure a 20 percent increase in giving, the successful transition from a pastoral- to program-size parish, or any other specific goal. The congregation's work with the focus points is an explicitly emergent process, shaped by the members' exploration of their core values and deepest concerns, by their mission commitments and aspirations. All of these must also be viewed within the unique contexts of their various connections and leadership resources. Of course, in some instances, specific outcomes or results are required or desired, either by certain stakeholders (judicatory staff, congregational leaders, or special interest groups) or by the congregation at large. While occasionally desirable, or even necessary, such focused objectives are more accurately characterized as Redevelopment and should be differentiated from a process of intentional interim ministry. These objectives should be made clear from the very beginning and detailed in the contracting process.

Third, as has been stressed repeatedly, the engagement of the focus points is ultimately the work of the congregation. This fact has two primary implications. First, the intentional interim minister must be ready, willing, and able to facilitate this process with a sense of responsibility for the scope and integrity of the process, but not for the specific outcome. This is often far more difficult than it initially sounds, and the psychospiritual maturity of the interim minister is crucial. The second implication is that the discernment and articulation of the outcome, together with its ultimate implementation is, and must be, the responsibility of the congregation, which will be called upon to embody it as it moves into the future. Far from being a "one and done" process that concludes with a specific event, the work of exploring the focus points is a continuous process that positions the congregation for the next portion of its journey in faith.

In the twelfth chapter of Genesis, Abram is called to set out on a journey of transition that has shaped all of our ministry. Presaging much of the work of the intentional interim minster, he receives the Word of the Lord, which instructs him, "Go . . . to a land that I will show you" (Gen. 12:1). Abram was given no clear destination, no implementation plan, no schedule, and no guarantee of "success." Nonetheless, he responded in faith to the call of mission. For all the changes in context and form, tools and language, it may be that the process of faithful transition has not changed through the millennia as much as we might think!

REFLECTION QUESTIONS

1. In your congregation, what are the most notable stories told for each of the focus points? It may be helpful actually to list the focus points, followed by the stories or incidents that relate to each one.
2. What beliefs or values seem to be expressed through the stories? Again, list them for each story or incident.

3. How have these beliefs and values shaped the congregation's present and recent past?

4. What patterns seem to emerge from this reflection process? There may be harmony or dissonance, convergence or divergence.

5. Do some of the focus points seem to be more robust or developed than others? If so, which ones?

6. As you reflect on the focus points, how might you help the congregation prepare for an emergent and dynamic future?

7. Would such actions be consistent with the congregation's overall core values?

Chapter Five

Transitional Ministry as an Opportunity to Lead

Beverly A. Thompson and George B. Thompson, Jr.

Every fall around our neck of the woods, a few billboards and a lot of small signs stuck along roadsides announce that it is time to experience the "corn maze." Late in the growing season, when fields of cornstalks have turned autumn brown, enterprising farmers design and then cut into the fields an honest-to-goodness maze. There is an entrance point and an exit, but between them lay lots of turns and dead ends. Visitors pay to follow a handheld map, being unable to see over or between the mature stalks of corn. Numbered stations are marked on the map. The goal is to see if you can get to all of the stations—and how quickly you can come out on the other end of the maze. Incorrectly reading the map, or hurrying and missing a turn, will cost you time, and—in your zeal to finish—you might miss one of the stations. For many who enter the maze, the fun comes in the adventure—you and a few of your pals relying on your wits, along with a little luck.

CORN MAZES, LABYRINTHS, AND YOUR CHURCH

Today's world can seem like a maze to congregations that are staring transition in the face. Indeed, any one of a number of external changes in its immediate community, the economy, or society can trigger a congregational transition. All too often, congregations deal with change either by resisting or reacting rather than by responding.[1] Trying to figure out what to do is often like entering a corn maze. Church members, pastors, and denominational officials alike can find themselves walking into one dead end after another, supposing that yet one more game plan or another might lead to the other side. You think that the process will be as simple as following the maze's map, locating one station after another. By treating transition as though it were a corn maze, congregations (and those who seek to help them) end up frustrated, getting nowhere, and running out of energy.

What would happen if congregations in transition were able instead to engage their circumstances like a labyrinth walk? The ancient practice of using a labyrinth to "walk" one's prayer contrasts significantly with that of walking a maze—even though both of them involve a design laid out on the ground. Whereas the pattern of the maze is intended to challenge and perplex its users, that of the labyrinth serves the purpose of opening up the walker to new insights about self, spirit, and God. Labyrinth paths are visible, and the way to travel through them is clearly but unobtrusively evident. Often, the paths go in loops or circles and eventually bring the walker to the center, where she or he remains for moments of quiet contemplation. As the walker moves from that center around the spiraling paths, back toward the entrance, she or he carries out into the world fresh awareness, hope, and energy.

For a number of years, our interest as teachers, coaches, and writers has been to understand and articulate authentic leadership—that is, to identify how both clergy and laity can learn how to lead. It occurs to us that especially when facing transition, pastors and congregations could use the labyrinth as a metaphor for leading. Perhaps corn mazes illustrate what typically happens to congregations when they realize that things are not the way they used to be. Getting through the maze might appear daunting, so the congregation's (and denomination's) officials grab whatever map is available and start running down lanes that offer little view ahead. We are persuaded that religious communities in the twenty-first century need new paradigms, one key element of which has to do with leadership. Those who engage in the special ministry of helping congregations during pastoral transition would do well to recognize the practical value of such paradigms.

THE HEART OF LEADING TODAY

Among both practitioners and scholars these days, a fresh angle and approach toward leadership is emerging. The practice of leadership does not occur merely by virtue of holding an office, being assigned certain responsibilities, demonstrating specific skills effectively, or seeking to exert one's will over others. Instead, we believe that *leading happens when a person or committed cadre assists an organization or community in discerning and following, with integrity, a fresh vision of some common good.* Such a compact statement about this critical concept, however, veils the complexity that is encompassed. Circumstances that trigger transition often are thrust upon us, but the decisions related to discerning and following vision require enduring intentionality. In other words, the "path" leading from acknowledgment of external change to embrace of transition to new congregational vision, energy, and achievement is not a straight or simple one.[2]

Tying the notion of leadership deliberately to following a "vision of some common good" suggests the goals, tasks, and even roles involved in pastoral transitions need ongoing monitoring. As we teach seminary students and work with pastors, the two of us are aware that common, traditional ideas about leadership still prevail. All too often, church folks at all levels assume that the pastoral *role*—the office itself—carries with it sufficient *authority* that the pastor is able to exercise *power* freely, in other words, to make things happen. Actions that follow from these assumptions about office, authority, and power more often than not get pastors in trouble, particularly when such actions fail to account for the congregation's own folkways and worldview. In an interim/transitional context, these stakes are raised. Tensions and conflict that can emerge from clashes between pastoral style and church folkways very likely will divert the transitional congregation from its necessary tasks. As a result, its ability to prepare for the next phase of its life and witness becomes compromised.

Our point here is that the success of a transitional pastor in contributing to a congregation's long-term well-being depends more on things like establishing trust and respect. This is an immediate and critical transition-pastoral task that must not be overlooked—and it requires constant sensitivity to the congregation's own energy. Trust and respect foster the transitional pastor's capacity to engage the congregation's "cultural capital" effectively;[3] gaining this capacity relies on the kind of commitment and behavior that is not defined in conventional terms of authority or power. She or he thus is in a stronger position to help the congregation engage in the kind of self-discovery that contributes to its health and witness for the long run. What such self-discovery might look like will be treated broadly subsequently.

Actually, what congregations need during pastoral transitions demonstrates in a particular way what this vision-based, culturally informed, trust-centered model of leading looks like in general. Any congregation thrives with faithful vitality and effectiveness when its vision is clear, articulated, and compelling. On the one hand, the tasks and skills necessary to help a congregation thrive are not distinctive to transitions. On the other hand, what *is* distinctive in transition is heightened opportunity. Congregations, especially their officers, enter a peculiar *kairos* during a pastoral absence to review, reflect, and refocus. This "kairos" moment of being "in between" provides the transitional pastor an opportunity to lead—to help "an organization or community discern and follow a fresh vision of some common good, with integrity." Three fresh concepts in particular have proven to us to be useful in gaining fresh clarity about the nature of transition and its potential for leadership. These three are "open-systems" thinking, an open-systems view of "growth and decline," and a nuanced but rich definition of "culture."

CONCEPTS FOR REDEFINING LEADERSHIP

Most of us reading this book grew up in a world in which people did not give a second thought to what kind of organizational paradigm permeated our thinking. The emergence of large corporations by the late nineteenth century led to the development and widespread application of a style of business that now is taken for granted. Specialized positions requiring specific training and experience; organizational charts defining hierarchical relationships, responsibilities, and accountability; the use of meetings for making decisions; documentation through minutes, reports, and memoranda; and other features of corporate life have become familiar to American society in general. Their influence as norms is readily recognizable in the way that governmental agencies and many religious denominations function, especially beyond the parish or local congregation.

This model of organizational life, sometimes identified in scholarly literature as the "rational system" approach,[4] focuses mainly inwardly: it assumes a "closed system." In a closed system, what receives an organization's primary energies are those elements that are within the direct control of the organization itself. Even variations of this bureaucratic, corporate model tend to function as closed systems.

In more recent decades, however, newer models of organizational life take account in a central way how an organization relates to its given *environment*. These open systems models are based on the principle that no organization can exist or continue indefinitely without intentionally considering the fundamental influence of the context in which the organization finds itself. When something in an organization's context changes, it creates a ripple effect on that organization, one that should not be ignored. In many respects, today's world is defined by change, much of it rapid—whether technological, social, or political. An open systems model is better suited for explaining what happens to organizations in our sometimes unstable world.

Think, for instance, of faith communities that were established in neighborhoods of large American cities. What happens to a congregation founded by, say, German-speaking Protestants, who after thirty years or so proudly construct a lovely stone building at a time when everyone in the neighborhood was "like them"? Years go by, the grandchildren of the German founders move to the suburbs, land values around the church begin to soften, and families from other continents speaking unfamiliar languages begin to move in. What are the aging members of this once-proud congregation to do? Urban neighborhoods all across America continue to experience dramatic changes like this one. The churches in such neighborhoods have virtually no control over what is going on around them, and yet the change influences them undeniably.

Shifting away from attending mainly to the organization's closed system to exploring its integral relationship with its context (open system) can help congregations think more realistically about engaging transition. Changes in a church's environment can appear dramatic, as in urban neighborhoods, but they also emerge more subtlety, too. Think, for instance, how distinctly different the world has been experienced by various generations: the Silents, who came of age in the 1940s and benefited from the postwar economic boom; the Boomers, whose idealism prompted civil unrest in the 1960s and feeds the polarization of national politics; the Xers, super tech savvy, who find a more expensive, complicated society than the one in which their grandparents grew up. Generational differences are only one of several ways in which environment changes. An interim period between pastors offers the congregation a chance to take a hard look at all the things that could be affecting its world.

Growing out of the concept of open systems is a second concept worth identifying. When churches think and talk about "growth" and "decline," they are usually referring to numbers. How many people attend Sunday services, go to Sunday school or educational programs, participate in youth ministry activities, pledge money to the budget, and so forth? How much money is coming in? How large are the facilities? How many more computers does the office staff need? What will it cost to replace the HVAC system? Clearly, keeping track of things that can be measured does have a certain value for congregations. However, in an open systems view, a different kind of question is even more critical: "How might changes in our world affect our vision and mission?"

This question redefines what we mean by "growth" and "decline." From the first concept—open systems—congregations learn to keep asking, "What's happening in our world?" This question opens up church members to begin to think about growth and decline in a different way. Instead of being based on numbers, growth and decline is a fluid notion, to be understood in terms of *the capacity of an organization to respond when the environment becomes unpredictable or to maintain its strength when the environment is steady.*[5] Typically, well-established congregations pay only modest attention to changes around them; they believe that because of satisfaction over their past successes, they can weather anything. While they suppose that their current strength can ride out a shifting environment, congregations at this point actually begin to erode, even if numbers still appear sound. This is a common but dangerous attitude, since it exposes a lack of capacity for responding to change. Thus, decline is under way, even before it is numerically obvious.

A third and newer concept for helping to reframe transitional ministry has to do with the rich world of *culture*. In common use, the word "culture" often is used to refer to things like classical music and art—as in "She has cultured taste." However, we are using the term in a different way here—to take into account features of congregational life that are both rich and subtle. When human beings set up communities (of every kind), culture is one of the results. It both expresses and preserves the community's world and life.

Simply stated, culture can be thought of in the broadest of terms, as "shared meaning and behavior."[6] Styles of dress, foods, expected behaviors, types of acceptable relationships, stories used to define the community, and the like all become woven into a tapestry of particular culture. Even beyond these more recognizable forms, however, culture also involves rich, almost cryptic, elements of meaning. These deeply held beliefs, submerged as they are below the surface of ready awareness, hold the community's energy and are the key to its own distinctive folkways. All of the observable elements of any culture are intricately tied, often in mysterious ways, to its submerged beliefs.[7]

We believe that anyone who seeks to lead must become an astute detective of culture. Paying attention to a congregation's specific cultural elements slowly but surely offers perceptive insights, illuminating congregational behavior in a way that nothing else can. The two of us have written at some length about how to use culture as an ally in congregational transition.[8] We ignore culture only to our frustration and failure.

RETHINKING RESULTS

These three concepts—adopting an open systems perspective, measuring growth and decline by the capacity to respond to change, and attending to the multifaceted world of culture—open up a new kind of paradigm from which to view the many complexities of congregational life. Using this paradigm, we can begin to appreciate why pastoral transitions hold such potential for authentic leadership. Hence, the two of us are proposing that the best possible outcomes for a congregation in pastoral transition would look something like the following.

Explore its own culture for the presence of "peculiar" forms of deep energy that will both support and impede the congregation in following its vision. Every congregation's life consists of some elements that also are recognizable in other congregations, as well as other elements that derive from its own specific history, context, and experience. Whatever they are, all of these elements survive because they become connected to the congregation's deeply grounded cultural foundation. The two of us have seen how beneficial it is for congregations to walk through a process of discovering the idiosyncratic nature of their own deep energy. The insights from such a discovery are powerful and long lasting; key among their benefits is to integrate them into the ongoing reflective and decision-making rhythms of the congregation's life. Transitional pastors are in a pivotal position for assisting congregations in developing this style of cultural attentiveness.

Re imagine and affirm a new, or fresh version of, congregational vision, by attending more deliberately not only to the congregation's internal characteristics but also to its external realities . "Vision" is a word that religious people use frequently but not necessarily with sufficient understanding. Vision represents, to use Lovett Weems's helpful phrase, "a picture of a preferred future,"[9] some ideal condition or way of being that captivates the community. Framed in this way, the value of vision is in calling the community ahead, toward something spiritually desirable that is yet to be.

It is possible that the vast majority of today's existing congregations came into being without any deliberate attention to vision. In many cases, however, a thoughtful review of its history (but not relying only on memories of longtime members) will yield clues to some significant theological and religious embers from its past. These can be rekindled as the congregation brings them into fruitful interaction with a renewed awareness of its context. What results from this kind of discovery is a "fresh version" of the particular congregation's vision.

Learn how to balance creatively the congregation 's attention to issues of long-term effectiveness and flexibility with attention to institutional needs that are short term and provide stability . Congregations tend to think primarily about shorter-term issues (e.g., budget, facilities maintenance, Sunday school teachers, etc.), often leaving longer-term decisions (vision clarity and strength, relationships with neighborhood, authentic assimilation of new members, congregation-wide spiritual development, etc.) to nebulous—if even deemed necessary—discussions for the future. Yet, keeping an eye on the future of church life and witness is part of what a clear and strong vision stimulates. Even so, vision by itself does not solve all of a church's challenges: it also brings all the various long-term functions and goals into tension with the short-term ones. Such tension is natural and cannot be avoided—although when it occurs, it sometimes is not recognized for what it represents. The point is not to make the tension "go away" but rather to help the congregation learn to interpret what the tension means within its current life. A cultural perspective on the congregation brings new insight to the idea that the conflict is not the issue. Congregations that learn how to practice this kind of discernment during their transitional period are better prepared to stay focused on vision when their next pastor arrives.

These three stated outcomes are more likely to occur if those who seek to lead are, as the Tao Te Ching suggests, both "soft" and "strong." Though water is soft and fluid, it "will wear away rock, which is rigid and cannot yield."[10] That is, the wise leader does not push against the resistance to change. Instead, she or he will learn to pay close attention, listening deeply—flowing like a gentle stream rather than fighting the rapids of resistance. The Tao claims that "if the leader were not like water, the leader would break. The ability to be soft makes the leader a leader."[11] This insight has numerous implications for the transitional pastor's way of handling his or her own discomfort, as well as that of the congregation's.

TRANSITION TASKS FOR LEADING

To lead the congregation toward these three named outcomes, the transitional pastor must recognize and oversee particular tasks. These tasks encompass the several issues affecting organizational transition that an open systems, cultural perspective on congregations suggests. In brief, these tasks follow:

- **To help to create conditions for the congregation to name the truth about itself.** In any transition, congregations benefit so much when they reflect carefully and intently enough about themselves to be able to come to terms with their real-life conditions. One way to do this is through exploring three simple but probing questions: Who are we (identity)? Why are we here (purpose)? Who is our neighbor/might our neighbor be (context)?[12] A discovery process based on the model outlined in this chapter yields similar insights, in a way in which congregational stakeholders do not feel judged or threatened.[13] This kind of breakthrough is a key to the congregation's strength, so undertaking it during pastoral transition can make all the difference in the long run.
- **To help manage members' apprehensions as the congregation begins to realize that it has entered "in-between times."** If they are to thrive, both individuals and communities need some measure of stability. Declining organizations usually resist anything they perceive as a threat to the status quo. Yet positive movement during any transition is not possible without the apple cart getting upset at least a little.[14] Transitional pastors realize that the anxiety represents the fear of the congregation losing not only the artifacts, but also those deeply held beliefs that represent the congregation's earlier successes. Preparing them for such apprehension, and not becoming the messenger who is "killed," can be a transitional pastor's most strenuous task, sometimes a desert through which both pastor and congregation travel toward the Promised Land.
- **To help the congregation discern a shared vision .** Because vision is so central to organizational vitality, creating momentum and clarity about vision is a key transitional task. Congregations in organizational and cultural decline do not realize that their next pastorate will work better if they do their vision work first. In transition, they might be capable of identify-

ing only a "fuzzy," rather than a "clear," vision[15] —but this much progress still can be useful. A transitional pastor is prepared to help the congregation walk through such a process.

- **To help the congregation take initial steps for following its fresh vision** . All too often, statements of vision—or even of mission—get produced, published—and then ignored. Yet, as Alfred North Whitehead once said, "Ideas won't keep. Something must be done about them."[16] Congregations that use their fresh vision to experiment with new ideas for worship, nurture, outreach, and the like can create momentum and confidence. A transitional pastor serves the congregation by assisting it in its experimentation and evaluation of new things. Learning how to review and decide what to continue and what to drop or revise will reinforce a valuable congregational skill.

- **To anticipate and help the congregation to handle its own natural resistance to changes that result from following fresh vision** . In this approach, resistance to change is seen as natural and typical. It should not be treated, as usually happens, as an occasion that polarizes the congregation. To lead, the transitional pastor keeps helping congregational officers and members to reframe what is happening. At the same time, however, officers need to be aware that not everyone will choose to stay. The goal in a congregational transition is not to keep everyone happy but to move into a new, divinely led future with clarity and grace.

As we hope you realize by now, undertaking these several transitional tasks calls for a distinct pastoral style. Such a style reminds us of the Tao Te Ching's comments about leadership as a midwife:

> The wise leader does not intervene unnecessarily. The leader's presence is felt, but often the group runs itself. . . . Do not intrude. Do not control. Do not force your own needs and insights into the foreground. . . . Imagine that you are a midwife; you are assisting at someone else's birth.[17]

Midwives realize that the energy required for the desired outcome resides not in themselves but in the one who is giving birth. Midwifing offers an instructive metaphor for leading during congregational transitions.

SKILLS AND DISPOSITIONS FOR THE TRANSITIONAL PASTOR

In the context of transitional ministry, then, what might midwifing look like? We believe that it will focus on certain dispositions, interweaving the capacities of learning and listening, engaging, attending, and discovering.

Learning and Listening

Listening is no simple task. Interim pastors and denominational officials have heard churches say all too often: "We've never done it this way; we just want to get on with this search and get our real pastor." All too often, congregations get impatient—and even fearful—about this in-between time. Yet it is through a disposition of deeply listening to members and officers that the transitional pastor learns more about the congregation—and therefore helps the congregation to learn more about itself. Both parties learn to pay attention not only to words but also to the intensity of what words might be masking. It is within the congregation's hidden, shared beliefs that the transitional pastor helps members to uncover their deep energy. She or he must deliberately withhold opinions and conclusions, allowing the members sometimes to wrestle through their uncertainty to greater insight and awareness.

Engaging

The congregation must sense that the transitional pastor is with them, has joined them on this journey, this labyrinth walk that at times might seem aimless or silly. Participating in church meals, picnics, and special events; visiting various church groups and auxiliaries; preaching sermons that comfort and affirm a community in uncertainty—these kinds of pastoral activities help develop the "cultural capital" necessary to walk together with the congregation through its wilderness. Beyond these wise, general pastoral tasks, the transitional pastor goes a step further. Without engaging a congregational team in a process of discovery, the transitional pastor is merely sending them into a maze. Instead, he or she should invite them, figuratively speaking, to walk a labyrinth. One technique for engaging them in such a walk is to pose big questions rather than jump in with answers every time a question is raised. Other techniques and practices are developed in our book, *Grace for the Journey: Practices and Possibilities for In-Between Times.*[18]

Attending

As the midwife metaphor suggests, the transitional pastor cannot bear the congregation's baby. It is the work of the members, as they enter the labyrinth of their future, to recognize the new life growing in their midst—and to prepare for its arrival. At times, they will need technical support with processes that at times might seem unnecessary. At other times, they will need old-fashioned spiritual encouragement. The effective transitional pastor's behavior, language, and overall disposition is as one who knows what is involved in the entire process, yet whose strategic contributions come along the sidelines.

Discovering

This chapter is based on the premise that every congregation in a transition must learn how to discover new insights about itself, over and over again. For this to happen, the congregation's transitional pastor must be skilled in, and committed to, group process. Here is where this chapter's shift in paradigms becomes most challenging, as members at times will prefer for the rubber band to snap back to its familiar shape. The disposition to engage, discussed above, is a "people" skill that during transitional ministry must be balanced with the essential need for discovery, which is a "task" skill. Here, the congregation's task is to unearth its deep energy, to face the often subtle danger of decline, and to relate in new ways to its wider community. This kind of work can be challenging and seem threatening. Transitional pastors must be prepared internally to manage the congregation's, and her or his own, anxiety in the midst of such discovery.[19]

"HOW LONG, O LORD?"

According to conventional wisdom, interim pastorates are thought to be most effective if they last between twelve and eighteen months. From the open systems, culture-based perspective of this chapter, transitional ministry requires more time. As with every other organization or community, religious culture does not change readily. What congregations have a difficult time realizing is how their unhealthy patterns go unexamined, thus assuring that they will be repeated. It is better for the congregation to take more time for an interim period—to treat it as the transition that it can become—especially following difficult circumstances or events. Transitional pastors who seek to lead need to take the long view and use specific skills to assist the congregation with the tasks that we have named here.

Transition offers a special opportunity for the congregation to nourish its collective spirit. The energy required to think, learn, decide, and behave in new ways activates the members' minds, emotions, and wills—but it rightfully goes further. Pastoral transition offers the congregation a deeply spiritual opportunity, whether the members initially perceive it as such or not. Especially for churches further in decline, the period between pastors offers the congregation its best chance to be revitalized, even transformed. New energy that emerges as renewal begins will feed the congregation's spiritual life and witness.

Judicatories that understand the need for rethinking transitional ministry will revise some of their practices and policies. In call traditions, judicatories will encourage, and sometimes require, two to three years between called pastors, or will opt for modified call processes designed for such purposes. Appointment traditions could add a specialized appointment process, designed for situations in which judicatory officials recognize issues of congregational transition (misconduct, conflict, death of pastor or other tragedy, etc.). Establishing new structures and processes would demonstrate the judicatory's commitment to the opportunity for authentic congregational renewal. In other words, the denomination recognizes the "kairos moment" of transition, during which authentic pastoral leadership could be exercised.

CHOOSING THE LABYRINTH AND THE MIDWIFE

The pleasure and reward of transition depends in part on traveling it with others. A community of faith cannot find its new day simply by letting one or two people make the decisions. Like navigating a maze, making a journey through transition calls forth your "wits"—that is, a capacity for being alert and focused on the task. Too, like the passage through the maze, this journey will lead to an unexpected turn or two.

Unlike mastering the maze, however, successfully working through transitions depends not on luck, but on grace. Thus, as with entering a labyrinth, a transition must be entered with expectancy, coupled with the conviction that the God who created us in the first place continues to lead and offer us new life. Transitional pastors hence serve (pardon the mix of metaphors) as midwives through the labyrinth. They help the congregation redefine and reframe what it faces, thus preparing it to give birth to something new and wonderful.

Such an opportunity carries much promise for authentic leadership. We trust that those who seek to assist congregations in transition will also seek to lead them. Through such an experience, pastor and congregation alike can continue to learn more about what it means to be God's people.

NOTES ON REFLECTION AND PRACTICE

Our book, *Grace for the Journey: Practices and Possibilities for In-Between Times*, contains a number of spiritual practices that are designed for use in congregational transition. This book is cited in this chapter's endnotes and elaborates on a number of the ideas here, although organized a little differently.

On the three stated outcomes of transitional ministry:

- Exploring the congregation's culture: See *Grace for the Journey*, chapter 2, "Naming Your Energy: Discovery and Truth-Telling," and chapter 4, "Digging Even Deeper: Sources of Congregational Energy." These two chapters engage a simple but powerful tool for beginning the congregation's cultural discovery.

- Developing fresh vision in light of both internal and external realities: Two simple processes can help jump-start the kind of conversation out of which vision may emerge. These two are the church walkaround and the neighborhood walkaround, both explained in *Grace for the Journey*, 43–45.
- Creatively balancing short-term results with long-term effectiveness: Today's congregations—in light of continuing changes at the local, national, and worldwide scales—often end up majoring in the minors. They tend to focus on maintaining familiar, comfortable things and are skeptical about new ideas or talk about the future. To keep the long term in focus, train yourself to ask the governing board and other church leaders questions that provoke conversation beyond the day-to-day details. Use their responses to build awareness of the need for a clear purpose that drives the details. Resist giving them "answers." Instead, stimulate their thinking with questions like "What might God's call on this church look like for the next ten years?" and "How do the changes you see in our world today help you imagine what God might be nudging this church to become?"

On the five transitional tasks: Most of the transitional tasks are addressed in *Grace for the Journey*. Vision discernment often is more challenging than it first seems. There is no simple, straight-line way to help a church move outside of its own comfort zone long enough to talk about where the church might be headed. The transitional pastor can help the congregation become clearer about its vision. For more details on process, consult George's book, *Futuring Your Church: Finding Your Vision and Making It Work*.

On skills and dispositions of the transitional pastor as midwife:

- Discuss in one of your first meetings with the congregation's governing board the congregation's experience with difficult experiences. To help board members become aware of what these situations represent in the church's life, ask open-ended questions (i.e., questions that cannot be answered with a yes or no) to move more deeply into the stories. Encourage leaders as much as possible to use descriptive, neutral language as a discipline for analysis and insight.
- Build upon board members' growing insights about the congregation to help them identify ways to deal with new things. What issues might arise during the pastoral transition period that might spark congregational anxiety? How can the board members use their knowledge of, and participation in, congregational life to provide a safe space during uncertainty?
- Design with the governing board a "covenant ceremony" for the transition period. Prepare appropriately and share that ceremony together. Be alert for other opportunities to use the ceremony in the congregation at large.

Help the board "own" the ceremony as a particular expression of this congregation's style and commitment.

- For you as the transitional pastor: How do you take care of yourself? Make a few quiet moments and write notes to yourself about your habits and rhythms—sleep, diet, exercise, spiritual nurture, work, and relationships. What healthy practices do you use for relaxing? How do you step back and keep focused on the bigger picture of what you seek to accomplish in your ministry?

Chapter Six

Leadership Transition within Immigrant and African American Churches

Bianca Duemling

In each cultural context leadership transition within churches is handled differently. Whereas transitional ministry is common in European American mainline churches, historically in neither immigrant churches[1] nor African American[2] churches is transitional ministry widely used. Additionally, the complexity of tradition, history, culture, social context, and minority status in a society has to be taken into account when analyzing leadership transition. No one model or framework fits all. Nevertheless, there are some patterns or common threads of leadership transition within immigrant churches and African American churches. The main focus of this chapter is on immigrant churches in the wider Protestant context and their models of leadership transition. Because African American churches are such a crucial part of the Christian landscape of the United States, I also will reflect on leadership transition within their context.

LEADERSHIP TRANSITION WITHIN IMMIGRANT CHURCHES

In the past five decades immigrant churches have been emerging all over the country. The Immigration and Nationality Act of 1965 and the following changes in immigration policies have been opening doors for an influx of new immigrants.[3] Most of these immigrants are Christians and form their own fellowships and churches.[4] In addition, immigrants from traditionally non-Christian countries who converted to Christianity in the United States attend these churches.[5] For example, roughly 75 percent of Korean

Americans and one-third of Chinese Americans are Christians, and most of them attend immigrant churches.[6] In Greater Boston, worship services are held in more than thirty languages representing more than 110 nationalities.[7]

Immigrant churches are primarily founded by individuals with a vision to provide a worship space for their people living in Diaspora. In many cases, the congregation's centeredness around the founding pastor or group is one among the many challenges immigrant churches face when handing over leadership to the next pastor. This challenge increases if the next generation to whom leadership is handed grew up in the United States. The culture of immigrant churches is also different from European American churches in other ways. The immigrant identity and experience, the disrupted paths of life, and the distance from family networks and cultural traditions affect the church culture and inform leadership practices.

Culture and the way culture affects leadership are complex. My frame of reference when discussing how culture affects leadership is the work of Geert Hofstede, a Dutch social psychologist, who did a pioneering study of cultures across modern nations. In his extensive research he has identified six cultural dimensions that affect society and hence, organizations and leadership.[8]

1. Power distance expresses the degree to which the less powerful members of a society accept and expect that power is distributed unequally, thus agreeing with an existing hierarchical order.
2. Individualism versus collectivism refers to whether people's self-image is defined in terms of "I" or "we" and how this affects their decision-making structure.
3. Masculinity versus femininity refers to whether a society at large is more competitive or more consensus oriented.
4. Uncertainty avoidance expresses the degree to which the members of a society feel uncomfortable with uncertainty and ambiguity.
5. Long-term versus short-term orientation reflects a society's search for virtue. Societies with a short-term orientation are generally normative in their thinking and have a strong concern with establishing the absolute Truth. In societies with a long-term orientation, people believe that truth depends very much on situation, context, and time. They show an ability to adapt traditions to changed conditions.
6. Indulgence versus restraint defines whether a society allows relatively free gratification or suppresses gratification and regulates it by means of strict social norms.[9]

Although leadership transition is a pressing issue in U.S. churches, few studies focusing on immigrant churches and leadership transition are available. Therefore, this chapter is based primarily on my experience working with immigrant churches over the past decade as well as on interviews with leaders of Haitian, Chinese, Korean, Cambodian, Indian, African (Liberian), and Hispanic immigrant churches in Greater Boston. The leaders interviewed are well connected among their people and can speak on behalf of the broader community. The analysis focuses on common tendencies within immigrant churches that transcend ethnic and cultural particularities.

THE CONTEXT AND CHALLENGES OF IMMIGRANT CONGREGATIONS

Migration, voluntary or not, dramatically affects all people who leave their home countries. It creates vulnerability and a vacuum in people's lives as they leave their families and their cultural and social contexts. Immigrant churches are established to meet spiritual but also emotional, social, and practical needs. They are a "home away from home." Within the Christian Diaspora, immigrant churches function as the most influential ethnic public sphere as well as places of worship.[10] In a nutshell, immigrant churches "provide the physical and social spaces in which those who share the same traditions, customs and languages can reproduce many aspects of their native cultures for themselves and attempt to pass them on to their children."[11] Immigrants also start their own churches because they are often excluded from existing congregations.[12] The experience of discrimination can be extreme. For example, a West African immigrant was denied the opportunity to shake hands during the passing of the peace, and another said that no one sat in his pew, which made him feel awkward. However, most discrimination is more subtle; for example, immigrants are welcomed as members but not granted any leadership responsibilities. Such an experience adds to their daily experience of exclusion, power imbalance, and discrimination, which increases the desire for a safe environment among fellow countrymen and -women.

The struggle to survive in a new, unfamiliar country inherent in an immigrant experience is one of the many challenges immigrant churches face. I have identified three major challenges that affect leadership transition: lack of financial and human resources, generational differences, and social and cultural diversity within monolingual and mono-ethnic churches.

Lack of Financial and Human Resources

Although many immigrants are educated, they often cannot find work in their professions due to a lack of language skills or recognition of their degrees. Despite working hard, they struggle to provide for their families. Financial challenges of individual members affect the ability of the congregation to purchase or even rent their own facilities. Moreover, they cannot financially support their pastor; therefore, many immigrant pastors are bivocational.

Lack of consistent meeting space and limited pastoral availability make it difficult to build stable organizational structures and invest in leadership development within the congregation. Additionally, immigrant communities tend to be transient and work varied hours, preventing members from exercising committed leadership, which again hinders congregational stability and growth.

The challenge is to increase financial and human resources that enable the church to build up a functional and stable organizational structure that can exist independently from a single pastor who is holding the congregation together. Such stability would in turn provide the congregational support and sustainability necessary before handing over leadership.

Generational Differences

Generational challenges within immigrant churches transcend ethnic groups. The parents' struggle for survival often leaves no time for understanding and addressing the challenges their children face. The children have to navigate the cultural values and expectations of their parents on the one hand and deal with the pressure of school and the American culture of their peers on the other. As immigrant churches primarily serve the needs of parents, the emotional needs of the young people are often neglected. In addition, many young people lack sufficient knowledge of their parents' native tongue to completely participate in the congregation's life. These challenges often result in the "Silent Exodus," which journalist Helen Lee describes: "At an alarming rate, many young believers . . . are now choosing to leave not only their home churches, but possibly their Christian faith as well."[13]

The challenge is to increase understanding of each generation's worldview and integrate the different needs into one congregation. Integrating the second generation into the immigrant congregation will provide a better foundation for survival beyond the first generation.

Social and Cultural Diversity within Monolingual or Mono-Ethnic Congregations

Although monolingual or mono-ethnic congregations look very homogeneous from the outside, they are socially and culturally diverse on the inside. Hispanic congregations, for example, often consist of members from different Latin American countries and cultures who like different kinds of food and worship styles. Conflicts easily arise if members perceive that the pastor favors people from his home country.

Members of Indian congregations share the same nationality but might not share the same mother tongue and tribal tradition, as they may come from different parts of India. Additionally, cultural differences exist between the more established immigrants and new arrivals. Even if they share the same language and nationality, an earlier immigrant's cultural values may be based on a home country of fifty years ago, whereas recent immigrants' values will be rooted in a more developed and modernized country. The challenge is to acknowledge and value the different cultures and their needs within an immigrant church that appears from the outside to be homogeneous. Otherwise, a leadership transition can easily lead to a split of the congregation along ethnic or tribal lines.

Although these challenges are common, they are experienced differently depending on the specific context of a congregation, as well as on how established a congregation and its members are. Mark Mullin, professor for Asian Studies, points out that immigrant churches go through a life cycle, and the degree of challenges a congregation faces varies depending on which stage the congregation is in. During the first stage, the needs of primarily the first generation are met, as the services and activities are dominated by the language and clergy from the old country. Individuals, hence the congregation as a whole, are often still very vulnerable and struggling to survive. Therefore, the challenges of immigrant churches in this first stage are closely connected to the lack of financial and human resources. During the second stage, congregations are more established, and organizational changes are made. For example, bilingual leaders are recruited and English ministries are launched. In this stage the immigrant churches are more likely to address the generational challenges. The third stage is marked by large-scale assimilation into the institutions of the host society as well as members' greater access to higher education and the job market, and, eventually, a certain degree of cultural assimilation.[14] At this stage the above described challenges are still present but not as essential as in the two earlier stages.

ORGANIZATIONAL STRUCTURES WITHIN IMMIGRANT CHURCHES

The organizational structure of immigrant churches—the decision-making structure, the governance structure, and leadership styles—depends on how a congregation was founded and developed, as well as its cultural background and denominational tradition. Most of the immigrant churches grow organically from relational networks, such as prayer groups or family-based gatherings. Either immigrant pastors receive their pastoral calls out of a secular job through which they serve their people in the Diaspora, or they are appointed by a group of people to spiritually lead the group. Gatherings start in people's homes, and then groups share church buildings or rent storefront shops. In the past few years churches and denominations are increasingly planting immigrant churches in a strategic fashion. Teams are commissioned and sent out with a given organizational structure. However, the majority of churches are developing relationally and organically.

There are three basic organizational structures observable within immigrant churches. Structures may be based on the senior pastor or a board or key church committee, or have a denominational focus.

Organizational Structure Based on the Senior Pastor

When the organizational structure is centered on the senior pastor, in most cases he or she is the founding pastor of the congregation and has a very specific vision for the ministry. The founding pastor gathers confidants or family members around him or her to grow and lead the church. The pastor holds the primary decision-making power and determines the direction and actions of the congregation. The structure is hierarchical and common within cultures with a high level of power distance.

Organizational Structure Focused on the Board[15]

Within a board-focused leadership structure, the power is not concentrated in a single person but rather in a tight-knit group of people. Helen R. Ebaugh and Janet S. Chafetz, professors of sociology, point out that immigrant religious institutions "were founded and built by groups of lay members who, in most cases, maintain substantial control over their institutions in later years. . . . In most cases, clergy were originally recruited by a group of lay members who had already established some sort of religious group or formal organization."[16] Lay leaders' ability to maintain control is enhanced, intentionally or unintentionally, by giving a pastor only time-limited contracts, which is common in such a leadership structure.

This model demonstrates a high level of participation and care for the congregation and, to a certain degree, shared decision-making power, depending on who is allowed onto the board. This organizational structure is not a congregational model where the entire membership calls a pastor or votes on key issues. Instead, the leadership is shared by just a few people. Depending on the maturity of a board, unhealthy dynamics can develop if board members have too much power and micromanage the pastor. Such a power imbalance or power distance is especially challenging for the pastor if the cultural background of the immigrant church is more hierarchical, but the power structure is reversed in the congregation.

Denomination-Focused Organizational Structure

The polity and doctrines of a denomination affect the organizational structure of a congregation. Some denominations have a loose structure, so the local church can make all decisions, while others are more rigid and leadership succession is laid out in the denominational polity. Immigrant churches can be connected to a denomination in either the United States or in their homeland. Some denominations, such as the Church of the Nazarene or the Presbyterian Church, have integrated immigrant churches into their structures. Another example is the Calvin Synod of the United Church of Christ, which is a nongeographic body comprising churches from the Hungarian Reformed Church.[17] Others, such as the Assemblies of God or the Christian and Missionary Alliance, have ethnic-based districts.

These organizational structures are described as "pure" models, but in practice, the structures can also be blended. For example, a denomination's organizational structure can be implemented with a focus on either a senior pastor or a board. Over time, leadership styles and structures can also adapt and develop. This can lead to tensions and contradictions between local churches and denominations, whether the denomination is based in the United States or in their homeland. One example is that in many Indian denominations, women and men historically sit separately from each other. This tradition is difficult to keep up in the North American context, especially for second-generation American Indians.

Each structure poses different challenges, depending on the specific context. However, neither the traditional organizational structures used in their homeland nor the American structures or traditions seem to be adequate for the unique situation of immigrant churches. Congregations are at once trying to preserve their cultural heritage and adapt to the host country. Few pastors are well prepared for leading an immigrant church, as neither seminary education in the homeland nor in the United States prepares pastors for the realities and unique challenges of immigrant churches.

UNIQUE CHALLENGES REGARDING THE IMMIGRANT PASTOR

There are unique challenges for an immigrant pastor that affect leadership transitions differently from those in European American churches. All pastors have to navigate a wide range of expectations from their members, but for immigrant pastors the challenges are significantly higher. The demands, needs, and vulnerability of the members of immigrant churches are often connected to emotional, social, and physical survival in a foreign country. The difficulties in raising their own children, the experience of discrimination, the struggle to pay the bills, and even the fear of deportation, along with the high demands members place on their pastors, all create significant stress. In some cases, a pastor is treated as a superhero who has all the answers for practical and spiritual problems. In Latino churches, for example, members view the pastor as a trustworthy father figure and seek him out

for guidance and emotional support in every possible matter. In his study on
Indian American churches, Raymond Brady Williams, emeritus professor in
the humanities, summarizes the reality of these immigrant pastors:

> The religious specialists for the immigrant church become not only symbolic
> mediators between earth and heaven, but also practical mediators between
> India and the United States, between parents and children, between the reli-
> giosity of an Indian past and the secularity of the American present, and
> between Christian immigrants and other churches.[18]

Another challenge for congregations is that immigration often involves a
loss of status, as former education and social identity have a decreased value
in the new American context. A leadership position in the church might offer
the only possibility for increasing one's own social status. This reality can be
very challenging for a congregation if pastors and other people in leadership
tie their individual social promotion or personal agenda to a church office.
The focus is then shifted from building the kingdom of God to building a
personal kingdom.

Another common issue regarding immigrant pastors has to do with the
difficulty they have retiring. There are several reasons for leadership transition. Perhaps the pastor is moving on, he is asked to go, or he dies. But often,
the pastor retires. In many Western countries pastors retire in their midsixties
and receive a pension from their denomination or congregation. However,
retirement and pension plans are not very common among immigrant
churches. A prevalent mental model among pastors of immigrant churches is
to "die with your shoes on." Thus, they serve their congregations until they
are too sick or die. Moreover, many first-generation immigrants work hard
and live sacrificially to secure a future for their children, so provision for
their own retirement is not a priority. This mental model is reflected in how
the congregations provide for their pastors. If the church employs a pastor, it
rarely includes a retirement package. As many pastors have no means to
provide for their living after leaving the church and their salary behind, they
tend to serve as long as possible. Such a tendency affects the process of
leadership transition, because it is motivated by the personal agenda of the
pastor and not what is best for the whole congregation. Furthermore, it influences the relationship with possible emerging leaders within the congregation and affects their leadership development, as they could be a threat to the
pastor's position.

The expectations of the members, an idealized perception of the pastor,
the pastor's desire for social validation and respect, and the unwillingness or
inability of the pastor to retire put pressure on the relationship between
clergy and laity. Additionally, unclear decision-making structures and the
pastor's dependency on a board can create an unhealthy environment for both

the congregation and the pastor. The environment can also be shaped by the personal agendas of lay leaders. These factors prevent constructive and honest dialogue regarding the future direction of the church and make it difficult to constructively address the issue of leadership transition.

TRANSITIONAL MINISTRY AND IMMIGRANT CHURCHES

Although different approaches to leadership transition can be found among immigrant churches, interim or transitional ministry is not a common one. The first reason is logistical. Effective transitional ministry depends on having an accessible pool of interim ministers provided by the respective denomination. Once a pastor leaves the church, the denomination sends an interim pastor who leads the congregation through the transition and helps them find a new permanent pastor. This process is not possible for many immigrant churches due to a general lack of indigenous leadership, particularly in traditionally non-Christian countries. Moreover, many immigrant churches are nondenominational and are not connected to a denominational structure that would provide interim pastors. In addition, immigrant churches often belong to very relational cultures, where the pastor is a key figure who needs to be known and trusted. It would be difficult to invite someone in for a short period of time. In case of a pastoral vacancy, either the congregation is run by the board until a new pastor is appointed, or the board invites pastors from other congregations to preach on Sundays. Generally, the pastors who enter the pulpit of a church in transition have personal connections to the congregation and are often already known by at least some of its members.

Although immigrant churches do not often use interim pastors or transitional specialists, transition in leadership is always a critical time for a congregation. Ideally, leadership transition is well planned ahead of time, and the pastor and congregation agree on the process. In new immigrant cultures, however, survival is often a defining element not only for individual members but for the whole congregation. Therefore, the focus of immigrant churches is mainly on immediate needs, such as obtaining a worship space or assisting members in need. Developing a long-term vision or a succession plan, especially if the congregation is not yet fully established, is not one of their priorities. In times of transition this drive for survival as well as the crucial role of the pastor can easily lead to a disintegration of the whole congregation and scatter the members, especially if the pastor did not depart on good terms.

Leadership transition is an opportunity for profound change. In the immigrant context the choice of leadership determines whether a congregation continually caters to the needs of the first-generation and newly arrived immigrants or adapts to the needs and reality of the second-generation or well-established generations. Transition generally, and change of direction specifically, bears high potential for conflict and church splits. Although there are no definitive studies yet, the observation of my interviewees is that a large percentage of leadership transitions are rough. Nevertheless, there are also encouraging examples of leadership transition within immigrant churches.

One example in the Greater Boston area is the Boston Chinese Evangelical Church (BCEC). BCEC was started in 1961 in Chinatown to reach the Cantonese-speaking Chinese with the Gospel. In the past fifty years BCEC has developed from a Cantonese-speaking to a multilingual congregation with two campuses and a strong English-speaking ministry. In this time BCEC has experienced two significant leadership transitions. Steven Chin became pastor in 2003 as the successor to Jacob Fung, who had served almost twenty-five years as the senior pastor of BCEC.[19] Before becoming the senior pastor, Chin was mentored by Pastor Fung and faithfully served at BCEC in different leadership positions for many years. Although he is an American-born Chinese, over the years he has gained trust and respect from the whole congregation. His relationship to the congregation made the leadership transition successful.

Although, the context and culture of a congregation affects the process of leadership transition, I was able to identify four approaches to leadership transition through my interviews: the senior leader chooses and mentors the successor, the leadership transition is orchestrated by the board, the congregational transition is orchestrated by denominational leaders, and the congregation transitions from missionary leadership to indigenous leadership. Some approaches to leadership transition are more inclined toward internal and others toward external successors. The approaches are presented as ideal models and can appear in various combinations.

The Senior Leader Chooses and Mentors the Successor

The seemingly most successful approach to leadership transition is for the senior pastor to choose and mentor his or her successor from within the congregation. BCEC is such an example. The transition process starts with identifying leadership potential in a person and then appointing him or her as assistant or associate pastor. Over time more leadership responsibilities are transferred to that person. Before his or her retirement or departure, the senior pastor recommends his or her assistant as successor. In family-based structures, often the son or other relatives are prepared to take over.

This way of leadership development and training is common among many immigrant cultures, where formal seminary education is not the first step into ministry and might not be a requirement for being a pastor at all. Daniel A. Rodriguez, professor of religion and Hispanic studies, says that for the Hispanic community, the local church is an organic seminary. He explains how this works in one context:

> Similar to David in the all-too-familiar episode in which he killed Goliath the Philistine, many aspiring Hispanic pastors must wrestle with the question of appropriate weapons or theological training needed to effectively engage the Goliath that terrorizes many at-risk urban barrios in the United States. . . . In response to the need for appropriate weapons to take on these giants, Bible colleges, Christian Universities and seminaries suggest putting on Saul's armor. . . . However, a growing number of modern day Hispanic giant killers are being encouraged to rely instead on the training and experience they can acquire at the feet of a pastor in the context of the local church. [20]

This approach has also been successfully applied within the Haitian community as well as in immigrant churches of various Asian and African cultures, where the senior pastor is highly respected and his choice for successor is accepted.

The strength of this approach is that the successor knows the congregation and is known by them. The endorsement of the successor transfers some of the authority and trust the senior pastor has earned to the successor. This enables a smoother transition, as the congregation does not feel abandoned or forced to adapt to the unknown. It is a very natural transition and based on mutual agreement. Another strength of intentional leadership development is that the senior pastor is focused on creating the next generation of leaders instead of trying to keep her job.

There are also weaknesses to this approach. The opportunity for change, such as revisiting the mission of a congregation and discussing its programs in light of new realities, can be missed. The transition time does not invite a fresh perspective from the outside. Moreover, there is the danger of partisanship, nepotism, and a lack of transparency and accountability if decisions are made only within a family unit or a closed circle of confidants. More suitable leaders can be left out because they do not belong to the family. This can lead to frustration among members and even result in church splits.

Leadership Transition Is Orchestrated by the Board

In this approach the board runs the business of the church; thus, the board is the key entity involved in leadership transition. Board members are in charge of searching for and appointing or calling, as well as dismissing, a pastor. In this process it is most common to appoint or call a pastor from the outside to fill the position. It is not unusual, especially if the congregation is well established, for the board to invite someone from their home country to immigrate to serve the church. Depending on the general leadership structure, the members of the congregation may be included or excluded from the decision-making process.

The strength of this approach is that an external pastor brings a new perspective. Furthermore, he or she has the opportunity to lead the congregation to a new level in their spiritual journey and to adapt programs to the new realities in changing cities. The weakness of this approach is that the pastor is dependent on the board and primarily caters to its needs because he or she does not want to lose the job, especially if the pastor requires a visa that is dependent on the position at the church. Conflict between the board and the pastor can lead to the dismissal of the pastor. Moreover, an external pastor does not know the congregational culture and its members. In addition, time-limited contracts, which are common in this setting, affect the pastor's level of investment in the congregation and the neighborhood.

Congregational Transition Is Orchestrated by Denominational Leaders

Some immigrant churches are part of a denomination whose bylaws determine the process of transition. In some cases the denominational leaders appoint and send a new pastor. The principle of rotation may be practiced, meaning that a congregation expects a new pastor every few years.

The strength of this approach is that leadership transition does not ignite a conflict around power, as there is a clear pathway for such a process. The weakness of this approach is that the new pastor does not know the congregation. Moreover, rotation is especially hard for immigrants, as they get attached to the pastor. When he or she is relocated, the loss can break their hearts.

The Congregation Transitions from Missionary to Indigenous Leadership

Some immigrant churches have been planted by European American missionary church planting teams to reach out to a particular ethnic group with a traditionally non-Christian background. Besides reaching out, the missionaries also intentionally train indigenous leaders among this group. Once the indigenous leadership has grown in their responsibilities and matured, the missionary leaders pass on their leadership to the indigenous leaders. This model is common among ethnic groups from a traditionally non-Christian background. For example, many Cambodian and Vietnamese churches were planted by Christian Missionary and Alliance European American missionaries and are now led by indigenous pastors.

The strength of this approach is that leadership development is engrained in the nature of the congregation. The congregation is supported by a denomination to allow it to become structurally stable, and the denomination walks alongside them in times of transition and struggle. The weakness of this approach is that if a Western style of leadership has been implemented, it inhibits indigenous leadership to flourish, especially if the European American leadership is not experienced in cross-cultural ministry.

The reality of immigrant churches is very different from that of European American mainline churches. Leadership transition is always a very sensitive issue for a congregation, but it seems that within immigrant churches there is a higher potential for conflict, drama, and church splits because of their more difficult and unstable situation. This preliminary study on leadership transition makes obvious that this issue deserves more extensive research to analyze its complexity and significance. In particular, three questions need further reflection: How can the whole body of Christ, especially European American churches, assist immigrant churches in their leadership transition without being patronizing? How does the lack of pension plans and other benefits affect the spiritual growth and development of a whole congregation? How can structures be established to address the challenges of the second-generation immigrants and their need for leadership development?

LEADERSHIP TRANSITION WITHIN AFRICAN AMERICAN CHURCHES

African American churches in transition present an entirely different set of issues and questions from those of immigrant churches. The history and development of the African American church is closely connected to African Americans' experience of slavery, the struggle of abolishing slavery, the civil rights movement, and fighting for equal participation in society. Even in the present day, racism informs the daily experience of the African American community. As in immigrant churches the history of a specific community and social context affect leadership transition. Furthermore, this is a particularly critical time for the African American community, because their churches, more than any mainline church culture, are facing a massive pastoral transition. According to Ralph Watkins, associate professor of society, religion, and Africana studies,

> [a]s we look at the African American church, what we find is that civil rights-era pastors are retiring, and the next generations are up to lead. Thus, African American churches are doing more than simply moving from one pastor to the next; in these transitions are generational-divide issues like never before.[21]

Just as I interviewed immigrant pastors from Greater Boston, I also interviewed several African American pastors from the area, representing different denominations, genders, and age diversity. I do not claim to speak for the

African American Christian community as a whole, as their experience also varies based on geographic location.

The African American church developed through a history of political and social struggle. While the American colonies were struggling for their freedom from their mother country, African slaves were under their subjugation. During these early years the African American church was shaped by the experience of degradation, despair, and disgrace coupled with a desire to be free. [22]

The major turning point in the development of African American Christianity that led to the emergence of the historic Black church tradition is connected to the pietism and religious revivalism of the "Great Awakenings." The character of revivalism was to engage not the intellect, but the hearts and emotions of the hearers through singing, physical movement, and spiritual rebirth. [23] African Americans were drawn by the Great Awakening's emphasis on the concept of a "priesthood of all believers." Hence, anyone who experienced a rebirth, and not only those with formal training, was able to preach the gospel. Through this experience the enslaved Africans were able to assume leadership and self-determination seldom held before this period. [24]

Another key development in the historic Black church tradition was the emerging influence of Methodism. First, the founders John Wesley and Francis Asbury believed that the Gospel was meant for all people, regardless of color. Second, the less hierarchical structure as well as the accepted role of traveling ministers allowed the members of the African American communities to preach in various churches. [25] Today, the African American Christian community consists of three major streams: the African American Methodist Churches, African American Baptist Churches, and African American Pentecostalism. With an estimated twenty to twenty-five million members combined, they represent the vast majority of the nation's African American Christians. Of course, millions of African American Christians belong to congregations in the Roman Catholic Church, smaller African American denominations, independent churches, and predominantly European American denominations. [26]

Although each of the denominations has its own doctrines and different theological emphases, the experience of slavery has given rise to a distinctive theology that transcends the other differences. According to historian Gayraud Wilmore, the African American church tradition is defined by three factors: "the quest for independence from white control; the revalorization of the image of Africa [and African people]; and the acceptance of protest and agitation as theological prerequisites for Black liberation and the liberation of all oppressed peoples." [27] The African American church was the first public institution led by the African American community itself; therefore, it has influenced the whole community beyond the ordinary church members. Anson Shupe, professor of sociology, and sociologist Janelle Eliasson-Nannini have observed that "[t]he Black Church has unquestionably been the most important macro and micro institution in historical African-American subculture."[28]

The African American church's roots in liberation theology and the social gospel encouraged these Christians to put their faith to work addressing the everyday needs of African Americans. By providing job training, housing, educational opportunities, and child care, the Black church has attempted to create access to the majority culture society. The high point of this civil involvement was clearly during the civil rights movement, when churches provided the meeting space, resources, and bodies necessary to undertake nonviolent, direct action.[29] Nevertheless, this tradition of social action continues until the present day and is expected from the pastoral staff of congregations as well as from the wider community.

THE SPECIAL ROLE OF THE AFRICAN AMERICAN PASTOR

The development of the African American church was always connected to charismatic leaders, who assumed a special role not only in church matters but in the wider community. Shupe and Eliasson-Nannini write:

> The black church has been a stable safe point in a changing, sometimes hostile, world and the black pastor has been the ship's captain whose perceived strength and leadership wisdom provides real help and succor for church members. . . . Moreover, the black pastor in the African American community has assumed both prophetic and administratively priestly positions in serving the role of gatekeeper to larger majority society.[30]

The pastor is seen as a religious and personal guide and mentor. His or her special role in people's lives and the personal emotional connection between pastor and people affect leadership transition and how it is experienced by the congregation. This connection to the pastor is very strong, especially when the members and the pastor have been part of the same congregation for many years, which is not uncommon in African American communities. The Peoples Baptist Church of Boston is one example of such long tenure. The present pastor, Wesley Roberts, is only the fourth pastor since 1915.[31] At Twelve Baptist Church in Roxbury, Massachusetts, Arthur Gerald, Jr., is also only the fourth pastor since 1894.[32]

LEADERSHIP TRANSITION

As mentioned previously, the African American church is mainly organized in denominations. Each of these denominations has a distinct process for

leadership transition or succession. Some denominations are more hierarchi-
cally structured than others. In the A.M.E. Church, for example, the bishop
reappoints the pastor to the congregations every year. Either the present
assignment is confirmed (this confirmation can continue for decades), or the
pastor is sent to another congregation. Within the African American Pentecostal movement, which includes many nondenominational churches, however, most of the congregations are autonomous and have their own structures and processes.

In many European American churches, mainline or evangelical, pastors
are most often invited from the outside to become the new senior pastor.
Within African American churches, especially larger ones, leadership development and the staffing of leadership positions within a congregation are
often the senior pastor's responsibility, and these pastors tend to look first
inside their congregation to find their successor. Because of the importance
of relationships and the special role of the pastor, according to several pastors
I interviewed, transitions are generally easier if the successor knows the
context, culture, and history of a church. Therefore, the pastor mentors the
congregation's own leaders, who can identify with the congregation's cultural and historical values.

The pastor's sons and daughters, biological or spiritual, are naturally the
first ones to be nurtured and developed; hence, they are high candidates for
succession, especially, if they have chosen pastoral ministry as their career.
Such an approach to leadership structure and transition commonly leads to a
succession from father/mother to son/daughter within the African American
community. This is particularly true if the senior pastor is also the founding
pastor of the church. Although the transition from father/mother to spiritual
or biological son/daughter is more widespread in the Pentecostal movement,
this model also exists in other denominations. Even in the A.M.E. Church,
where the bishop appoints the pastor, this process does not prevent the senior
pastor from mentoring potential leaders, who may then go to seminary, become ordained, and end up on staff in the church where they grew up—with
the option to become the successor to their mentor. The relational connection
to the congregation and the senior pastor is ideally one of the driving forces
of leadership transition. I emphasize *ideally*, because the reality poses challenges that can prevent churches from pursuing the model of relational connection.

Although analysis of my interviews suggests that a successor from within
a congregation is more likely to be successful, opinions about whether leadership transition is smoother within denominational than within nondenominational churches varies. One pastor emphasized that transition is a critical
juncture and that the denomination provides guidance for the transition. His
observation is that nondenominational churches are too senior-pastor centered; hence, once the senior pastor leaves, there is a risk of the church being

damaged. Another pastor commented that leadership transition in a nonde-nominational church has more potential to be smooth, because the senior pastor can prepare the church for the transition and has the freedom to lead the way, knowing what the congregation needs.

CHALLENGES RELATING TO LEADERSHIP TRANSITION

Leadership transition is challenging in every congregation, especially if the reasons for the transition involve trauma, such as the sudden death of the pastor or pastoral misconduct.[33] Besides congregation-specific particular-ities, the African American church as a whole faces several challenges. The analysis of the interviews with the African American leaders led me to iden-tify five challenges that congregations commonly face in leadership transi-tion: the congregation's centering itself on the senior pastor, the lack of preparation for leadership transition, a shortage of new pastors, generational drift, and a lack of resources. These challenges are connected, and one may cause the other.

The Senior Pastor–Centered Church

As discussed previously, there are certain advantages in a leadership transi-tion that is orchestrated by the senior pastor. However, the challenges such a transition poses should not be underestimated, as they can have a negative impact if a church is run like a family business. If the family connection is the deciding factor in succession, the successor might not be the most suit-able candidate.

Another challenge in a senior pastor–centered church is that members' loyalty lies with the personality of the pastor and not within the congregation and their mission. This might lead to an exodus of congregants when the senior pastor leaves, which has financial and social impact on the congrega-tion as a whole.

Lack of Preparation for Leadership Transition

Many formerly thriving African American churches are aging, the pastor growing old with the members of the congregation. One of the hazards of a long-term pastorate is the failure to train younger leaders and develop a good succession plan. A lack of resources often causes leaders to focus on today's pressing needs and not to think about the future. Thus, preparing the congre-gation for the pastor's retirement and readying members to welcome and provide a fair financial package for an incoming pastor is hardly the first priority. This lack of preparedness for leadership transition is closely con-nected with the next challenge.

A Shortage of New Pastors

Several pastors I interviewed emphasized the lack of young leaders to take over smaller congregations. First, not enough young African Americans go to seminary and choose a pastoral career. Second, many of the young seminary graduates look for positions in larger churches that can pay them a realistic salary, or, third, they plant their own churches.

These three realities make it very difficult for smaller congregations with mainly aging congregants to find a successor if their senior pastor leaves. These congregations do not have the resources to provide for a young pastor (who may have accumulated significant debt during his schooling) and his family.

Generational Drift

As mentioned previously many African American churches are rapidly aging and still very traditional. The new generation of pastors has grown up in a different context and with a different vision, which can lead to generational challenges and conflicts, especially if the church board is tied to the traditions. Therefore, the prospect of leading an older congregation through revitalization and change is not very tempting for most young seminary graduates.

A Lack of Resources

The pastors I interviewed agreed that leadership transition would be easier if there were more resources available. Many African American churches are located in poorer communities and focus on reaching out to marginalized people. These congregations have fewer financial and human resources than do congregations with higher-income members. In such cases the financial constraints, not necessarily who would be the best fit, can be the most decisive factor when choosing the next leader.

INTERIM PASTORS AND TRANSITIONAL MINISTRY

The concept of interim pastors is known within the African American church as it applies to situations when a pastor unexpectedly resigns or dies. In such a case an interim pastor is sent by the denomination or invited by the departing pastor or the board. However, the understanding of the role of an interim pastor is very different from that of intentional interim ministry, where the interim pastor stays for a set period of time to guide the congregation through transition. The interim pastors within the African American community are either between assignments or serving as associate pastors at another church, and they have been asked by the pastor, board, or denomination to fill in. These pastors are not specifically trained to be interim pastors. It is also rare that an African American pastor would have a career as an interim pastor and move to one interim pastorate after another. More commonly, the interim pastor is asked by the congregation or denomination to stay permanently if the fit proves to be good.

A recent and prominent example is the leadership transition at Roxbury Presbyterian Church in Boston. The departing pastor, Hurmon Hamilton, asked his friend Liz Walker, who worked with the youth at Bethel A.M.E. in Boston, whether she would step in for a few weeks until Roxbury found a new pastor. The few weeks expanded, and recently Walker was asked to lead the church permanently, although she belonged to another denomination. Walker accepted and is now training for ordination in the Presbyterian denomination.[34] This example shows the importance of personal relationships and the endorsement of the departing pastor in the process of leadership transition.

The special role of the African American pastor and the usually long-term commitment pastors make to a congregation do not create a culture conducive to transitional ministry. Moreover, most predominantly African American denominations are not set up to support transitional ministry. Nevertheless, several pastors in the Greater Boston area emphasize that only planning ahead and leaving well will give a church a foundation for sustainability and long-term growth.[35]

LEADERSHIP TRANSITION: A CONCLUSION

The history and culture of immigrant churches and African American churches are distinct. Additionally each congregation faces specific challenges. Nevertheless, there are similarities that distinguish these congregations from European American mainline churches. In both communities, churches are places of spiritual and emotional empowerment, and safety in the face of discrimination and struggles for survival in a society where people of color are marginalized. Moreover, the pastor is seen as a prophetic leader and plays a significant role in the congregants' lives. He or she is more than just a spiritual agent; he or she holds the community together and gives advice and guidance in all matters of life. The relationship between clergy and laity is an important factor in leadership transition. For both the immigrant churches and the African American churches, the smoothest transition takes place when the senior pastor chooses and mentors his successor, although this model can be risky because it can lack transparency and smack of nepotism. The biggest difference in the way leadership transition takes place lies in the organizational structure. There is a strong denominational structure among the African American community, while the immigrant churches are more organically grown and structured.

Neither immigrant nor African American churches practice intentional transitional ministry as it is described elsewhere in this book. The reasons for that are on the one hand cultural, such as the strong relational ties between clergy and laity, and the important role the pastor plays in congregants' lives. On the other hand, structural and logistical issues, such as a lack of leaders, are reasons a transitional ministry is not common. However, both immigrant and African American churches do sometimes experience in times of transition the need for interim pastors to step in and fill a pastoral vacancy. Listening to the interviewees and drawing on my experience, however, I see both a need for pastors to receive training to be good interim pastors, but even more, a need to prepare congregations for leadership transition.

REFLECTION QUESTIONS

1. How does culture affect leadership transition?
2. What are the challenges of immigrant churches that affect leadership transition?
3. How does the context for African American churches and immigrant churches differ from that of European American mainline churches, even though they are located in the same neighborhood?
4. What is the most successful model of leadership transition that you have witnessed in immigrant churches? Why was it successful?
5. Why is transitional leadership uncommon in immigrant churches and African American churches?

II

New Models and Methods

Chapter Seven

Revitalization, Renewal, or Redevelopment during the Interim

Michael Piazza

As we enter a new era of ministry wherein the culture and the church are changing at breakneck speed, revitalization, renewal, and redevelopment need to be an essential piece of transitional ministry. In the past when North America was still in the throes of "Christendom," this season in the life of a church was seen as a time to allow the congregation to grieve and release its former pastor and then prepare for the arrival of the next one. Loren Mead, who provided the intellectual soil for the beginning of interim ministry as a specialization, found that the time between pastors was the most fertile for a church's members to look together in the mirror at themselves and to take stock of changes needed in leadership, vision, mission, and life. Some congregations have gladly entered into this time of reflection, and others have resisted, being content with maintenance.

THE HIGH COST OF LOSING MOMENTUM

At the current pace of life in the real world today, however, maintenance alone cannot be sustained. Church history is replete with stories of churches that were thriving until an effective pastor retired or moved away. The subsequent decline often is attributed to the successor's being less skilled or gifted than was the previous pastor. That does happen. A number of former pastors I have interviewed, however, identify a loss of momentum during the interim period as the reason so much of their work became undone. John Maxwell, who was once a successful pastor in San Diego, says, "A train travelling fifty-five mph on a railroad track can crash through a five-foot-thick steel-reinforced concrete wall without stopping. That same train won't be able to move if you put a one-inch block of wood in front of the wheels."

The loss of momentum in even vital congregations is often caused by putting on hold critical decisions, changes, and functions in the absence of a lead pastor. The interim ministry and congregational leaders might assume the members of the church need to take time to do the work of grieving, for example, failing to recognize that pastors today fill a role much different from those of just a couple of decades ago. In vital and growing churches, the pastor likely served as CEO as much as spiritual leader. The pastor's vision, management skills, and energizing presence will be greatly missed, but in these settings, an effective pastor elicits more respect than personal affection, so the classic family dynamics are absent or much less significant. Members' attachment to the pastor in vibrant churches is often less than interim ministers may assume, and, therefore, the grief is much less significant.

Interims can come into these situations understanding their role as caregivers in a transitional process. Attempting to be a "healing" presence when healing is not really needed can contribute to the loss of vitality, however. It also can negatively affect the pastoral search process. Healthy adults may enjoy having a caregiver, even though they are at a developmental stage when they do not need one and should instead be the ones giving the care. Shifting the congregation's focus during an interim to an internal one, rather than maintaining the external focus that created congregational vitality, can affect the culture and halt growth, diminish the source of energy and self-esteem, and weaken what has probably been a compelling vision.

In my experience, even medium and large churches that have had vital, thriving ministries—that have stretched themselves to do more, serve more, and be more—can lose that momentum if those flames aren't continually fanned and too much time is spent on introspection. In fact, ironically, such churches may be particularly at risk. While the extent of their community outreach is likely what has distinguished them from numerous declining mainline churches in their community, they have also probably pushed themselves to the edge of their resources. Such churches cannot afford even a small loss of momentum or vibrancy.

The fact that a congregation is vital and growing is an indication that it is a pretty healthy place. If the pastor has been an exceptionally dynamic and effective leader, however, the vacuum her or his departure creates is an inevitable reality. Further, the larger the church, the greater the likely impact of a loss of momentum, so the more urgent the need for alternatives. Consequently, pastors of larger churches especially are looking seriously at a succession model of transition. (See chapter 8 of this volume, which lays out this model in detail.) Approaches to succession planning vary:

- Many congregations begin seeking a successor before the current pastor's tenure is complete so that the current pastor might mentor the incoming pastor for at least a short period.
- Several churches that I work with have hired associate pastors who will be trained deliberately to lead a multistaff church. The assumption is that the congregation *may* select that person as the successor or, at the very least, that person will be prepared to be selected by another congregation.
- In some settings a co-pastor model is temporarily implemented with a clear delineation of responsibilities. After months, or perhaps even a couple of years of serving together, the longtime pastor's role gradually decreases so his or her absence will have minimal impact when he or she steps out of the picture.

These models are imperfect, but they are experiments motivated by a desire to avoid the stagnation and decline that can happen in a vibrant church when a long-term pastor leaves. In mainline denominations, where a wave of retirements is imminent, conversations about potential succession models especially need to happen in medium to larger churches where a pastoral transition is about to take place.

PREPARING FOR RENEWAL

Given the realities of our day, interim leaders need to see their role as "renewing pastor" and the time of transition as a season for growth and revitalization. In the past the best that a stable, stagnant, or declining congregation (as well as the judicatory or entering interim pastor) might hope for was maintenance of the status quo. In the Christian faith, resurrection is a very rare occurrence, but many have had the experience of being "born again." Transitional ministers must retool their approach from being hospice chaplains for a church suffering a loss to becoming midwives of hope for a bright new future born out of this season of change. While the interim pastor may not be present at this rebirth, she or he certainly can lay the groundwork for that miracle by dealing directly with issues contributing to loss of momentum or even decline. These issues include:

- An absence of self-awareness. Few churches are aware that they have declined into the fourth quadrant of their life cycle. (See pages 191–193 for a detailed description of "quadrant.") Renting their facility to a school or having a significant endowment can keep a congregation in denial until the chance of renewal grows very slim. There is no fifth quadrant. Holding up a clear mirror is the first step toward stemming decline. Using tools such as appreciative inquiry or bringing in a consultant to help with honest evaluation is critical. None of us enjoy bringing bad news to people we like, but any journey must begin from where we are, not where we have been or where we are pretending to be. Truth telling must be a primary role for interim ministry.

- A lack of a transformational vision and mission. A vital role for many interim pastors is to lead the congregation through a process to discover a transformational vision and mission. Unfortunately, unless a clear and compelling vision is present, the congregation may very well search for a new pastor who is much like the last pastor, who perhaps was presiding over their death. By facilitating a courageous visioning process, the interim may help the congregation seek out a different kind of pastor. Without a clear vision, the church members can see only their past, and they make their selection based on the past rather than on the future. As our friends in Alcoholics Anonymous often remark, however, doing the same thing while expecting different results is the very definition of crazy. Even if fully developing a new vision and mission is not possible, beginning this work may help them recognize that change is both possible and probably essential.

- Burdensome systems and structures. One thing many churches have in common, especially if they are in their fourth quarter, is an excess of structures, bylaws, systems, and policies. Many churches have more pages of governance than they have members. These have been encrusting the church for many years and now are crushing the very life out of the community. Challenging those systems is vital. Dynamic and growing churches empower people for ministry and are relentlessly permission giving. Like the human skeleton, the polity, governance, management, structure, and systems of the church should be vigorous and effective. They should support the life and activity of the body. They should function smoothly without calling attention to themselves. They should be healthy but invisible support systems for all the good the body of Christ can do. Raising this issue is critical. Even if a new governance system cannot be implemented during the interim, we can increase the likelihood that the settled pastor will be able to make changes. If the interim is effective, none of the changes a permanent pastor suggests should come as a surprise.

- Stagnant worship. Inevitably a declining church is worshipping the same way it has for decades. If that style of worship were effective, it would be attracting new people. Changing worship is a tough thing to do. While the interim pastor might be tempted to leave that for the settled pastor (and that may seem the logical thing to do), doing so also makes the new pastor pay the full price. A courageous transitional minister knows she or he is leaving and that being beloved isn't necessary. Even if the settled pastor changes worship after the interim has left, the price the settled pastor pays will be much lower because of the interim's courage. Introducing new liturgy and order, different music styles, weekly communion, multimedia technology, lessons from contemporary literature or movies, and so forth will make the congregation more ready for the changes that must come if it is to survive long into the twenty-first century. Helping church members move toward worshipping with their hearts as well as their heads will make a service much more attractive to visitors. People rarely visit churches wanting to know more about God. They come longing for an encounter with the holy that might transform their lives.

- Viewing evangelism as a low priority. FTVs (first-time visitors) must become VIPs. If any church is to have a future, it will come from attracting, retaining, and ultimately integrating new people. Recognizing this truth and implementing it are two different things. The ultimate test for the members of the congregation is, are they willing to craft worship to meet the needs and desires of new people, or will they insist it stay as they like it? The shift to focusing on those who are not yet there will require persistent teachings about what it means to be a church and relentless reality checks about what the future will be like if they do not start attracting and retaining new folks who have different needs and expectations. Discovering new ways to use social media and other low-cost means of advertising is a critical first step to attracting people.

  Before we begin to try that, though, we must consider every aspect of visitors' experience. Where will they park? How will they find their way into the building? What will it look or smell like? Who will greet them? What about the service will touch them and make them want more? How warm will the welcome be? Will they see a place for them and their family in this community? Growing a church is simple: get people to come, get them to come back, get them to stay. It is not easy, though. If it were, the church would be growing. Since congregations are probably not growing, however, things must change, and getting church members to see new people as their only hope for the future is the hardest part. Mainline churches simply do not have a birthrate sufficient to sustain their future. Seeing *everything*—from the building, to the welcome, to the restrooms, to the bulletin, to the worship—through the eyes of first-time visitors is critical. The congregation will expect the new pastor to be oriented to serving the current congregation. That works *only* if the congregation is outwardly oriented.

- Self-absorption. Most churches in America believe in the truth of Jesus's instruction that our mission is "to serve, not to be served." However, simply ask church members for whom their worship is designed, and you will discover the truth. If the interim can help a church's members "take off their bibs and put on their aprons," the interim will take a major step toward transformation. A church should look at every aspect of its programs and ministries and whether those elements are designed to serve others rather than self and ask whether members are functioning as hosts or guests. Almost all people outside of the church will tell you they want to volunteer for something that will make a difference. Sadly, the church may be the last place where they think that might happen. How do we make the local church the charity of choice? We can do good work more efficiently than almost any charity. We have buildings that often are paid for, we underpay staff, and our administrative overhead is minimal. The trouble is that the public sees us as a charity that serves itself rather than a portal where one might come to serve the poor, the hurting, the estranged. A congregation can make an incredible difference in the community and beyond if it spends its energy on working for peace, healing creation, and serving the poor rather than maintaining a building and having committee meetings. People who are not particularly religious find externally focused churches to be places they can support.

Dozens of issues require attention if interim pastors are going to serve as ministers of revitalization. This is an awful lot of work for an interim period; however, given the speed of life and the rate of decline in most churches, it is immoral for congregations in interim to simply allow the decline to continue for two years. We may not fully accomplish any of these things, but beginning them will hand the new pastor a much greater opportunity for success.

FOUR PRINCIPLES OF RENEWAL

At the Center for Progressive Renewal, we have uncovered four key principles of renewal that may be helpful in framing transitional work. We may be tempted to think implementing these principles should be the work of a settled pastor, and in some situations that might be true. However, understanding these principles and helping a congregation gain clarity about them is a critical component in the work of transition.

Renewal Should Be Perpetual

It would be lovely to believe that we simply could go into a church and apply renewal principles and the church then would grow into a bright and glorious future with its new pastor. That is certainly a noble and worthy goal, but it is also a fantasy.

Because the rate of change has accelerated so greatly in our lifetimes, the reality is we cannot "fix" anything, but we are always fixing. Worship doesn't need to be *changed*; it needs to be *changing*. Teaching members of a congregation this principle is important. They may be willing to do the hard work of changing things, but then they want to leave the work behind and move on. Congregations are instinctively change averse, and congregations in the fourth quadrant of their life cycles are so resistant to change that the likelihood of conflict (primarily about what should and should not be changed) is high. Churches therefore avoid change. The challenge of the interim period is to help a congregation shift from seeing itself as a "rock"—unchanging, stable, and perpetual—to being a lab for spiritual experimentation.

We recommend that churches write into a new pastor's covenant that she or he is *required* to make at least twelve mistakes a year and one of them needs to be major. At the annual meeting, the pastor must report on the twelve mistakes. The church should recruit leaders for various ministries by making the same demands. The only requirement for being the church is grace, and we must create an atmosphere in which grace is not only possible but necessary. In a spiritual lab, experiments are essential, and there will be many failures. Creating a dynamic in which change, growth, and grace are the critical vital signs for the church's future is a great gift to give a new pastor. It is the only hope the church has for finding a place in a culture changing so rapidly and continuously.

In planning a Christmas Eve service recently, the worship team of the small church I pastor talked about beloved traditions. Someone observed, ironically, if we want to have the same impact on the new members of the congregation that those traditions had on the old, we need to do things completely differently and create new traditions. Renewal should be perpetual, and creating a permission-giving culture in which that is possible releases a people to be responsive to Spirit and responsible for the community we are called to serve.

Renewal Is Incremental

The theory behind this observation that renewal is incremental is what the Center for Progressive Renewal calls the "Step-Fix Theory." In simplest terms, this means that with each step in growth, development, or revitalization, things have changed and now certain additional things must be fixed or changed.

For example, the way that a church that averages 125 people in attendance does coffee hour must be very different from how a seventy-five-person congregation might gather. Space becomes an issue, and the purpose of the time must be reconsidered. Generic coffee and cheap store-bought cookies might have sufficed for a congregation that long had been the same size and used the time after service simply for neighbors to reconnect every week, as it had for years. Now, with new people, this gathering must serve to build new community. Younger people come expecting higher-quality refreshments, and they probably bring children who do not drink coffee. The failure to fix even a function this simple can send a strong signal to new people that *they* are joining *us* and this is simply how *we* do it and *they* will have to adapt. Refreshments have become important.

The church has taken a step forward by significantly increasing attendance, and now a whole range of things probably must be fixed. A new or renewed vision will require a new supporting structure and systems that function differently. This must be fixed before the next step can be taken. Frequently, new or revitalizing churches reach a plateau and feel as though they have gotten stuck. This assessment might be correct, but it might also be a perfectly normal developmental stage. Which it is depends on our response. When we make progress but then our growth or renewal pauses, we may not even notice, and that can be deadly. What is healthy is recognizing this developmental pause as an opportunity to "fix" what needs to be different at this new developmental stage. If we can use this pause to address new needs, we can lay the foundation for the next step.

Churches that have long been stable (read "stagnant") do not tend to think this way. Progress is a source of joy and celebration, and rare is the leader who can notice what changes are needed to sustain the new level, let alone move on to the next. It is important not to see the church as "having arrived" with the new stage. That will result inevitably in the church's sliding backward or, at best, being in another season of stagnation. The leader's role here is to help other leaders assess what needs to be changed in order to adapt to where the congregation is *and* where it is going.

If a church has gone from seventy-five to 125 in attendance, members have great reason to celebrate, which is important and should not be neglected. However, while the community is celebrating and being affirmed, the leader's job is also to ask, "What is needed to be a 150- or 200-person worshipping congregation?" The effective leader will be thinking at least two developmental stages ahead and considering what a church at that stage will need to do differently. You see, you must fix the step you find yourself on, but you must fix it in a way that enables your church to take the next two steps. An aphorism I often use is "Two steps ahead is leadership; three is martyrdom." Facilitating the changes needed to grow from one hundred in attendance to 125 or even 150 can be seen as visionary, and you will find support. Growing from 100 to 175 or 200 requires changes that are stark, and resistance will damage your leadership ability. This is a time to remember that good leaders don't tell all that they know or think.

An interim minister can't fix everything, so it is critical to determine which changes can make an impact on renewal and which areas simply can be ignored. Don't invest your limited energy in areas that will not support revitalization or are not hindering it. There is an art to knowing how to ignore. Rather than trying to end a program or ministry that is not strong or healthy, a wiser strategy may be to try ignoring it to death. Your absence may be enough to let something die a natural death, so long as your presence is making a positive difference in other areas. Ignoring something to death is a fine art. Fix what you can, and ignore the rest. Done strategically that will be sufficient for a church to be transformed.

Renewal Is Exponential

Renewal is about multiplication, not addition. We can't simply add on to what a church is doing. That will not have sufficient impact to transform a stagnant church. Most mainline churches are so encrusted with the rust of their history, tradition, fears, and failures that getting them moving again requires extraordinary energy. Simple addition is not usually sufficient. If we can put our energy into a few areas where the impact can be multiplied, the outcome can be transformational.

Perhaps this mathematics illustration can make this idea clearer:

$3 \times 3 \times 3 \times 3 \times 3 = 243$

$4 \times 4 \times 4 \times 4 \times 4 = 1,024$

Notice that the difference between three and four is only one. That is not particularly significant if your approach is adding to what you are doing already. However, the cumulative difference between 243 and 1,024 is remarkable.

You cannot fix all that needs to be addressed during your interim time. Carefully select four or five areas where your gifts and the church's needs intersect. Don't try to add to what the church is doing in those areas; try to transform who they are in those areas. Select areas where the positive impact of change can be multiplied throughout the system.

A former church I served always had collected food for those in need at Thanksgiving. It was a pleasant thing to do, and several families were helped. The first year after I arrived, I saw several things about this process that needed to be fixed. With little effort, the congregation could serve many more people much more effectively. I was tempted to try to fix it. Instead, I invited the team members who led this ministry over to my house for dinner. I cooked the same food items they collected in the Thanksgiving baskets as a way of saying thank you. We spent the meal sharing the joy that they experienced in doing the ministry and talked of how rewarding it was. Later, over coffee and pumpkin pie, I facilitated a conversation about how I'd like to figure out a way to share their experience with the entire congregation. How could we get everyone involved in the work of feeding those less fortunate? It was nearly midnight when everyone left. They had dozens of ideas about how to do more at Thanksgiving, but also projects we could do at Christmas and Easter, during the summer, and with school supplies.

What was clear in these conversations was that most of the folks were there to serve, but a couple of people were leaders. Less than a week later, I took a staff member and those two leaders to lunch. I talked to them about my dream to make community service the defining ministry of our church. Again, I asked them for ideas about how this might be. They had many. I asked if it was acceptable for me to put their ideas together in a strategic plan and send it to them for input. They were honored. On the drive back to the church, I explained to the staff member that my goal was for community outreach to become his full-time job. My goal was for him to:

- Get as many people as possible involved in as many different ways of serving as possible;
- Ensure that everything we did was documented and got publicized in the congregation, until, when asked about their church, all members would be able to describe everything their church does for those in need;
- Recruit every new member to get involved in these ministries and to get all the small groups to adopt projects; and
- Give 100 percent of this ministry away to the "lay" leaders of the congregation so that he could manage much more than if he tried to lead it all. His job was not to *do* anything, but to resource everything.

Finally, I hoped that on Christmas Eve two years from that day we would report to the members of the congregation that *they* gave away more than one million dollars in food, services, resources, money, and the like.

I could have tried to fix only the Thanksgiving food basket program, but I strategically managed to multiply the impact of that ministry through the entire church. It transformed the congregation's identity, its reputation in the community, and the lives of the hundreds of people who got involved and invited their neighbors to help. In the end, it became a great source of evangelism, and, on Christmas Eve two years later, we reported that the church had given away more than 1.3 million dollars in goods and services in one year. As the staff member talked about all that had been done, we showed images of those who had worked so hard and those we had served. By the end of the presentation, there was not a dry eye in the sanctuary, and that congregation was never the same. No one ever has to try to persuade them that they are there to serve, not to be served.

Think strategically about how your efforts and energy can have an impact that is multiplied throughout the entire church.

Renewal Is Environmental

We have observed that churches are not renewed so much by specific changes they make, but by their ability to effect climate change. Shifting from doing things to meet the needs of the members to doing everything to meet the needs of others is a prime example of climate change. When a church shifts to seeing every member as a minister and host, the transformation is so significant the environment has changed.

Nothing is more critical to revitalization than helping progressive churches recapture a sense of urgency about their future. David Ruhe, senior pastor of Plymouth United Church of Christ in Des Moines, Iowa, has led a thriving urban mainline congregation for almost two decades. The church has added a contemporary service that attracts more than two hundred people. It has a youth choir that is larger than the average church in America. David was asked in an interview what he thought was the most significant lesson mainline churches needed to learn. He answered, "If the mainline church is to have any future in this country, it must recover a sense of *urgency*."

It is clear that evangelical churches have that in abundance. Armed with the threat of an eternity spent in hell, they care deeply about those who are lost, but mainline churches do not understand hell in the same way. We have clearly seen the hells to which people have been consigned, and we have a word of hope for the hells of their despair and grace for the hells of their shame. We have eternal purpose for those who have lost their way. What must be recaptured is the same passion and urgency for saving people from these hells as the evangelical and fundamentalist churches have for saving people from eternal damnation. Kindling this passionate sense of urgency can transform the culture of the church, which, in turn, can transform the culture of the surrounding community. One principle I would love to teach every mainline church, especially in regard to worship, is something that was said of literary and social critic Irving Howe: "Enthusiasm is not the enemy of intellect." Recovering passion, enthusiasm, and a sense of urgency is a critical environmental change for a church that hopes to be renewed.

Creating an environment of service, hospitality, compassion, healing, celebration, empowerment, or hope can change every component of a church. The congregation that decided to make community service its defining ministry is an example of a church that created a climate that defined everything else about the church. Structures and systems all aligned to support and empower the church's serving those in significant need.

An interim pastor has amazing power to change the environment of a local church. The congregation has lost its pastor and now must grapple with who it really is and why any new pastor would choose to serve it. With a bit of courage, many shifts can be made that will create a culture for hospitality, growth, and passionate service. Creating a change in the culture of a church is an amazing gift to the success of the future pastor. It provides the hope of new life for a congregation that has been stagnant for too long and on the edge of death.

If an interim can turn a stronger, healthier, and more impassioned church over to a new pastor, she or he will have done a heroic service to the church of Jesus Christ. The world needs the mainline progressive church and the inclusive, passionate hope we have to offer. While an interim cannot ensure the success of the new pastor, the interim can certainly give the new pastor the best possible chance to lead an old church into a new future. Our call is to be midwives of hope, and for that, the church will be grateful.

REFLECTION QUESTIONS

1. How would renaming "transitional minister" to "renewal leader" change your approach to this ministry?
2. Giving a congregation hope is always a key function for a transitional minister. How can you help a congregation see that life for it can be even better, without diminishing the work of the departing leader?
3. What excites you about the possibility of a church growing in health and vitality? What challenges you? What perplexes you?

Chapter Eight

Another Option

Pastoral Succession

Anthony B. Robinson

Loren Mead and Alice Mann and their colleagues, whose research in the late 1960s and early 1970s led to the creation of interim ministry as a particular and specialized ministry, were surely right in their key insight: times of leadership transition are especially important and potentially transformational moments in the life of a congregation. Such transitions almost inevitably raise important questions and stir fresh conversations. For many congregations, engaging a specifically trained interim minister is a good option for leveraging the possibilities of this time.

But is the interim ministry model the only one to be considered for such transitional moments? Are there situations in which other models might work and be even wiser choices? There are. For a growing number of congregations, another option to consider is pastoral succession.

What is "pastoral succession"? It means the outgoing pastor is directly succeeded by a new (hopefully long-term) pastor. There is with pastoral succession no intervening interim period or intentional interim ministry. Sometimes the new pastor, the successor, has been on-site for a time. Indeed, he or she may be an associate minister who has been chosen with the understanding that in a certain amount of time—say two to three years—the associate will become the new senior or lead pastor. Other times the overlap between the outgoing and incoming pastor is a shorter period, as much as six months or as little as two weeks. And sometimes there is no overlap between the two at all. But in all of these models, an outgoing pastor is succeeded by a new pastor directly, without an interim period.

Can this work? The answer is yes, it can work. Indeed, it has worked well in a number of churches. Two of the churches where it has worked well are

Plymouth Church UCC in Lincoln, Nebraska, and Plymouth Church UCC in Des Moines, Iowa. In Lincoln, Jim Keck succeeded Otis Young, who stayed around in a background role that Keck found comfortable and supportive. Young was also very much involved in the search process that brought Keck to Lincoln. In Des Moines it was similar but different. Outgoing senior minister Jim Gilliam left the church and community immediately after successor David Ruhe arrived. And Gilliam was not a part of the search committee that called his successor.

Is such a pastoral succession model right for all churches? No. Where it is right, will it always work? No. One notable church where it was tried but did not work was Fourth Presbyterian in Chicago. Joanna Adams was called to Fourth with the understanding that she would follow John Buchanan. Adams ended up leaving long before Buchanan retired from Fourth.

There is no model for changing pastoral leaders that comes with an iron-clad, money-back guarantee. The vagaries of people and institutions remain many and various. But pastoral succession is a viable alternative that may make good sense for some congregations. In the bulk of this chapter I want to explore ten factors that are critically important if a pastoral succession is to work.

WHY PASTORAL SUCCESSION?

But before getting into those ten factors, let's ask another question. Why pastoral succession? Why not—at least in some cases—use the now common interim ministry model? What is to be gained?

Partly, the answer reflects on the way interim ministry has developed and is practiced. Many interim ministers are very, very good at what they do. But not all are. Some carry with them baggage from past disappointments. Others appear to insist on the formulaic "five tasks of interim ministry" in a way that may override the reality of a particular congregation or context. As a result, some congregations have had disappointing, even disastrous, experiences with an interim minister and are reluctant to risk that model again. (Such unfortunate experiences can of course also apply to settled pastors—that the new settled pastor is not competent or fails to read the context or goes off the rails in some other way.)

Another factor suggesting congregations consider the possibility of pastoral succession is that interim ministry periods seem to be growing longer, up to two and three years in some cases. Again, in some situations that is perhaps necessary. Some congregations have some tough issues to work through and some hard questions to face, and may be better served by an effective interim. If, however, a congregation is healthy and vital and has been making changes and adjustments—even reforms—as it goes, then it may be ready to enter a new chapter without an interim period. Such congregations may fear that having an interim would be a bit like going "off-line" for an extended period, with consequent loss of momentum and strength. And they may be right.

Still, there are dangers in electing for pastoral succession and avoiding the possibly more reflective and intentional period of an interim. People may imagine that their congregation can change leaders the way Pony Express riders used to change horses, without breaking stride or losing time. Or they may invoke what they call the "business model": "In my company we just get a head hunter and get someone in here in three months." While there are some ways in which churches and businesses are similar, there are also important differences. Church members are not, for example, employees.

The idea of no fuss, no muss, no disruption is appealing, but it could mask a temptation better resisted—to avoid hard questions and real change. But while hard questions and real change cannot, and should not, be avoided, there's no guarantee that an interim ministry will lead a congregation there either. An intentional pastoral succession may engage the important questions and evolutionary change required equally effectively.

TEN FACTORS FOR SUCCESS

What is necessary if the pastoral succession model is to be effective, if it is to "work" and work well? Based on my own research and observation of churches that have used this model, I see ten critical factors that need to be in place for pastoral succession to work. They include the following.

Key factor one: The church in question needs to be a healthy one. The congregation needs to be one in which there is vitality, where there has been an absence of serious or chronic conflict, and where the pastoral ministry of the outgoing pastor has been a strong one. But be careful here. Many congregations would describe themselves as "healthy," but are they really? Often congregations mistake being on a plateau and consequent stability with health. The two are not the same, however. If the trend lines over a ten- or twenty-year period indicate membership, attendance, and giving have stayed about the same, that may not suggest health. Nor is health equivalent to historic prominence or reputation in the community. Things may be going south in a congregation even if its reputation is one of importance, prominence, or even "greatness."

While there is no simple index or completely adequate measure of congregational health, some of the markers I look for are the following: First, worship is alive. There is a sense of expectation in worship, a feeling of excitement. Second, the church has a couple of strong "flagship" ministries that are changing lives and for which it is known in the community. Third, chronic, low-level conflict is absent. The church has experienced conflict around some issues, *and it has been successful in resolving conflict and moving on.* Fourth, there is some level of growth in membership, attendance, and giving, and as important, newer people (those who have been members for two to five years) are finding their way into leadership. Fifth, lay leadership is strong and includes a significant number of mature, nonanxious people. Sixth and finally, people love their church and are enthusiastic about sharing it with others. All these markers—and certainly there are more—are signs of congregational health. For pastoral succession to work, a congregation needs to be healthy. It would be helpful to have a consultant or a judicatory official come in and make such an assessment, thus providing a balcony view or third set of eyes. Such an assessment should involve real time and effort and not be a quick once-over.

Key factor two: The outgoing pastor is able to be open to and allow planning or lead time for the impending change. Allowing such open discussion of impending transition and planning time might mean the outgoing pastor is retiring. Or there may be cases when the pastor's move to another kind of position (say the academic world) affords such lead time. In any event, the outgoing minister is able to be open with his or her leaders and congregation about the impending change, and there is sufficient time (at least a year prior to the conclusion of the current pastorate) to conduct an open and intentional public process of transition.

Often when clergy are moving from one church to another, such a change is kept under wraps, both by the clergy person and by prospective congregations. Such discretion or confidentiality may be unavoidable in many cases. But it does mean news of a pastor's move to another church may come suddenly and thus provide a shorter window between the time of that announcement and the actual change. When this is the case, the pastoral succession model is probably not a good choice or perhaps even a possible option.

It is noteworthy that some recent studies, such as *The Elephant in the Boardroom: Speaking the Unspoken about Pastoral Transitions*, by Carolyn Weese and Russell Crabtree, argue that churches lose a lot of ground because the pastor searches for a new call in secret. And some denominations—for example, the Lutheran Church–Missouri Synod and United Methodists—do not operate this way.

But usually when a pastor receives a new call, the pastor gives the church sixty to ninety days' notice. At that time everything is put on hold so that she or he can wind down her or his ministry, find an interim pastor, and begin putting a search committee together. Weese and Crabtree argue that every church should have a contingency plan in place to make a smooth pastoral transition in the event of an emergency or unexpected departure of the current pastor, including costs, consultant resources, and strategies to keep momentum going. They argue, as well, that pastors need to keep leaders apprised of their vocational intentions. While such ideas are certainly worthy of consideration, they may also prove easier said than done!

But if a pastor has served a church for ten or twenty years and is planning to retire or has accepted a position as, say, a seminary president to begin a year from now, then pastoral succession is an option that may be right. Such conditions tend to mean that pastoral succession is more likely in larger congregations where a pastor may have stayed for a longer pastorate and from which she or he does retire. And in many ways the larger church is appropriate for a pastoral succession, as in such congregations, a pastor's leadership role is especially crucial. Complex, larger congregations do not function well without someone at the helm who is effective.

Key factor three: The church has experienced constant, evolutionary change. Many of the strongest churches are strong because they are continually evaluating their ministry and mission and making changes as they go. They are familiar with change. They are accustomed to significant change. They expect it. They like it. Moreover, such congregations experience change as *evolutionary, not revolutionary*. That is, changes feel like next steps. They may be challenging and demanding. But they are continuous, not discontinuous, with the nature and mission of the church.

In some situations, there has been so little intentional and evolutionary change over a long period that something like a revolution may be the only way forward. Dramatic change is needed in staff, program, facility, vision, and mission. When that is the case, it is probably wise to have an interim who plows and prepares the hardened ground for a new pastor—and even then it will likely be tough going. This is the situation for countless congregations of the once mainline today. They are not so much stable as stuck. They don't just need a change of pastor. They need a change—often a dramatic one—in the culture of the congregation. Again, if that is the case, it is probably wise to have an effective interim who prepares the way.

If, however, a congregation has made honest self-evaluation and periodic shifts in the culture of the congregation part of its life, then it is in a better position to employ a pastoral succession model.

Key factor four: The outgoing pastor is a mature person who manages his or her ego well and really does want pastoral succession to work. Of course, "mature person" is like "healthy congregation"—a description most aspire to and would probably apply to themselves. In this case, it means a couple of things. The outgoing pastor gets the concept of "boundaries" and has good ones. He or she understands that he or she is no longer the church's pastor and surrenders that role and responsibility in the lives of people and the church. Such a person doesn't play games—that is, raising an eyebrow or shrugging the shoulders in just the right way or at just the right moment to plant suspicion about his or her successor. This probably also means that the outgoing pastor has something else to go to, something else to which she or he is ready to devote her or his time and energies. She or he isn't going off to "do nothing" but has spent some time discerning her or his next calling even if she or he is officially retired.

Again, I would not tend simply to accept an outgoing pastor's own self-evaluation or word that he or she will mind his or her boundaries. I would suggest that this person be counseled, even evaluated, for her or his capacity to keep good boundaries by a couple of people, perhaps an outside consultant and a judicatory executive. Ask them if they think this pastor is a good candidate for this kind of transition. Make sure that with the help of such people, your outgoing pastor has thought through contingencies like whether she or he will remain in the community and worship at the church, and how she or he will handle requests to perform funerals or weddings.

If the outgoing pastor has a sense he or she has "done his or her work" at that church, that is, that he or she has taught what he or she was called to teach and learned what he or she was called to learn and is now ready for something else, such sense of completion bodes well for a pastoral succession.

The outgoing pastor must be willing and able to publically "bless" his or her successor. This may happen on one memorable occasion, such as a special service of transition, but more likely it will happen on a number of occasions, when the outgoing pastor lauds, expresses confidence in, and defers to his or her successor. And finally, the outgoing pastor will return, when invited, to the church and will participate cheerfully and constructively on such occasions.

Key factor five: The incoming pastor is a mature person who manages his or her ego well and really does want pastoral succession to work. Again, "mature person" is probably how most of us would wish to refer to ourselves. But some are more mature than others. Such maturity probably means the incoming pastor has significant pastoral experience under his or her belt. She or he sees her- or himself not as a "new messiah" but as building on the work and standing on the shoulders of others who have also done good ministry.

And again, I wouldn't just take someone's own say-so in assessing such maturity and ego strength. I'd engage an outside consultant as well as a judicatory person to talk with the prospective successor and evaluate her or his fit and fitness for this kind of succession.

A mature successor will be comfortable speaking of his or her predecessor and doing so in positive ways. He or she will also allow members of the congregation to speak of his or her predecessor in honest and appreciative ways without being threatened or uneasy.

Just as the outgoing pastor will "bless" his or her successor, so the incoming pastor will bless her or his predecessor by referring to her or his ministry, affirming it, and inviting that person to be present and engaged on appropriate special occasions, such as the celebration of church anniversaries, dedication of a particular memorial, or retirement of another staff member who has served with both.

Key factor six: There is a good match between the out going and in coming pastors in terms of theology and approach to pastoral ministry. Such a match is not, to make the point negatively, like Barack Obama succeeding George W. Bush. This is more like Timothy succeeding Paul.

To be sure, there will be differences between the two pastoral leaders. They are likely of different generations and have been influenced by different formative events, teachers, and theologians. But again, the differences are more evolutionary than revolutionary. Beyond such continuities, there is also genuine mutual respect and affection. The two people like each other. They are not in competition but are colleagues in ministry.

In some cases of which I am aware, the outgoing pastor has played a role in the search process for his or her successor, even serving on the search committee. In other cases, the outgoing pastor does not play such a role, but is available for conversation with candidates as they weigh their decisions.

Key factor seven: The congregation understands the pastoral succession process and buys in. Congregational understanding and buy-in with respect to pastoral succession probably means that the congregation's leaders have looked at several options for the transition and have informed the congregation of their process. Further, leaders have described the nature of pastoral succession, its advantages and risks, and why they recommend it, as well as the specifics of the process for their church. They allow for comment and input from the congregation and create a way in which the congregation may register its support for this method.

While such a process of input and decision making may be forgotten with passing time, I would suggest making an effort to say, "Because we are doing pastoral succession now does not mean that will always be the method we employ."

Key factor eight: Even though there isn't one single model for how an outgoing pastor functions after leaving her or his position, there is discussion and clarity about what that person's role and expectations will be post-transition , before the actual change occurs. In some cases, the outgoing pastor remains in the community, participates in worship as a member of the congregation, and may be invited to teach an occasional class or co-officiate at a memorial service. In other instances, the outgoing pastor leaves town, resettles elsewhere, and returns to visit the church only when invited to do so. Denominational rules and guidelines are sometimes a factor in which of these, or some other variation, happens. The point is to talk about, think through, and plan for the role of the former pastor in advance of her or his retirement.

The specifics depend on the needs and plans of the outgoing pastor and his or her family, the incoming pastor, and the congregation. But the contours of the outgoing pastor's role should be discussed and agreed upon *in advance* of the change.

Key factor nine: The role the out going pastor assumes in preparing for the incoming pastor before the in coming pastor arrives or moves into the senior position is another critical factor in successful pastoral transitions. Pastors who have thrived in the successor role point to a number of things their predecessors did to make their lives easier. First, they identified someone on the staff to train, orient, and answer the questions of the incoming pastor. If there was an overlap period, this adviser might be the outgoing pastor. If not, it might be a church business administrator or senior associate. Or, it might be some combination of both.

Another thing an outgoing pastor can do for a successor is help a difficult or noncontributing staff member to find the door, whether to retirement or a new position elsewhere. It's a whole lot better for the incoming pastor not to be the fall guy on this one.

Third, the outgoing pastor can make sure that associate ministers who stay on understand that they are not the new senior minister, even if for a time they know more than the new person. Associate pastors who continue through a pastoral succession also need to be mature people who understand and mind boundaries and who do not play games with their own loyalties or those of the congregation.

Finally, an outgoing pastor can help by introducing his or her successor to some of the leaders in the wider community and again giving his or her blessing to that person's presence and role in the wider community.

Key factor ten: The new pastor must be able to preach effectively. Preaching remains the single most important task, among all the tasks of a pastor. It is the role in which the largest number of people experience their new pastor and in which they perceive both his or her caring and competence.

If a person who succeeds an effective and beloved former pastor is not effective in the pulpit, there won't be too much else that can be done to compensate for that lack. Of course, the new person will have a different style and voice in the pulpit. That is expected, even desirable. But hers or his must be a strong voice, one that engages and inspires the congregation.

CONCLUSION

While I am sure that others could come up with additional factors, these ten are worth paying serious attention to if your church is considering such a path for pastoral transition. Pastoral succession is not right for every church in transition. But it is a good option for some.

REFLECTION QUESTIONS

1. What do you think are the pluses and minuses of this model? What are potential hazards and opportunities for success?
2. Have you ever seen this model used before? If so, what were the outcomes?
3. Might this model work for your church? Why or why not?

Chapter Nine

An Appreciative Inquiry Paradigm for Transitional Ministry

Rob Voyle

Many years ago I was very miserable. I saw many spiritual directors and therapists who basically wanted to know why I was miserable. We turned over every rock and uncovered all sorts of bad history, pain, and rejection. Yet all that got me was a better informed misery. The little good it did was in helping me reach a place of acceptance. I discovered I had very good reasons for being miserable, and so I stopped hating myself for being miserable, which was a significant relief, but I was still fundamentally miserable.

What really helped at that time was a clinical pastoral education supervisor, George Markham, who was radically uninterested in my misery, or changing it, or getting rid of it. What George was interested in was "How did Rob do happy?" and "How can Rob do more of that?" I discovered that you cannot be happy by working on being less miserable.

Much of religion and psychology shares an interest in trying to determine what is wrong with humanity and why we suffer so many afflictions. Religion gives us catalogs of sin, as in the book of Leviticus, while psychology has given us catalogs of human misery, such as the *Diagnostic and Statistical Manual of Mental Disorders*. Yet they give no hint of how to resolve these miseries, nor do they provide an equally robust classification of human joys or life-giving qualities. While religion and psychology use different language, both focus on what is wrong and promote the idea that the path to peace is to "come to terms with" the dark forces, whether they be sin, id impulses, neurosis, traumatic history, or bad learning. Despite degrees in theology and psychology, however, I have never been quite sure what it means to "come to terms" with the past or the darkness that dwells within us. I am surprised now that in all the courses I took for my doctorate in psychology, I heard only one lecture on the nature of a healthy person but spent many hours learning to classify human misery.

Yet within the world of contemplative spirituality there is another perspective that suggests that rather than come to terms with the dark, we need to turn on the light. When children are afraid of the dark, we don't turn off the dark. We don't need to spend time analyzing the darkness or where it came from, or eloquently describing its subtle shades and nuances, or romanticizing the darkness, or fighting the monsters that roam in the darkness. We just need to turn on the light! And in the words of Martin Buber, if we teach the child to see and carry the light that is within her or him, she or he need never be afraid of the darkness.[1]

A similar voice can also be found in the field of positive psychology, which seeks to discover a person's strengths and explore how these strengths can be used to help the person create his or her preferred future. Here is an example of a therapist whom I would place in the positive psychology school working with a young boy who is very afraid of dogs.

Therapist: So I understand you are afraid of dogs?

(*Boy nods head and shivers.*)

Therapist: So, here is what we are going to do. We are going to go down to the pound, and you won't need to be afraid, because I will be with you and all the dogs are in cages.

(*Later at the pound.*)

Therapist: Now here is what we are going to do. We are going to walk around the pound; and I want you to find the most frightened puppy in the pound, and you are going to take the puppy home and teach the puppy not to be afraid.

(*End of therapy.*)[2]

Notice that there is no exploration of the origins or the impact of the phobia on the child's life. Nor is there any need for the boy to have insight into the origin or nature of the phobia. There is simply a problem and a strategy to create a solution.

Many of the approaches to transitional ministry seem to mirror my own personal experience of trying to dealing with my misery. Congregations often find themselves in transition because of problems with their former pastor, and they manifest a variety of miseries. Conventional wisdom suggests that before these congregations can have a successful relationship with their next minister, they need to "come to terms" with their history and gain insight into how they were part of the cause of these problems. Some of these congregations will spend considerable sums of money to hire consultants to analyze the problems and write reports explaining the origins of the problems from a variety of perspectives. Yet, despite the detailed analysis and eloquent descriptions of the problems, little—if anything—actually changes within the system, because the focus has been on the cause of the problem and not on creating a solution.

When interim ministry began, it was focused on troubled congregations and used as its primary tool what psychology had to offer at that time. It relied heavily, if not myopically, upon the "family systems" model of Murray Bowen to understand the systemic nature of congregations. Other "family" approaches, such as the strategic family therapy model of Jay Haley or Conjoint Family therapy of Virginia Satir, were ignored. Likewise "systems thinking" was reduced to "family systems," and other systemic approaches, such as Peter Senge's learning organization, were largely ignored. In many ways, transitional ministry has generally used a "fix the pathology" model. I believe, however, that since we will spend the rest of our lives in the future, what we need to come to terms with is the future and not the past. We need to learn how to let the light shine in our congregations and to turn that light toward our future. We are not agents of less death, less darkness, less disease, or less dysfunction. We are agents of the Gospel and love, power that transforms lives and congregations.

THE APPRECIATIVE WAY

During my early days as an interim minister I became increasingly frustrated with the less-death model of transitional ministry and began searching for an alternative. I tired of sitting with other clergy as they described the bride of Christ as codependent, dysfunctional, toxic, and unhealthy clergy killers, and regaled one another with stories of how dysfunctional their congregations were. It was in my search for an alternative that I was introduced to the world of Appreciative Inquiry.

Appreciative Inquiry was developed by David Cooperrider at Case Western Reserve University in the mid-1980s.[3] As part of his doctoral studies, Cooperrider was conducting a traditional organization development consulting exercise at the Cleveland Clinic. His approach, based on the best wisdom of the day, was to conduct an assessment of the organization to determine "what's wrong" in the organization. Once this diagnosis had been achieved, then "treatment" could be applied to the causes of the problem. This approach was based on the assumption that development occurs through the continual solving of problems.

As Cooperrider gathered his data, he became amazed at the high level of cooperation, innovation, and organizational effectiveness at the clinic. His academic adviser, Suresh Srivastva, observed Cooperrider's excitement in these discoveries and encouraged him to explore what was enabling such high levels of collaborative performance. The focus of the assessment was changed from "what's wrong" to "what's working." Cooperrider discovered that the more people shared stories about what was working and life-giving in the organization, the more these life-giving realities grew. Understanding this way of growing what works, rather than focusing on preventing what doesn't work, became the focus of his research. Cooperrider called this approach Appreciative Inquiry.

Appreciative Inquiry is characterized by people sharing stories about their best experience of the organization or the activity being developed, and then on the basis of these stories dreaming and envisioning a future that builds on those experiences. Sharing best experiences and life-giving values typically evokes considerable positive emotion, which in turn liberates the creative potential in the group.[4]

Appreciative Inquiry has been used extensively in a variety of contexts, such as businesses, churches, and relief agencies, in wide-scale community development, and as a foundation of executive and personal coaching. In many situations its use has resulted in systemic transformation rather than only incremental change and development.

Many practitioners in the field, myself included, have found that Appreciative Inquiry is more than just another organization development technique. It is a different way of being and doing in the world that has an impact on all aspects of life and work. Because of this, and because of its parallels with other positive approaches I valued, my wife, Kim, and I created the Appreciative Way, our synthesis of Appreciative Inquiry, the change work of Milton Erickson[5] and Steve Andreas,[6] and Eastern and Western contemplative spirituality.

To describe the application of the Appreciative Way to the work of transitional ministry, I will outline three assumptions that are foundational to the Appreciative Way and then the eight assumptions of Appreciative Inquiry. Each assumption informs the others, and in many situations they overlap to create an organic whole rather than provide discrete concepts.

Appreciative Way Assumption A: At the heart of the universe is love, which is the source of our existence and our purpose for being. On the Sunday after the 9/11 attack on the World Trade Center, Chris Rankin-Williams, my parish associate at the time, said in his sermon: "The challenge of this life is not to stay alive; the challenge of this life is to stay in love." If your goal is to stay alive, you will lose, because we all will die. The real choice is about how we live until that day. From my experience, we get two options: we can live either in love or in fear. From an evolutionary, biological perspective, living in fear is the default position. We have many more neurons scanning our environment for life-threatening dangers than we have scanning for beauty, joy, love, or other life-enhancing possibilities. Consequently, living in love is an acquired and often challenging habit.

In the English language we often talk of being "in love." This language points to the reality that love is not something I do to you and you do to me, but that somehow in each other's company we find ourselves connected to that which is greater than either of us. This is the heart of contemplative spirituality. We do not need to earn love or make love happen; rather, we need to wake up to the love that already is and allow ourselves to be held by and filled with this love. When loving or getting love is the focus of our activity, we will actually live in fear, afraid that we may never gain love or, having gained it, we will lose it. Awakening to the reality that we are already enfolded in eternal loving-kindness liberates us from this fundamental fear and sets us free to manifest that eternal love in this temporal world. Calling people to live in this love rather than fear is the fundamental essence of all ministry. You and I are unique expressions of God's love in this temporal world, and living in love is our heritage as the people of God. When we create ministry strategies, we need to ensure that our strategies are an expression of that love.

Implications for Transitional Ministry

We do not need to "bring God or God's love to people." We need to help people wake up to the love that already exists and join God in what God is doing. People will not change, at least in the direction we want them to change, because we frighten them, judge them, or hate them. People will change only because we love them. As we work with congregations in transition, one of the big challenges is maintaining and working from a place of love. It is easy to become afraid, frustrated, and distracted from love when congregations act in unloving ways. For transitional ministers, belonging to a loving community beyond the congregation we are currently serving may be an important resource if we are to keep our focus on love when ministering in unloving congregations.

Appreciative Way Assumption B: The deepest longing of the human heart is for acceptance, and the only changes that will be sustainable are those that result in greater self-acceptance and acceptance from and for others. While acceptance is the deepest longing of the human heart, we often experience life as a state of alienation. We experience alienation from our self, our abilities, and our deepest potential; from our neighbor; and from God, the source of our existence. Jesus's cry from the cross, "My God, my God, why have you forsaken me?" (Mark 15:34), is one of the deepest expressions of the alienation that is in every human heart. The practical consequence of this alienation is that we are unable to create a life worth living.

All human problems have their basis in alienation. We do not need to spend time considering the origins of the alienation, however. Rather, we need to focus our attention on reconciliation and collaboration. With respect to God, we can focus on the atonement, God's response to humanity's alienation. Rather than trying to understand how the mystery of our "at-one-ment" has taken place in Christ, I suggest people start with the extravagant acceptance of God's infinite love—and then wonder how they can join God in making that timeless grace of acceptance a reality for others.

Within organizations we need to ensure that our change processes and outcomes result in greater acceptance throughout the systems. Processes that are inherently alienating, despite the facilitator's best of intentions, are not likely to result in sustainable outcomes. We cannot fight for peace. Teaching people to fight fairly keeps alive the notion of fighting and sustains a mentality that we will always have winners and losers. We must pursue justice and blessing for all if we are to create a peaceful world.

Organizational psychologists have often borrowed the medical model of assess, diagnose, and treat when working with systems. The model may be appropriate when treating an individual with a bacterial infection and the bacteria must be "alienated" from the person's body. However, it is not appropriate when dealing with human systems. Diagnosis is a sophisticated word for judgment and blame, and when used with social systems, regardless of the intention, it will be experienced as alienating. Some people in the system will always feel blamed and experience alienation, which will not incline their hearts toward life-giving outcomes. Likewise, the word "treatment" when applied to human systems evokes a sense of arrogance and condescension. Rather than assess, diagnose, and treat in the Appreciative Way, we first join with the system to help the system discover its life-giving potential and then dream of and design ways to manifest that potential in the world.

While I believe our deepest longing is for acceptance, I also view acceptance as a safe foundation from which to seek and create solutions. If I could, I would add two additional phrases to the serenity prayer: "God, grant me the serenity to accept the things I cannot change, the courage to change the things I can, *the curiosity to discover how to do things many claim cannot be done*, and the wisdom to know the difference *and where to begin.*"

Implications for Transitional Ministry

The deepest longing within individual members of a congregation and the congregation as a whole is for acceptance. That acceptance may be from God, from another member, from the wider church, or from the world in which they find themselves. All problems within the congregation have their origins in alienation; all solutions have their origin in acceptance. As transition ministers we need to be agents of acceptance and not less alienation.

In conflicted situations, the parties often engage in behaviors that disenfranchise or alienate others. Since alienation is antithetical to the reconciling ways of God, it is impossible to discover God's will by using strategies that result in alienation. We have not been entrusted with a ministry of conflict management; we have been entrusted with the ministry of reconciliation. Eloquently describing levels of conflict may make clergy or expert facilitators feel better, but does little to resolve the conflict. We need to be agents of reconciliation, not less conflict. Teaching people how to forgive and not just that they need to forgive will be essential if we are to go beyond managing the conflict to create reconciliation and communities of acceptance that are actively involved in the work of God.

To know and feel accepted, people need to have these four aspects of their lives validated:

1. All need their existence, their presence, to be seen and affirmed by the community.
2. All have a voice and need to have their story listened to and heard by the community.
3. All have talents that need to be received as unique contributions to the well-being of the community.
4. All have specific dreams and hope for a better tomorrow that the community needs to affirm and bless.

During transitional times we can keep these factors in mind as we work to create cultures of reconciliation and acceptance. The Appreciative Inquiry process—shared storytelling, listening, dreaming, and aligning people's strengths with core purposes—by its very nature fulfills the four needs for acceptance and creates cultures of acceptance that are more likely to result in outcomes that are inherently reconciling and sustainable.

Appreciative Way Assumption C: At any given moment, people are doing the best they know how to in that context. In other words, underlying all behavior is a positive intention.[7] Often this assumption is difficult for people to accept, especially when the behavior in question is violent or disrespectful. This assumption does not mean that we approve of the other's behavior or that we do not hold people responsible for their behavior. We do acknowledge, however, that even when people do know that they "should" do something better, contextual factors may restrict a person's ability to choose an appropriate response. For example, a person who typically tells the truth may resort to lying when faced with the threat of injury or great loss. At that point, immediate safety concerns may take precedence over the long-term damage to the person's integrity. This explanation is not to condone lying, but it is one way of understanding why, in some situations, generally honest people may lie.

From a biblical perspective, Jesus's plea from the cross, "Father, forgive them, for they don't know what they are doing" (Luke 23:34), expresses the truth of this assumption. Jesus did not attribute evil to the people who sought and carried out his execution; rather, he attributed their actions to ignorance. In their ignorance they believed that Jesus was a menace and their lives would be better if he were dead. Their desire to live peaceably, free from the chaos Jesus was causing, was part of their positive intention. Unfortunately, as in many instances, a negative strategy was used in the pursuit of a positive intention.

The assumption that positive intentions underlie behavior may require that we explore several layers of intention to find the positive one. Notice the behavior itself is not the positive intention. The positive intention wasn't to kill Jesus; the positive intention was to live in peace. While the behavior is unacceptable, the underlying positive intention is one we could affirm. We do not condone behavior that denigrates or destroys humanity. Rather, we find the positive intention underlying that destructive behavior and then encourage respectful, life-giving alternative behaviors to achieve that intention.

A strategy people, and the church in particular, have used when dealing with problematic behavior is to shame or make the perpetrator feel guilty for his or her behavior. Unfortunately, shame rarely creates sustainable change. When shamed, people feel small and vulnerable rather than strong and equipped to resolve a problem. When a person is continually shamed over a period of time, the shamed person will be motivated to destroy those who are shaming her or him. As the apostle Paul attests in his letter to the Romans, hating a behavior and trying not to do it actually makes it worse and does not bring healing and transformation (Romans 7:15–25). We cannot enjoy a grace-filled life by focusing our attention on having less sin in our lives. In fact, being shamed and hating our sinful nature is a guaranteed way to stay miserable, alienated, and trapped in the sin we hate. Paul concludes his reflections on the power of sin, "Who will rescue me from this body of death? Thanks be to God through Jesus Christ our Lord!" (vv. 24–25). The way to a grace-filled life is not the path of trying to have less sin, but turning one's attention to the grace of God that is already present in Jesus.

Implications for Transitional Ministry

The Gospel message is fundamentally about the infinite loving acceptance of God as it has been made known to us in Jesus. Transitional ministers need to express that acceptance toward the congregation. This congregation is doing the best it knows how, even when that best is not very good. When confronting problems, we need to remain open and curious to discover and join with the positive intention behind problematic behaviors rather than focusing on and joining with the problem. From my experience, congregations don't change because we judge them and hold them in contempt or shame them for their failings. Judgment, blame, and shame keep congregations, like Paul, in disempowered cycles of doing and hating. In the world of Appreciative Inquiry, such cycles are called "negative spirals of enfeeblement," and no matter what we try, they only get worse. I have found that "stepping back" and seeing a congregation and individual members as having a positive intent helps me create a foundation for loving them, which keeps me open and curious to discover what God may be up to in their midst.

These three assumptions—that the heart of the universe is love, that people's deepest longing is for acceptance, and that positive intention underlies all behavior—form a foundation from which I understand all of life and create the core of the Appreciative Way. The assumptions of Appreciative Inquiry are also central elements of my understanding of the Appreciative Way.

ASSUMPTIONS OF APPRECIATIVE INQUIRY

In *The Thin Book of Appreciative Inquiry*, author and Appreciative Inquiry practitioner Sue Hammond lists eight assumptions that form the foundation of Appreciative Inquiry thought and practice.

1. In every society, organization, or group, something works.
2. What we focus on becomes our reality.
3. Reality is created in the moment, and there are multiple realities.
4. The act of asking questions of an organization or group influences the group in some way.
5. People have more confidence and comfort to journey to the future (the unknown) when they carry forward parts of the past (the known).
6. If we carry parts of the past forward, they should be what is best about the past.
7. It is important to value differences.
8. The language we use creates our reality.[8]

Assumption 1. In every society, organization, or group, something works. Sometimes, especially after a traumatic experience, those suffering have difficulty imagining that anything is working. I was once trying to explain this first assumption to members of a small congregation that had experienced a considerable decline in membership and finances. They told me things were so bad that nothing worked, and as an example, they said they couldn't get anyone to volunteer for altar guild duty. I asked them what they were inviting people to volunteer for, and they said, "Polishing the brass, pressing linens, and basically getting ready for Sunday." Since they said nothing was working, I became curious about their congregational life and engaged them in the following conversation:

"You say nothing works here, so I am curious. Did you have Eucharist on Sunday?"

"Yes," they replied.

"Were there candles on the altar?"

"Yes," they replied.

"Were the candles lit?"

"Yes."

"Were there flowers on the altar?" (I had walked through the sanctuary to get to the meeting room and had seen the flowers.)

"Yes."

"Was there bread and wine on the altar?"

"Yes."

"Now I am really curious! You say nothing works, yet you had Eucharist, with bread and wine, and there were flowers on the altar and the candles were lit. If nothing is working, how did all that happen?"

"Oh, that's Helen," they chorused.

"So what you are telling me is that Helen works! We need to find Helen and discover what she knows that you really need to know."

We found Helen and I asked her what she did at the church, to which she replied:

"I have the best job. I get to come down to church on Saturday and prepare a place for God and people to sit down and have a meal together."

When we heard this, I suggested to the leaders, "Rather than asking people to come down and polish brass and press linens, why not invite people to come down to the church to prepare a place for people to sit down and have a meal with God?"

What had happened in this congregation was that the members had become obsessed with what was not working, and in that frustrated obsession they were blind to the good that was happening. Granted, there may have been little besides Helen that was working. But if they are to have a future, they need to build the future on what is working rather than trying to build the future on having less of what is not working.

Implications for Transitional Ministry

In my transitional ministry work, my first sermon was always titled, "What in God's name is going on here?" I would dramatically ask that question at the beginning of the sermon and pause, especially if there had been misconduct or conflict that had led to the pastor's departure. I would then say: "Whatever you are thinking in answer to that question probably is none of my or our business, because it wasn't happening in God's name. Our task is to discover the things that are happening in God's name and joining with God in doing more of it."

To discover what in God's name is going on, I use appreciative interviewing and storytelling focused on their best experiences of their church, for it is when we are at our best that we most closely approximate the image of God that we were created to be. In this storytelling of life-giving times in the congregation the people can discern God's presence and articulate their congregation's purpose and core values, which in turn become the foundation for cocreating their preferred future.

Assumption 2. What we focus on becomes our reality. We are confronted with millions of stimuli during the course of a day, and it would be overwhelming to pay attention to them all. Through the course of our lives we have learned to filter or screen for certain information and ignore other things. Over time, this filtering process becomes an unconscious habit that typically serves us well, as we automatically focus our attention on information that we have discovered is important in making decisions to achieve our objectives. On the other hand, these unconscious habits can create blind spots that limit our potential to respond creatively and compassionately to the world around us, especially when that world is changing and we are locked into seeing reality as it was, and not as it currently is.

Observing something isn't benign. To observe something means that we have begun to engage with what we are observing, and in this engagement we begin to affect it. Golfers know the negative impact of focus all too well. If a golfer is admonished just before hitting the ball, "Don't hit it into the trees," the golfer is likely to look up, focus on the trees, and then hit the ball straight into them. As they focus on the trees, the trees become their reality.

Focus is not only an individual process but also a group process. Different groups will focus on specific things within the community. Police officers will look for criminals and signs of crime, while psychologists and mental health workers will look for people with psychological problems. Transitional clergy, steeped in pathology-focused psychology, will look for and find all manner of dysfunction and troubles in the belief that is their responsibility to solve all these problems before the next pastor arrives. Alternatively, transitional clergy steeped in positive psychology, such as Appreciative Inquiry, will focus their attention on empowering a congregation to develop its strengths to cocreate the congregation's future.

We can choose what we focus on and attend to. Throughout the Scriptures the words "behold" or "see" and other phrases are used to focus people's attention on the things of God. For example, "See what love God has given us, that we should be called children of God" (1 John 3:1), or Paul's admonishment: "Finally, beloved, whatever is true, whatever is honorable, whatever is just, whatever is pure, whatever is pleasing, whatever is commendable, if there is any excellence and if there is anything worthy of praise, think about these things" (Phil. 4:8).

Since we can choose what we focus on, and what we focus on becomes our reality, it is important to choose to focus on those things that bring us closer to the reality we want to live in. Jesus demonstrated the power of focus throughout his ministry. He kept his focus on the kingdom of God, yet the reality of the people around him was the kingdom of Rome. When "multiple realities," such as the kingdom of God and the kingdom of Rome, are present, asking, "Which reality do you want to live in?" and then focusing attention on that reality makes sense. It will grow in our consciousness and become truer to us. This is what Jesus did with his proclamation of the kingdom of God. The more Jesus talked of the kingdom of God, the reality that was still to come in its complete fullness, the more it grew in the hearers' awareness.

Jesus also demonstrated the power of focus when responding to an individual's pastoral concern. Jesus remained focused on his desired outcome and not the current reality of the person. He did not waste time worrying about the causes of problems, nor did he spend time trying to get people to have insight into their problems. For example, in the story of the man born blind, the disciples asked, "Whose sin, his own or his parents, caused him to be blind?" Jesus dismissed those possibilities and instead saw in the man's blindness an opportunity for God's glory to be manifested (John 9:1–3). Likewise, in the story of the woman at the well, Jesus never explored why she had multiple husbands, nor did he require that she gain insight into her interpersonal problems. Instead, he used ambiguous language to evoke confusion and melt the certainty of her worldview to help the woman come to a whole new understanding of the nature of life (John 4:7–30).

As these two stories indicate, choosing to focus on outcomes does not mean that we need to engage in ostrich-like avoidance or denial. There are many miserable things in the world that we do need to attend to—but how we focus is critical. Rather than focus on the origins of the problem, we can focus on the problem from the perspective of its solution.

Implications for Transitional Ministry

Because all action begins with focus, what the transitional minister and the congregation in transition focus on will be critical. In situations where there has been turmoil or conflict, the congregation is likely to be very distracted by multiple obsessions and concerns that typically have little to do with creating a godly future. Reorienting the congregation to its core purpose and values will be an essential part of the work of the transitional ministry to create a unified foundation for the congregation's future.

Problems easily distract us and get us focusing on things we don't want. What can be particularly frustrating is that minor irritants can become major distractions and interfere with our enjoyment of life. In the Gospel Jesus taught us to leave the weeds in the field, because our attempts to pull them out would also damage the good crop that we want (Matt. 13:24–30). I have seen too much damage done to the vibrant parts of a congregation by efforts to pull out a few weeds. As any gardener knows, the best way to prevent weeds is to plant and grow the healthy plants we do want. They will crowd out the weeds. Paying attention to and affirming what is life giving will cause those realities to grow at the expense of those realities we do not want.

We also need to be careful with the labels we use to describe our congregations and the groups within the congregations. How we focus on these groups will affect what we call forth from them. When a congregation is labeled a "clergy killer," it is likely to repeat those patterns. Yet, no congregation is only one thing. If we want to call forth the best from people, we need to use language that evokes their best rather than their worst.

"Elephants in the room" are those issues or realities that we all know are present, so they cannot be ignored, but that no one will discuss. To intentionally not talk of something requires that we keep it in focus so that we are sure to avoid it. Being well nourished by negative attention, most "elephants" grow and overwhelm the emotional space so that eventually there is no real conversation. Rather than forcing people to engage in the conversation, which would be an act of emotional violence, we need to step back from the issue and have a conversation about what would make people feel safe enough to have the conversation. For some, creating norms of behavior and respect may provide enough safety. In other situations, the presence of an external facilitator may be required to create sufficient safety. Only when the community has been made safe will the people be able to freely have a conversation about the "elephant" and resolve the unspoken issue.

Assumption 3. Reality is created in the moment, and there are multiple realities. Appreciative Inquiry makes considerable use of the philosophy and practice of social constructionism. In its absolute form, social constructionism posits that there is no objective reality, but individuals and groups construct an understanding of reality that then becomes the reality that they live in and experience.

Personally, I am not a social construction absolutist. However, I think while there is an objective reality, human beings do socially construct an understanding of that reality. We deal with reality not directly, but through our senses and subjective interpretation of our perceptions. Even when we are being "objective" or "literal," we are using language, which is an intellectual abstraction or metaphoric communication about the reality we are experiencing. As we focus on a particular understanding of reality, that view will in turn shape us in self-confirming patterns.

Within the church, considerable argument occurs over whose map of God is true. Because our understanding of God affects deep, existential issues, such as life, death, and the possibility of an afterlife, having our map of God challenged can be very anxiety provoking. Understanding that the map is just the map and not the territory will help in making communities safer for people to enter into dialogue with those with whom they disagree.

I am no longer interested in whose map of God is true or right. I do however pay attention to the fruit or outcome of the map. As someone who has planted bare-root fruit trees, I have learned that the only way really to know what I planted is to wait for the fruit and not simply rely on a label attached to the tree when I planted it.

What is the fruit of your theology or "map" of God? Does your understanding of God lead naturally to love, acceptance, reverence, caring for the poor, doing justice, and other behaviors we would associate with the followers of Jesus? If your understanding of God leads to fear, hatred, and war, and perpetuates injustice, then I would suggest that you may want to change your map.

Implications for Transitional Ministry

A significant task of transitional ministry is to help the congregation develop or affirm its self-understanding. From a social constructionist perspective, a congregation's self-understanding is created through the telling of stories. Different groups within the congregation, such as the early or later service attendees, will often have different understandings of the congregation. Some congregations may believe that they are failing, while others may believe they can do anything they put their mind to. Both beliefs will be based on the stories that people tell about their congregation.

The shared narrative of a congregation is not written in stone; it is shared in human hearts and minds. As such, it can always be changed, and often it will need to be changed to create a positive outcome. For example, imagine two small, dying congregations that decide to merge. The key narrative in both congregations is "We are a small, dying church." When they merge the narrative will still be "We are a slightly larger dying congregation." Until the "dying congregation" narrative is changed, the congregation will continue to decline, and research suggests that most merged congregations will quickly become the size of the larger of the original congregations rather than grow beyond the combined congregations' size. Knowing how to change a congregation's narrative is essential for effective transitional ministry.

When leading congregations in transition, leaders must ensure that the congregation's narrative is transformed to be consistent with the congregation's desired purpose and goals. If the narrative is inconsistent with a goal, the desired outcome will not be sustainable, and people will return to manifesting their former narrative. This is the struggle Moses had in leading the people out of Egypt. The people came out of Egypt with a slave narrative, to which they were easily tempted to return when confronted by the hardship of journeying through the wilderness (Numbers 11:4–6). The people wandered in the wilderness for forty years before the "people of God" narrative took sustainable root in their consciousness. Within a congregation there will be many narratives about the past. Rather than working to create a shared historical narrative, the transitional minister needs to focus attention on developing a shared future narrative that the people can grow into. Jesus's preaching of the kingdom of God is an example of creating and sustaining focus on the future narrative rather than on the historical narrative of the people of Israel.

One way to change the narrative is to change the perspective from which the narrative is told. For example, a congregation that has undergone great turmoil during and following leadership misconduct will typically tell a victim narrative. They will focus on all the bad things that were done and the bad consequences of those actions, reinforcing victim consciousness. Well-intentioned transitional ministers will want the congregation to tell these stories rather than keep them secret. While keeping them secret is a real problem, incessant telling of the victim story, however, will reinforce victim consciousness and perpetuate other victim experiences.

What is often missing in the repetitive telling of victim narratives is the survivor story. How did the congregation survive? What in the congregation was so valuable that people didn't leave when the bad thing occurred? Many victims of trauma do not know they survived. Helping them to discover how they survived will be essential to helping them move out of victim consciousness and into the world of survivors. These two stories need to be told together, for just as repeated telling of the victim narrative will reinforce victim consciousness, allowing people to talk only about how they survived will foster denial. We can't have a survivor narrative without a victim narrative.

When the two stories are told, a third story, the thriver narrative, can begin to emerge. It is the story of how even in the midst of tragedy God is still present and life is still being offered. The victim story is the Bad Friday story. The survivor story is the bewildering "we survived, but so what?" Holy Saturday story. The thriver story is the Easter story; it turns Bad Friday into Good Friday and opens the possibility of a whole new reality. Preparing a congregation to write the next chapter in its thriver story is at the heart of transitional ministry.

Assumption 4. The act of asking questions of an organization or group influences the group. This assumption only hints at the great power of questions. According to the classical Newtonian scientific method, an objective observer can ask questions without influencing what is observed. While that claim may be true in large-scale material science, it is not true in quantum physics or the social sciences. Because an electron or subatomic particle is so small and never stationary, observing it alters it in some way. The same is true in social science research. The act of observing someone will change both the observer and the person being observed.

Since every question moves the members of a group in some way, we need to begin asking questions that move them in the direction we want them to move. Do we want them to move into bigger and deeper problems, or do we want them to move into the abundant life that Jesus promised? If we want them to experience more problems, then we need to keep asking them about their problems. If we want them to move in the direction of life, then we need to ask them questions about what is life giving.

To create powerful questions, we need to pay attention to the outcome of the questions and not simply to the verbal responses. The word "appreciate" has multiple meanings: to pay attention to, to value, to grow. When we inquire by asking appreciative questions, all these meanings come into play. The person or group pays attention to something, that which is attended to will be valued and will grow in their awareness, and the person or group is likely to be motivated to pursue more of what is valued. From this nonobjective perspective we design appreciative questions to motivate, inspire, energize, and mobilize people for action, not just to elicit information.

Imagine a search process in which a consultant asks a group of people these questions in the following order:

1. What is working well around here?
2. What is not working well around here?
3. What do you want in your next pastor?

The first question is an Appreciative Inquiry question and will lead the group into a creative, loving mind-set that will allow them to explore possibilities and think in generative ways. The second question will call forth blame, defensiveness, and feelings of alienation. This leads to negative emotions and a negative mental state that I call "funky brain." Research shows that in this state, people will be unable to think outside of the rut they are in, they are likely to be prejudiced and intolerant of others, and their intuition is more likely to be inaccurate.[9] Unfortunately the third question is too often asked of a group of people who have been led into funky brain, which now gets to decide the qualities of the next pastor! When people are in this state, they will describe what they don't want in a pastor rather than what they do want, as in, "We don't want a pastor like the last one!" But people's knowing what they don't want will not help them discover what they do need to create their desired future.

Rather than simply ignoring the problems that might exist, I would ask these questions in a different manner.

1. What is working well around here?
2. What do you want more of in the future?
3. What do you need in your next pastor to help you achieve that?

The second question is now focused on the future. If a problem did exist, it would be reframed into what they want more of rather than on what they don't want. The future-focused question also allows for the possibility that what they want more of are things that are already working well. Regardless of whether the answer is about reframed problems or things that are already working well, the question will begin to evoke images of things they desire, which will keep them in a creative mental state. The third question moves the focus from simply the pastor's role in the congregation to the collective mission of the community.

Implications for Transitional Ministry

Powerful questions are an essential part of the transitional minister's tool kit and can set the stage for the ministry from its very beginning. Imagine meeting with a church board as part of a transitional ministry "job interview" and being told you could ask only one question. What would that question be? From my experience in teaching transitional ministers, they will ask one of the following two questions:

• What would a successful transitional ministry in the congregation look like?
• What problems do you need to address before the new pastor arrives?

The first question will point people in the direction of creating a successful ministry; the second will direct the people's attention toward problems and make them the focus. The first question doesn't avoid problems but frames the ministry, including problem solving, in the context of success and will move people in that direction rather than in the direction of problems.

One of the common tasks of transitional ministry is to help the congregation clarify and define its identity and mission in a "parish profile" to be used in the search for a new pastor. Frequently, an anonymous survey of all the members is conducted. I have in the past written computer software to help congregations do such surveys. I now find them counterproductive and no longer develop them or support their use. My first objection is that surveys produce abstract data that do not motivate or inspire action. In contrast an appreciative inquiry storytelling process will not only provide data but will also motivate and inspire people to action. Why did Christianity flourish? Did it flourish because eleven guys got together in a room and took an anonymous vote, and ten voted for the resurrection? Or did Christianity flourish because people shared their stories about encountering the risen Lord and how that transformed their lives? Christianity has never been about what 51 percent of the people think. Throughout the history of Christianity, people have been inspired and motivated by the telling of stories.

My other major objection to anonymous surveys is that they violate one of the core values of Christianity: that in Christian community we are known by name. Because anonymous surveys violate our core values, they will disrupt community rather than grow it. Anonymity seems to give people license to unleash their vitriol but it provides no way to enter into dialogue with the person and resolve the issue. If problems do exist we need to work on making the community safe for people to openly discuss their concerns rather than rely on a cloak of anonymity that will diminish the community. While many churches are now accepting only signed surveys, which may appease my objection to anonymity, I still find them of questionable value, because they reduce the mystery of human existence to data points and percentages.

Assumption 5. People have more confidence and comfort to journey to the future (the unknown) when they carry forward parts of the past with them.

Assumption 6. If we carry parts of the past forward, they should be what is best about the past. Because Assumption 6 follows naturally from Assumption 5, I will review them together. These two assumptions describe how Appreciative Inquiry and the Appreciative Way relate to time. The future, where we will spend the rest of our lives, is calling us. While we can't change one iota of our past, we do get to decide what from our past we will use to inform our present and our future. Even when our past has been painful or difficult, we can build our future on the personal resources we used to survive those events and not on working to create less of the difficult times. Consequently we do not ignore the past and our history. We can choose to leave behind what is unhelpful and build our future on the best of our past.

Transitions are by their nature times of change, yet when it comes to change I agree with Stephen Gilligan, who said: "People don't want to be changed; they want to be blessed."[10] From my perspective, a blessing is a final state that is more valuable than the starting state plus the cost of the time, money, effort, or other resources required to achieve it. If we want our efforts to result in sustainable change, the change needs to be experienced as a blessing. Inviting people to engage in the change process rather than simply imposing a change on them will help people see the value in the change and own their part in achieving the change.

People resist change for three reasons:

1. They cannot perceive the value of the outcome.
2. They do not perceive the outcome is worth the effort or resources required to achieve it.
3. The change is imposed upon them without their input.

Regardless of the merits of the change, imposed change is an insult to the dignity of the person and will evoke resistance. Only a fool would gladly go to a place of lesser value or spend more resources on something that has minimal value or willingly allow someone to denigrate their essential dignity. Notice that a "perception" of the change's value rather than the actual value leads to resistance. For example, the rich, young ruler (Mark 10:17–22) could not perceive that the value of following Jesus was worth giving away all of his possessions, and so he resisted following Jesus. For whatever reason, Jesus was not able to alter this perception, but he looked on the ruler with love and respected his freedom rather than judging, condemning, or rebuking him. In contrast, James and John perceived that following Jesus was more valuable than being fishermen, and so they followed Jesus (Matthew 4:18–22). Jesus also strategically embedded the language and value of fishing in their future of "following him" by telling them that they would become "fishers of people."

Implications for Transitional Ministry

Too often I see transitional ministers acting like cowboys or cowgirls who believe they are sent by God or their denomination to "break" the congregation of its bad habits. These actions are often disrespectful and spiritually violent, evoking resistance rather than facilitating blessing. All sustainable change is an "inside job," however. Jesus did not come and inflict salvation on us. He came and lived as one of us, and as one of us he led us into the kingdom of God, where we know him as Lord and Savior. Transitional ministers need to incarnationally join a congregation at those places that are life giving and valued by the congregation. Once we have joined with them and are "on the inside," we need to ensure that as we make changes, the congregation's values are respected, enriched, and experienced as a blessing. When we find congregational values that we cannot value ourselves, we need, in a spirit of curiosity, to explore what deeper values these values are based on to discover their positive intent and discern a value that we can also value. If we cannot find a shared value, then we should probably leave, just as Jesus taught us when he said: "When you go to a town say peace to the town, if the peace is not returned leave" (Matt. 10:11–14).

Assumption 7. It is important to value differences. Just as people focus on different things within a congregation, they will also value different things. Some parishioners will value the quiet of a chapel service, whereas others will value the fellowship and community feeling of a larger service in the main sanctuary. To make changes and to create a vision for the future, the individual differences need to be valued and incorporated into the life of the congregation. If the differences are not valued, the seeds of resentment and future conflict will have been sown.

While valuing differences is important, it is not simply an end in itself. One of the things I consistently hear in congregations is that they "value their diversity." However, we cannot create community on the basis of diversity. We create community on the basis of what diverse people have in common— their "common unity." Creating a "common unity" doesn't mean that we overlook the diversity, but rather, out of radical respect for our differences, we create a safe and sacred space where we can discover our deeper commonalities. Exploring these common values and life-giving realities creates the "umbrella" under which the diversity is embraced and sustained. These values become the lifeblood of the community.

Valuing diversity also requires that we engage the entire congregation in defining these life-giving values. Top-down, hierarchical approaches violate the integrity of a congregation's experience and deny the incarnational reality that God is already present and working in the congregation. The task of ministry is not to bring God to people, but to help people discover how God is already present with them and how they can join God in what God is already doing.

Implications for Transitional Ministry

Because Jesus valued the differences in the people he encountered, he did not rely on only one method of healing in his ministry. The Gospels are full of stories about the varieties of ways he encountered people, entered their unique worlds, and created strategies of healing and transformation. Using Jesus as a model, I reject the one-size-fits-all approaches that impose a process from outside of the congregation.

Most rules about transitions, such as prohibitions against hiring an associate as the senior pastor or calling the new pastor while the incumbent is still in place, were designed to prevent bad things from happening. Sadly, such rules don't ensure that good things will happen. Rather than relying on rules that may deprive a congregation of a genuine blessing, we need to discern the mind of Christ as we engage with congregations in their uniqueness.

The rule against calling a new pastor while the incumbent is still present compounds the challenge of determining how long an interim should be. In many cases the traditional eighteen-month interim is either too short or too long. When significant culture change is required following conflict or trauma, three years may be a better time frame in which to resolve the issues and equip the congregation to engage in a search. On the other hand a highly motivated and effective parish does not need a long transition and in some situations could benefit from calling its pastor while the incumbent is still in place. This would be especially true in highly energized congregations where a pastor is retiring and could easily give a year's notice and invite the congregation to engage in a search during that time. As we join a congregation we need to ask, "What does this congregation, in its uniqueness, need to get it to where it needs to be?" And then we can invent a ministry that meets its need rather than rely on a formulaic adherence to a prescribed model of development.

Valuing differences needs to be foundational for congregations conducting a self-study and preparing a profile. At a very practical level we need to create processes that allow people from subgroups within a congregation to share their stories with people from other subgroups. In the appreciative interviewing process, Cooperrider recommends "the unlikely pairing of opposites." For example, people from the early service would interview people from the later service, men interview women, conservatives interview liberals, newcomers interview old-timers, and so on. From this practical expression of valuing differences, we can discern the commonalities and God-given purpose that hold the diverse groups together. As noted previously this is something that surveys cannot do. Averaging groups and other statistical analysis tend to blur and devalue individual differences. To truly value differences and honor the "valuing of diversity," we need to invite the entire community into dialogue and dreaming of a shared future.

Assumption 8. The language we use creates our reality. Language is not simply a benign tool we use to describe our experience. Our language focuses our attention, and as previously discussed, our focus affects the reality we experience. Appreciative Inquiry pays particular attention to the impact on ourselves and others of the language we use to describe our experiences. We also use language to ask questions, and the structure of questions can have a profound impact on both the asker and the asked, and in many cases constrains or predetermines the answers. For example in the previous examples about transition rules, we could ask either of these questions:

1. Is it right for the associate to be considered as the senior pastor?
2. Under what circumstances would it be appropriate for "this associate" to be considered as "this congregation's" next senior pastor?

The first question will elicit a yes or no response that does little to explore the issues and inform the decision. It relies on experiences in the past rather than on the current reality of the associate pastor and the congregation. The second question invites conversation that is more likely to facilitate a creative response to their current experience.

Beyond simply being descriptive, words also influence us and motivate people to act. Words can hurt, heal, incite violence, or inspire love. The language we use to describe our reality can put enormous constraints on our ability to move forward into our preferred future.

The language of "church growth" presents a problem. In training programs I often talk in general terms of the church and then after a few minutes ask: "Now, as I have been using the word 'church,' what image came into your minds?" Over 75 percent of the laity and approximately 50 percent of the clergy will report "a building," with the rest seeing people engaged in some form of community activity. Herein lies a serious problem: buildings don't grow, at least in any organic way that makes sense. When we want to inspire and motivate behavior in a person, the first step is to create an image of the desired behavior. Since for many people, "church growth" is unimaginable, the language will not inspire action.

When I work with congregations I listen for the words people use to describe their congregation. Congregations of fewer than one hundred fifty Sunday worshippers are most likely to say what they value about their church is that they are a family. Congregations of over three hundred Sunday worshippers rarely use the word "family" to describe themselves. Rather, they use the word "community." Members of congregations between one hundred fifty and three hundred Sunday worshippers will give mixed responses, some valuing that they are a family and others that they are a community. Compared to small and large congregations, these midsized congregations often show more volatility when transitioning between pastors, with pendulum-like swings between "family"-oriented clergy and "community"-oriented clergy and with people from the "other" group being disenfranchised. When the goal is to grow these communities of faith, it is important to honor the "family" values, perhaps by creating house churches or other opportunities for intimacy, while also provocatively using the "community" language for their desired future. Continually referring to the congregation only as a family or seeing the congregation exclusively through the lens of a "family system," however, will ensure that the family remains small.

Likewise in appreciative processes, we find the best of the past using the language of the future to inspire our current activity. For example if "community" and "mission" is the language of our preferred future, we would frame our question: "Tell me a story about your best experience of being a community, when you joined together with fellow parishioners to respond to a need in the wider community." Even if those experiences are few, they can form the foundation of a strategy for doing them again with more intention and focus. Since people have done them at least once, they are less likely to say, "We can't do that," because they have a memory of doing it in the past.

Implications for Transitional Ministry

The impact of language is contextual and changes over the course of time, so words that were helpful in the past may no longer inspire creative action. Transitional ministers need to consistently pay attention to the outcome and not to the intention of the language they and the congregation use. In particular they need to align their language with the congregation's deepest values and their desired future. Excessive use of therapeutic language or "family" language will constrain the scope of action and create unseen barriers to ministry and growth.

I find the language of "family systems," which has formed the basis of most transitional ministry, counterproductive, especially when it comes to growing our communities of faith. At clergy training programs in North America, I often say and ask participants the following question: "Imagine you are having an extended-family Thanksgiving gathering. Tell me how many people are gathered in the room."

Rarely will people imagine more than twenty people at this highly valued family event. Occasionally, perhaps 5 percent of the time, participants might say fifty, and in twelve years of asking, only one person has had over one hundred. What this means is that the language of "family" typically evokes a group of fewer than twenty people, an image that does not accurately reflect even small congregations, let alone moderate- or corporate-sized churches. Using inaccurate language will radically constrain our ability to find our bearings and plot a course for the future. In contrast, calling the congregation a learning community or a missional community (or some other action it deeply values) will call the congregation more deeply into becoming that community.

CONCLUSION

Ministry models steeped in the medical model of cause and effect, judgment and blame, and reducing things to their alienated parts rather than beholding and reconciling the whole are not consistent with the way of Jesus and will not serve us well as we proclaim his Gospel, whether in a transitional ministry or a settled pastorate. Fortunately there are new models of being, such as the Appreciative Way, which offers both an alternative model for transitional ministry and practical strategies for leading change and transformation that have a deep resonance with the Gospel. The Appreciative Way provides a love-based, life-giving paradigm rather than a fear-based, less-death paradigm that we can use as followers of Jesus and agents of transformation with congregations in transition.

REFLECTION QUESTIONS

1. Appreciative Way Assumption A: At the heart of the universe is love, which is the source of our existence and our purpose for being.

- For individuals: Where have you been most aware of love in action this past month?
- For congregations: Where have we been most aware of God's love within our community of faith this past month?

2. Appreciative Way Assumption B: The deepest longing of the human heart is for acceptance, and the only changes that will be sustainable are those that result in greater self-acceptance and acceptance from and for others.

- For congregations: Tell me a story of a time when you were seen, listened to, contributed to, and had your dreams blessed by your community of faith?

3. Appreciative Way Assumption C: At any given moment, people are doing the best they know how to in that context.

- For individuals: Think of someone who is really driving you crazy. Now ponder on this assumption that he or she is doing the best he or she knows how to do. When you view him or her from this perspective, notice any changes in your internal experience and whether you feel more resourceful in dealing with him or her.

4. Assumption 1. In every society, organization, or group, something works.

- For congregations: What do we do well? What is really working well in our community of faith? What enables and empowers that activity? What would happen if we applied those same strategies to another aspect of our community life?

5. Assumption 2. What we focus on becomes our reality.

- For individuals: When you walk into a novel situation where does your attention go? When you enter a familiar situation where does your attention go? Do you focus on what is wrong, or are you curious about what is working well? Is your attention different in novel and familiar contexts?
- For church boards: Think back over the past few months of board activity. What have you spent the most time and effort on? Where is your board's focus of attention?

6. Assumption 3. Reality is created in the moment, and there are multiple realities.

• For individuals: Think of somebody who has a very different understanding of the nature of God than you do. Rather than wonder who is right, step back and observe the fruit of your beliefs and her or his beliefs. Which of you is more loving toward God, your neighbor, and yourself?

7. Assumption 4. The act of asking questions of an organization or group influences the group in some way.

• For groups and individuals: Think of a problem situation where the goal is to have less of something undesirable. Now ask yourself or one another: What would I/we like more of? Which question leaves you more resourceful and hopeful: What do we want less of? or What do we want more of?

8. Assumption 5. People have more confidence and comfort to journey to the future (the unknown) when they carry forward parts of the past (the known). Assumption 6. If we carry parts of the past forward, they should be what is best about the past.

• For groups and individuals: What are we carrying from our past? Does carrying it give us a better future? What do I/we need to put it down if it is unhelpful?

9. Assumption 7. It is important to value differences.

• For individuals: Who is your role model for respecting the dignity of every human being? What is the challenge group that you need to grow in respecting their dignity? What is your role model able to do that you find difficult? What do you need to do to grow in being and acting like your role model?

10. Assumption 8. The language we use creates our reality.

• For church boards: What language do you use to describe your community of faith? What are the implications of that language? For example, churches, as in buildings, rarely grow, and congregations congregate, which is static rather than active or missional. What would more effective and empowering language to describe your community of faith and the action you would like to engage in?

Chapter Ten

A Trauma Treatment Model for Interim Work with Chronically Dysfunctional Congregations

Deborah J. Pope-Lance

Some congregations repeatedly wrestle with the same problems, but nothing changes. Interim ministry in these congregations can be extremely frustrating. The usual remedies—conducting healthy congregation workshops, hiring outside consultations, calling a succession of able-enough clergy—bring no permanent fix to their chronic struggle. Interims' efforts to address problems are openly opposed, merely tolerated, or simply ignored. Improvements are temporary. Often the crankiest, most troubled members govern, while those more mature and self-differentiated who might serve as the immune cells essential in a healthy congregation[1] grow weary and withdraw. What is going on in these congregations? Why do they struggle repeatedly and still not thrive? How might interim ministers think about these congregations in a new way? What new model might provide strategies for reducing clergy frustration, ending their chronic struggles, and effecting lasting change?

FAILURE TO THRIVE

A discovery by a group of clergy who met regularly for mutual support provides a clue.[2] The ministers had joined the support group because they were unusually stressed and frustrated. Despite considerable experience and past successes, they all felt inadequate to meet the challenges of their current ministry. The strain had affected their health, unsettled their families, and led some to consider leaving the ministry. Meeting together, they discovered some striking similarities in their congregations.

147

Each congregation was thought to have had promise, but these hopes remained unfulfilled. Each congregation was disturbingly ineffective at governing itself. Each seemed to lack a capacity to make decisions, follow procedures, set appropriate boundaries, establish lines of responsibility, secure their buildings, protect themselves from risk, welcome new members, run successful canvasses, or disagree without divisive upset. Differences were sharply drawn. Conflict escalated quickly and often resolved only when one side or the other left the congregation. Members routinely treated each other badly. Nearly all the congregations had a reputation for being hard on ministers. Members and leaders were overly critical and highly reactive to the person of the minister. Minister–congregant relationships were often perplexing and volatile. Many of the congregations had been served by a series of minsters whose short tenures and unhappy departures were otherwise unremarkable. And all had suffered for many years from what may best be described as a failure to thrive.

"Failure to thrive" is a phrase used in medicine to describe a condition found in young children and frail elderly. When children whose rate of growth, despite proper care and adequate nutrition, does not meet the expected growth rate of children their age, they are diagnosed with failure to thrive. In the elderly, a gradual decline in physical or cognitive function that occurs without adequate explanation is described as a failure to thrive. Whether young or old, those who fail to thrive appear to lack the capacity to adapt, grow, and survive.

Many contemporary congregations are stressed by changes in their surrounding communities and the larger world. (See chapter 3 in this volume, "The Changing Landscape of the American Church.") Some congregations, stressed by these same changes, manage well enough. A few even prosper. But other congregations do not and many do not survive. Why? Clearly, congregations have different resources. Some possess more skilled leaders or larger endowments. Others have more difficult problems—older buildings or more vulnerable populations. Nevertheless, some deeply challenged congregations remain intact, surviving or even to thriving, while in others, something appears to have compromised their capacity to adapt and grow in the face of far less significant stresses.

Why congregations, full of nice, capable people fail to thrive remained unclear until the ministers in the group discovered that all their congregations had a similar history. In every congregation, a past minister had engaged in misconduct. Typically the misconduct was sexual in nature, but sometimes it involved breaches of confidentiality, neglect of duty, theft of money, misuse of property, and betrayals of trust. In some congregations, the experience was recent; in others, long ago. In some, the events were a secret; in others, they were widely known. In some, serious conflict had erupted after the misconduct. In others, the misconducting minister simply departed without explanation. Regardless of these variations, each congregation had experienced its minister's misconduct as a devastating violation[3] and afterward had exhibited a persistent failure to thrive.

Other types of trauma also occur in congregations.[4] Public acts of violence—random armed assaults, bombings, or arson—do happen in congregations and inflict serious injury and loss of life. Unforeseen accidents caused, for example, by building failures, earthquakes, or human error cause irreparable damage and terrible grief. Intense interpersonal conflict, arising from controversy or exacerbated by human behavior, can escalate quickly, injuring people and shattering lives much like a bomb. These other sudden, hurtful, and intense violations also have a traumatic effect on a congregation. In the aftermath of these traumas, congregations struggle to address their injuries and losses. Some barely manage to survive.

The significance of a congregation's past in the evolution of its present challenges has long been recognized.[5] The first of the traditional five tasks of interim ministry—making sense of a congregation's history[6] —is informed by this recognition, as is the widely held belief that a congregation cannot know where it is going unless it understands where it has been. But these ministers, serving congregations with similar histories, recognized something more. They recognized that their congregations' failure to thrive in the present was rooted in the trauma of these past violations. Now, in the present, their inability to adapt and grow, and their chronic dysfunction, pervasive distrust, uncivil behavior, frequent conflict, and difficult relations with ministers were the persistent evidence of past trauma.

When interim ministers understand the experience of violence, intense conflict, or clergy misconduct as a trauma in the life of the congregation, what is required to address trauma's often persistent effect becomes clear. Resources developed to address psychological trauma in individuals can be applied to traumatized congregations. A trauma model provides a new perspective with which interim ministers might discern different priorities and strategies to navigate the chaos of chronically dysfunctional congregations. Even in congregations without known trauma histories but with chronic patterns of dysfunction, difficult ministries, or inexplicable failure to thrive, the treatment model provides a novel, effective approach. Employing these priorities and strategies, the adverse effect of trauma on a congregation, among these a chronic failure to thrive, can be reduced.

WHAT IS TRAUMA?

Trauma is the effect of an extreme difficult or unpleasant experience. This effect can cause a person to have mental or emotional problems for some time afterward. Traumatic experiences can be brought on by severe weather, an accident, an act of violence, or by any event that threatens the physical safety, living conditions, and assumed meaning of those who experience it. Soldiers, for example, who daily witness gruesome acts of violence and whose lives are routinely threatened, can suffer acute emotional distress long after leaving the battlefield. The emotional problems caused by traumatic experience were first recognized in soldiers returning from war. What was called "battle fatigue" in World War II, "shell shock" in World War I, and "soldier's heart" in the Civil War came to be identified in the aftermath of the Vietnam war as "post-traumatic stress disorder" (PTSD). Since then, PTSD has also been diagnosed in noncombatants, in mourners after complicated loss, and in survivors of assault, domestic abuse, political oppression, and civil unrest.

Trauma affects all aspects of an individual's functioning. Traumatic injury is not only physical and emotional and not only evidenced in dysfunctional or self-destructive behavior. The impact of trauma, especially as evidenced in PTSD, is more accurately described as biopsychosocial.[7] Neurological research, for example, has shown that trauma physically alters the brain structures of survivors.[8] Studies of communal experiences of trauma identify changes in social structures and relationships.[9]

Trauma's impact is most evident in a broad array of psychological symptoms. These include difficulties with concentration, intrusive thoughts, compulsive behaviors, panic attacks, and recurrent nightmares. Symptomatic individuals report irritability, agitation, anger, acute anxiety, depression, and sleep disturbance. Some display exaggerated startle responses or hypersensitivity to normal sights, sounds, or smells, especially when aspects of present experience resemble the trauma experience. Hypersensitivity can lead to distortions in thinking and feeling, inaccurate recollection, and sensations that the past trauma is being reexperienced in the present. A soldier back from war hears among the normal sounds on a city street an automobile loudly backfire and is triggered by this explosive sound to reexperience the imminent threat of enemy bombs and react by diving into an alley for safety. Similarly, some trauma survivors, when thinking about a trauma in the past, report dissociating or feeling disconnected from what is happening in the present. This dissociation generates gaps in survivors' memories.

Psychologists view these symptoms as normal reactions to the extremity of trauma and consider them sufficiently predictable that even in the absence of a known history of trauma, their presence may be considered reliable evidence of a past trauma. Persistent, chronic symptoms are evidence of a survivor's ongoing struggle to cope in trauma's aftermath. Coping strategies, such as obsessive attention to tiny details, evolve over time and become automatic. When normal pretrauma conditions return and these coping strategies are no longer necessary, they nevertheless persist as chronic symptoms that impair daily functioning and threaten survivors' well-being.

Normal responses to trauma vary in individual survivors. Some survivors cannot remember what happened. Yet others can describe their experience in impressive detail. Some reexperience the trauma in nightmares or in daytime flashbacks. Some do not. Some compulsively replicate aspects of the trauma experience when the dynamics of present situations or relationships resemble those of the trauma, increasing their distress and reinforcing symptoms. Others do not. Some survivors, overwhelmed by chronic symptoms and unmanageable lives, become passive and careless, while others are obsessive and hypervigilant. Some suffer from lifelong emotional distress and self-destructive behavior. A few others report that after the trauma, their lives gained renewed purpose.

Why some people are more deeply or permanently affected by trauma than others or why only some have a greater risk for developing the more acute symptoms of PTSD remains unclear. Differences in personal resources—resilience, self-esteem, and knowledge—may be a factor. Likely other factors—a person's proximity to the event, the extent of disruption to daily routine, the severity of physical injury, and the amount of time required for recovery—make a difference. Survivors isolated from others have a higher risk for developing PTSD, while survivors who receive compassionate support—security, medical care, and basic necessities—from others and who as a result feel safe, do not fear further injury, and do not lack food or shelter appear to suffer less severe or persistent distress.

Trauma survivors frequently are conflicted about their experience. They are seemingly caught between a wish to forget the trauma ever happened and a compulsion to describe its outrageous horrors to all who will listen. Those who witness a trauma from a safe distance (in time or geography) can also be conflicted, silencing survivors with comments such as "I'm sure it wasn't as bad as you say" or "In time you'll be fine." This ambivalence exacerbates symptoms, raises the risk for PTSD, and increases resistance to treatment. Companions who are knowledgeable about trauma and PTSD may be better equipped to support survivors as they try to make sense of what has happened.

A THREE-PHASE TRAUMA TREATMENT MODEL

Trauma's emotional impact is primarily treated through psychotherapy. Many psychotherapeutic treatment models exist, but generally psychotherapy is a process in which a person, talking with a trained psychological clinician, is helped to reflect on the experience and condition and to resolve problems in ways that allow him or her to adapt and grow. In psychotherapy, a survivor describes the trauma experience and aftermath to a nonanxious, empathetic, compassionate, and nonjudgmental therapist. Through this process, survivors find ways to lower their anxiety and increase their capacity to manage the conflicting emotions that are typical after trauma and to resolve difficulties caused by symptomatic behaviors. For some survivors, psychotherapeutic treatment is augmented with medications that reduce acute distress and improve self-control so that survivors may engage effectively in psychotherapy. Specific psychotherapeutic treatment models have been developed to encourage survivors to remember, reflect on, and reprocess a traumatic experience.

Many models are organized in phases, each attending to specific tasks in the healing process. In a model developed by Judith Herman, [10] the first phase focuses on safety, symptom reduction, and stabilization. The second phase supports survivors to reconstruct the traumatic story, process memories and emotions, and name and grieve losses. The third phase encourages survivors to discern some meaning in their experience of trauma and to integrate that meaning into their lives. Throughout all phases, survivors are empowered, to the fullest extent their current capacities allow, to take control of their treatment and their lives.

During phase one of treatment, survivors are the most distressed, in denial, and vulnerable. A therapist seeks to establish a safe environment in which a survivor feels both protected from further injury and respectfully heard. Essential to this task is clear acknowledgment that what has happened—the sudden unexpected event or experience, the consequent distress, and persistent symptoms—taken all together, constitute a trauma. In bearing witness to the trauma, a therapist normalizes a survivors' experience. Dissociated thoughts, crazy behaviors, and distressing emotions are transformed into predictable responses and vague recollections into accessible, discussable memories. A therapist helps a survivor find ways to manage the day-to-day upset these thoughts, behaviors, and emotions can cause, but she or he does so without rescuing or taking over. A neutral therapeutic stance encourages a survivor to take back control of his or her life and to resolve emotional conflicts rather than display them as symptoms. Against a nonneutral therapist, survivors may tenaciously embrace only one side of their emotional conflict and remain distressed. A neutral therapist is not indifferent but rather does not offer an opinion as to what survivors should choose to do now in the aftermath of the trauma.

Phase two focuses on remembering and mourning. Now the goal of treatment is to move from absent or vague memories of what happened to a clear, full story of the trauma experience. The therapist companions the survivor on the journey. Clearer memory increases a survivor's awareness of what has been lost and allows these losses to be named and grieved. A psychotherapist helps survivors to understand grieving these losses as an act of courage and a bold choice to adapt, grow, and heal.

Phase three of the model focuses on helping survivors regain trust in themselves, others, and life. During this phase, survivors become increasingly able to reengage in ordinary life, albeit a life after trauma. As survivors come to understand themselves—their thoughts and feelings, their insights and intuitions—their capacity to manage recurrent symptoms, to protect themselves against further injury, and to make choices that are in their best interest increases. Confidence in their own capacities allows survivors to trust themselves and choose to be the person they wish to be. Reconciled to the past, in charge of the present, and committed to a future of their own choosing, survivors become more willing to trust and rebuild social connections with others. Survivors who discern meaning in a trauma experience and integrate that meaning into how they live now have the best therapeutic outcomes. Some survivors become activists, working to prevent the type of trauma they experienced. Others contribute to the common good in some unrelated way, transforming the meaning of a personal tragedy into a public resolve to make the world a better place.

This three-phase psychological treatment model can be employed as a model for interim work in congregations with a history of trauma. Interim ministers think about their work in phases and focus on specific tasks in each phase.

PHASE ONE: ACKNOWLEDGING THE TRAUMA, RESTORING ORDER

Phase one of the model directs an interim minister, whether in the immediate aftermath of trauma or after years of chronic dysfunction, to focus first on acknowledging the trauma, establishing safety, and stabilizing congregational operations.

Acknowledging the trauma—quickly, publicly, and safely—is essential to the recovery of individual trauma survivors.[11] Similarly, acknowledging a congregation's experience and naming it as trauma is essential to minimizing the persistent, adverse impact the experience can have on a congregation. Ideally the acknowledgment will be made in a communal, public way—a letter mailed, a Sunday announcement made, a meeting held. Basic information is conveyed, questions are answered, and members are given time to talk together. These acknowledgments need not be graphic or exhaustive. Simple, gracious language, such as "After these recent events" or "Given what we have been through," is clear and honest and lowers anxiety. Lowering anxiety reduces distress and improves both individual and group functioning. When an investigation is pending or survivors' identities need to be confidential, some information may be withheld. In this situation, a straightforward statement—"This is what we know at this point, and we will keep you informed as we learn more"—is clear and honest and conveys compassion to all. Subsequent gatherings will convey new information as it becomes available and provide further opportunity for members to be together.

Some denominations have developed trauma response teams to be deployed to congregations in the immediate wake of a trauma. Composed of trained, empathetic companions, teams offer crisis counseling, restore order, and provide support. Their presence clearly states that what has happened in the life of this congregation constitutes a trauma. Although these teams generally are deployed in the wake of violence or natural disasters, they could be deployed in the aftermath of other types of trauma. After intense conflict or clergy misconduct, trauma response teams could provide the early intervention that has been shown in early treatment of individuals to reduce symptom severity and improve recovery.

When a denominational response team is not available, local community members can be brought together to form a response team. Psychotherapists and emergency responders can provide immediate assistance and crisis counseling. Ministers and lay pastoral teams from nearby congregations can offer pastoral care. Other volunteers can help maintain basic operations, providing, among other services, administrative support, media response, and most importantly, communal worship. This community-formed trauma response team, like a standing denominational team, can also facilitate a trauma debriefing.

A trauma debriefing is a structured opportunity for congregants to learn the known facts and to process the reality of the event. Different formats have been suggested for organizing trauma debriefings. In general, a trauma debriefing occurs within hours or days of a trauma event—for example, after the fire is put out, a minister's departure is announced, or intense conflict has ended. Even if all the facts are not yet available, participants will benefit from being together, hearing each other's feelings, and sharing concerns. Congregational leaders and denominational officials should be present and visible, participating not as facilitators but in their customary roles. A bishop, for example, whose role as bishop includes investigating misconduct allegations, might report on how the investigation will progress. A congregation president who received the fire chief's phone call might report on the status of the arson investigation. An assistant minister might offer prayers for the injured. But a trauma team member who is not the bishop, the president, or the pastor should be the person who facilitates the gathering.

Individuals process difficult experiences at different rates. Some members will need more opportunities than others to process the experience. Some will prefer different formats—one-to-one appointments with a counselor; small, facilitated group process; or weekly or monthly drop-in gatherings. Some groups, such as staff, board members, or survivors, may be served best by separate, dedicated opportunities to talk. Some congregations may be best served by holding periodic gatherings for some years and others by scheduling a meeting only when new information comes to light or new losses are discerned. Some congregations will benefit from educational opportunities, such as programs on trauma and its effects on individuals and communities. Congregations that have experienced the trauma of a minister's misconduct will benefit from learning more about ministerial roles and relationships and about the ethical standards and state laws governing ministerial practice.

Restoring Order

Another task in phase one of this trauma treatment model, restoring order, directs an interim minister to focus on stabilizing the congregation's basic operations. In the immediate aftermath of trauma, a congregation is in crisis. When trauma occurred in the distant past, a congregation likely has been in crisis for some time. Basic services have been neglected, buildings poorly tended, and mission unfulfilled. Loss of members and income have diminished program support and worship participation. Concern for the simple survival of a congregation post trauma is well founded. An interim minister who effectively sees to the fulfillment of members' pastoral needs and restores trust in its clergy fosters commitment to the congregation and cultivates confidence in its future viability. Greater confidence and less chaos will reduce anxiety and foster a sense of stability, leading members to participate in and support the congregation going forward.

Encouraging the use of best governing practices is a routine interim strategy that can significantly help address the extraordinary challenges of a traumatized congregation. Congregations that experienced traumas in the distant past have commonly been and remain poorly managed. Helping leaders learn to use best practices, for example, to manage the congregation's finances, personnel, and committees, creates order amid chaos and instills a confidence that leaders can manage their congregation well. A specific governing practice may be considered "best" because it is in keeping with applicable polity, puts into action a congregation's beliefs and values, has proved effective in other congregations of similar size or complexity, or is required by current standards in the business of congregations.

Chronic, poor management is not caused only by congregational leader's ignorance of best practices, however. More often it is caused by leaders' inconsistently or rarely following the good-enough practices already in place. For healthy congregational functioning, the content (or the what) of a practice is less important than the process (or the how) by which it is followed. Practices are best and generate a healthier congregation when they are based on agreements, clearly stated, consistently followed, and updated when necessary. An interim minister who focuses on helping a congregation operate in a manner consistent with its established practices and in keeping with its expressed mission effects a significant move toward health and recovery after trauma.

An essential strategy—highlighted by Friedman, Steinke, and others—for fostering best or healthy practices is to focus on process rather than on outcomes. When an interim asks questions—about *how* decisions are made, for example, or about *how* the bylaws address this issue, rather than focusing on *what* the correct decision or proper resolution is—leaders will be encouraged to consider how their actual practice compares with their intended practice. Discerning inconsistencies will provoke leaders to rewrite bylaws and policies to reflect more accurately their intended practice. When an interim minister helps leaders and members to reflect on their intended practice, leaders will be better able to articulate those values they wish to express in their relationships with one another.

These articulated values may be used to form a behavioral covenant and establish a values-based standard of interaction to which everyone agrees and can be held accountable. Accountability to a behavioral covenant fosters respect and civil discourse among members, reduces the frequency of conflict common in congregations after trauma, and increases an interim minister's capacity to manage the frustrations and challenges of working with post-trauma congregations. Basically, accountability to a behavioral covenant is good boundary maintenance. Boundaries are any of the rules, roles, and relationships that form the culture of a congregation. A boundary is violated when these rules, roles, and relationships are not honored. In congregations, good boundary maintenance reduces anxiety and improves everyone's functioning.

Congregations with trauma histories develop routine coping strategies to survive the immediate aftermath of a trauma. Common among these coping strategies is boundary-violating behavior. A small group, for example, decides to keep secret the truth about the trauma, fearing that if members knew, they would be distressed and withhold support. Now, months or years later, a cultural norm has evolved that encourages keeping secret information that should not be. Or sometimes a cultural norm evolves based on the controlling, boundary-violating leadership style typically seen in misconducting clergy. Even after a misconducting minister's departure, a pattern of boundary-violating behavior remains the cultural norm.

For an interim minister serving a congregation where boundary-violating behavior has become the norm, good boundary maintenance is a painstaking, repetitive task. Every interaction may contain violations. An interim may have to repeatedly restore boundaries or, unable to attend to every violation, selectively address those that he or she can do so effectively and without causing undue distress. Coaching leaders and members in how to communicate in direct, truthful, clear, and transparent ways will change a culture of secrecy into one of openness and honesty. Providing regular evaluation and assessment will encourage accountability and commitment. These changes will lead to greater comfort with difference and skill at consensus building. Interims who model good boundaries in their own conduct will move the cultural norms toward healthier patterns of interaction.

Limiting Acknowledgment of Trauma

In the immediate aftermath of trauma, congregation leaders may attempt to limit public acknowledgment or discussion of a trauma. These attempts are similar to the denial observed in individual survivors of trauma who are as yet unable to accept what has happened to them. Understandably, leaders may believe for a variety of reasons that limiting acknowledgment and discussion is a wise strategy. Where recent intense conflict has led to the departure of members and loss of funds, leaders may fear that talking publicly will rekindle conflict and further endanger the congregation. Where violence has occurred, leaders may be reasonably concerned about retaliation or further unrest. Where ministerial misconduct has been rumored, leaders may fear being sued or not wish to jeopardize a denominational or criminal investigation. Or when a minister has resigned "for the sake of the church" but remained in the area, leaders may fear that disclosing the events that led to his or her departure will provoke further bad behavior.

Leaders' efforts to limit public discussion slow the work of recovery. Still, interim ministers must respect their reluctance. Dismissing them or forcibly trying to compel them to see or do something that they are not yet able to see or do likely will increase their resistance and generate additional problems. Feeling disrespected by an interim, leaders may not support or trust the interim. Or constantly at odds with the interim, leaders may undermine the interim's work or try to fire the interim minister. In the presence of strong resistance to public discussion, interims must work at a slower, more prudent pace, much the way a psychotherapist calibrates the pace of a survivor's treatment so that it remains in keeping with what a survivor can presently manage. A slower pace is better than a survivor's withdrawal from treatment or, in a congregation, than having leaders withdraw their support and trust. In this interim work, pace is not as important as direction. Acknowledgment of a past trauma is not a single event but an ongoing process. In individual therapy, the process of acknowledging a trauma may go on for years. A congregation may take a generation before congregants, individually and together, can fully accept and make sense of what has happened.

PHASE TWO: REMEMBERING AND MOURNING

Phase two of the trauma treatment model focuses on remembering and mourning. As in individual therapy, the long-term goal for a congregation in phase two is to work from denial or vague memories to clearer recall and acknowledgment of a trauma so that losses can be named and mourning can begin. Like a psychotherapist treating an individual survivor, an interim minister serves as ally and advocate, respectfully and compassionately guiding congregants from a reluctant but growing awareness of what happened to a fuller, clearer telling of the story. An interim leader who can occasion the uncovering of a congregation's forgotten or never acknowledged trauma story creates an opportunity for congregants to name and grieve their losses.

Gradually and compassionately the story is pieced together, including the story of how the congregation survived, what it lost and learned, and how the trauma experience has changed the congregation. Piecing together what happened may require a thorough inquiry undertaken by a group of trusted and level-headed members or denominational representatives. An inquiry takes time, as records need to be reviewed and survivors and witnesses interviewed. After a thorough inquiry, some things will be clearer and others will remain unknown or not yet verified and therefore not yet public. A brief, simple summary of the inquiry is prepared and distributed to the congregation, and a meeting is held to discuss it, ask questions, express feelings, and share concerns.

During an interim, difficult issues from the past often come up without any deliberate effort on the part of the interim. Perhaps they come up because sufficient time has passed and members feel safe or resolved enough to speak of them. Perhaps the interim minister is seen as different, as more trustworthy, a better listener, or more gracious than previous ministers, and members finally are comfortable enough to break their silence. More frequently, especially when acknowledgment of a past trauma has been prohibited or limited, something may need to be done to encourage the story to be told. A history time line process can create a comfortable, accepting context that often evokes new revelations. Listening circles can connect members with others whose experience were similar and lead them together to a clearer understanding of what happened.

Serving a congregation with an undisclosed trauma history is not an exercise in tough love but an opportunity to offer pastoral care and gifts of grace. The primary task of any interim minister is to be the congregation's pastor, whether or not disclosure occurs and regardless of members' reluctance to acknowledge their congregation's history. Pastoring congregants requires an interim to minister to people where they are, in the aftermath of a literally unspeakable trauma, until they are ready to know and accept what has happened.

Pastoring congregants who hold varying if divergent perspectives is challenging. Interims must maintain an appearance of neutrality sufficient to allow them to serve as every member's pastor and no one's opposition. Members, for example, who believe a former minister was wrongly accused or poorly treated may feel betrayed by an interim who resolutely refers to a former minister's misconduct. Members, angry that their side lost in an intense conflict, may be put off by an interim minister who appears to side with those on the other side of the conflict.

Mourning Loss

After a trauma, individual perspectives on what has been lost may vary widely, but the experience of loss is shared. Everyone grieves. Focusing on this common experience will help interim ministers find ways to minister to members whose divergent perspectives evoke diverse reactions. An interim minister can say to one member, for example, without appearing to take sides, "I am sorry for your loss. I know the former minister was important to you and your family." And to another member, the interim might offer, "I'm sorry for your loss. I know this congregation means a lot to you, and seeing it go through these difficulties is hard for you." Both statements are true. Each focuses on the common experience of loss. Each allows a congregant to feel pastored by the interim minister. Over time the interim's calling attention to what congregants have in common—surviving a grievous loss—will lessen congregants' reactivity and nurture their capacity to see and accept the truth of what happened.

Supporting congregants as they mourn is the traditional work of clergy and a primary purpose of religious community. Elizabeth Kübler-Ross's work on death and dying is well known to clergy. Kübler-Ross theorized that a person who faces death or significant loss passes through five emotional stages of grief—denial, anger, bargaining, depression, and acceptance.[12] When these five stages of grief are worked through, Kübler-Ross observed, people endure loss with less upset and move on afterward without persistent distress. When losses remain unacknowledged and these five stages are unresolved, the work of grief remains undone. People who do not fully grieve experience more emotional or physical problems and greater difficulty in finding meaning and purpose in their lives.

PHASE THREE: RESTORING TRUST AND RENEWING PURPOSE

Phase three of the model focuses on helping survivors reclaim a sense of control in their lives and a capacity to trust themselves, others, and life. A sense of control allows survivors to discern what the meaning of the trauma will be for them and where this meaning will lead them. In charge of their present and reconciled to their past, survivors can commit to the future. The task of interim work in a congregation after trauma based on phase three of the treatment model is to help a congregation let go of what was before and embrace, with renewed meaning and purpose, what is now and what can yet be.

Trauma robs survivors of the power they once had to make their own choices and control their own lives. Because of this loss of control, survivors may appear helpless or indecisive. Trauma robs congregations of self-direction, too. In the aftermath of trauma, congregational members and leaders also may appear helpless, unable to manage and willing to do whatever any outside expert tells them to do.

The trauma treatment model cautions psychotherapists not to patronize or try to rescue survivors, but rather display a consistent neutrality about the choices survivors must make to move forward. This respectful neutrality allows survivors to resume control over their own lives. In a similar way, the model cautions interim ministers not to tell leaders what to do and to remain neutral regarding whatever dilemmas or decisions a congregation must consider. An interim's neutrality empowers leaders and members to take (back) control of the congregation.

This neutrality is especially important in the aftermath of traumas precipitated by a previous minister's misconduct if lasting cultural change is to be made. In ministerial misconduct, ministers abuse their pastoral role, using it not as intended, that is, for the fulfillment of pastoral duties, but rather for the satisfaction of their own personal needs. This misuse betrays a congregation's trust and causes harm to individual members and the community. In order to misuse the pastoral role and avoid being discovered, a misconducting minister manipulates leaders and members and controls what can happen in the congregation. In this way, the trauma inflicted by a misconducting minister is best understood as occurring in many relationships over a time and not as a particular event or behavior. Over time misconduct robs a congregation of self-direction, allows the minister unquestioned control, fosters a sense of helplessness, and changes the cultural norms of a congregation. A misconducted congregation comes to operate in ways that undermine the control leaders might have not only to stop misconduct, but also to create a healthy, thriving congregation. An interim minister who tells a previously misconducted congregation what leaders and members should or should not do risks replicating the manipulative, controlling pattern of the misconducting predecessor. However well intended, this replication will reinforce the dysfunctional patterns generated by the trauma of the misconducting previous minister and greatly reduce the opportunity to effect lasting change.

The complex dynamics of pastoral relationships are what make interim work in congregations post-trauma challenging and stressful. The seeming helplessness can lead interim ministers to overfunction. The constant reactivity can provoke interims to overexpress their frustration in angry outbursts at congregants. The stress of managing these and other dynamics can make interim work hazardous to one's health and a family's well-being. To limit these adverse effects and keep a post-trauma congregation focused on its own work and not the person of the minister, calling or appointing several interim ministers to serve for a year or less may be a better option than working with one interim who serves for multiple years. Still, regardless of their length of tenure, interim ministers must strive not to overreact or take personally the sometimes extreme emotions in post-trauma congregations directed at the person of the minister. Interim ministers who can conduct themselves with integrity, in ways worthy of trust and respect—for example, who do what they say they will do; are compassionate, polite, and nonanxious; act in ways appropriate to the pastoral office; and are able to avoid being the cause of congregational controversy or embarrassment—will be able to keep the work focused on the congregation and not on themselves. Through their own trustworthy example, interim ministers foster a climate of trust that rebuilds trust in ministers and allows congregants to reclaim trust in themselves, in others, and in life.

Renewing Purpose

A congregation that has experienced the trauma of extreme violence, intense conflict, or clergy misconduct, like an individual after trauma, is different from what it was before the experience. An interim minister's task, based on phase three of the model, is to help leaders and members discern that difference, to integrate its meaning in the longer, varied story of the congregation, and to discover where it will lead. Just as a psychotherapist helps individual survivors understand the meaning of an experience of trauma in the survivor's and others' lives, interim ministers help a congregation understand the meaning of its experience of trauma and discern how because of this meaning the congregation is now different.

One way to accomplish this task is to invite reflection on questions such as the following:

- What sort of congregation were you before?
- How did your beliefs and faith direct you?
- What matters ultimately to you now?
- How are you or your congregation different now that this has happened?
- How will you be together now?
- What will you do?
- How might you become the congregation you want to be?
- What must you do to thrive?

These questions can be addressed in a variety of ways. Small and large facilitated group discussions can provide opportunities for members to talk about the issues the questions raise. Groups gathered for other purposes—for example, for Bible study, religious education, mutual support, prayer and spiritual direction—can pause to explore these questions. Leadership trainings and governing board and committee meetings will provide brief or periodic opportunities to stop and reflect on these questions.

A congregation is a community of faith-filled people drawn together by common religious beliefs for worship and service. Helping a congregation articulate the meaning of a trauma experience and then integrate this meaning into the congregation's story is essentially a theological task. An interim minister can support these theological tasks by providing opportunities for individual and communal expressions of belief, revisiting the foundations of this congregation's faith tradition, relearning the history of the religious beliefs, and rediscovering the values and purposes that continue to inspire service. What of these has the experience of trauma changed? Which are less compelling and which more compelling? Which support their living out and serving the faith of this religious community?

CONCLUSION

Many congregations in the aftermath of traumas caused by violence, intense conflict, or clergy misconduct suffer significant adverse effects and may, like individual trauma victims, remain volatile and symptomatic, and require deliberate and strategic efforts for years to recover. A trauma treatment model provides a focus for these ongoing efforts. It also strongly suggests that a congregation that can openly discuss its experience of trauma, can name and grieve its losses, and can discern a meaning in the experience that brings new purpose will fare better, move on in healthy, faith-filled ways, and even thrive. The most important work of an interim leader is not to complete that effort but to help a congregation set itself in the direction of recovery.

DISCUSSION QUESTIONS

1. Have you ever served or observed a church that has experienced trauma? How did the congregation respond and behave afterwards?
2. What do you think of Pope-Lance's thesis that churches that "fail to thrive" likely have some trauma in their history? What other factors might contribute to dysfunction?
3. What is your assessment of the three phase model? Have you seen it work either as individual phases or as a whole? What makes it effective?

Chapter Eleven

Hospice Care for Struggling Congregations

Gretchen J. Switzer

Walter stood trembling in the midst of the old, wooden pews. He surveyed the faded, threadbare red carpet in the center aisle where the choir once processed every Sunday morning. He could almost hear the full strains of the organ pipes and feel the vibration as he had for sixty-five years from "his pew." But now there was only silence, punctuated by an occasional creak from the wind outside. Where would Walter go now? What would he do with his free time now that he wouldn't be needed to take care of repairs and restorations in this church? As his wife would say disparagingly, he had spent nearly all his time here since he retired. He was the only one who knew just where to kick the boiler to get the heat to come on. It was only Walter who could pick the lock on the pastor's office door when that scatterbrained young reverend would lock himself out. He had polished these pews once a week for decades, making sure they shone brightly all the time. And when he needed to rest, Walter would sit down on the chancel steps and see if he could hear God speaking to him. He would open his heart as wide as he could and just talk to Jesus about whatever was on his mind.

But tomorrow, the papers would be signed, the money would change hands, and this would no longer be his church. Walter felt as lost as he had ever felt in his seventy-five years. Where would he visit with God now? In what other place could he feel so needed? Where else could he know he was making such an important contribution? The church was his life. How could he understand himself apart from it?

Among the many situations into which a transitional minister may be placed these days is that of walking with a congregation that has said good-bye to a former pastor and is now facing profound life-and-death decisions

163

about its church's future. Transitional ministers are entering into the lives of congregations undergoing drastic downturns more frequently than ever before. The contemporary challenges presented by the diminishing of religious congregations in the United States is made especially difficult by the fact that pastoral leaders in general have not been taught to do ministry in a context of disintegration. Those who pastor churches during transitions, however, are in a unique position to address the multifaceted grieving process that accompanies the loss of a church.

Sometimes, ministers who specialize in guiding churches as they disband are called in after the decision to close has already been made. More often, however, a transitional minister enters into the life of a struggling congregation when it is just beginning to grapple with the idea that there may be no way for it to move together into the future or when it is so stuck in denial that it needs a compassionate, yet well-differentiated leader to challenge it to face reality.[1]

In my book *Finishing with Grace*, my coauthor, Linda Hilliard, and I explore these issues in a much deeper way than can be done in one chapter. We closed a church together and struggled with the fact that there were few practical resources to guide a congregation through such a thing, so we wrote *Finishing with Grace* as a manual for pastors and congregations facing these situations. The book delves deeply into many more specific issues.[2]

When I first began grappling with these issues, I thought in terms of churches "closing," institutions ceasing to exist. I dealt largely with the logistics of such a process. As I have connected with more congregations and church professionals, however, I have discovered that the image of "hospice care" is a much more valuable one. This is because the hospice philosophy initially assumes that some deaths are inevitable. In many situations, the issue is not whether a church is going to close, but how it will choose to live its final days and say its good-byes when disbanding has become the only option.

No matter when the transitional specialist enters into the life of the community of faith, the primary focus of his or her ministry will be to help individual church members and the congregation as a whole to mourn in healthy, helpful ways. The community of faith can be thought of as an individual facing a dire illness. Even before a terminal diagnosis is finally made, there is a certain amount of what many grief specialists call "anticipatory grief." From the moment that closing and disbanding is mentioned as a viable option, members of the church community begin to consider the profound emotion and spiritual challenge of such a turn of events. As time goes on and that option appears more and more likely, the grief begins to boil within. From the moment the decision is eventually made to close, that body, the church, begins to understand itself as the victim of a terminal illness and responds not unlike a hospice patient who has been given only a few months to live. It is at this juncture that ministry in and to a dying church takes on the nature of hospice care and the effective interim minister adopts the role of hospice chaplain.

FIVE ATTACHMENTS OF CONGREGATIONS

For hospice care in a church to be effective, we must begin to understand the unique nature of corporate ecclesiastical grief. There are five attachments unique to communities of faith that should be addressed by the transitional minister in these circumstances.

Attachment to a Static God

When we envision God, many of us picture a solid, immoveable force. One of the aspects of God we most treasure is that God is always there. God is the one thing in our life we can count on not to change. We rely on God to remain the same no matter how we, or the world, might be altered. The difficulty with this theology is that it creates a faith that can easily become resistant to new concepts, renewed passions, unexpected directions, or "bold decisions."[3] It's never occurred to us before that God might call our church to a new and different life, that God might want us in a new space or a new place, or that God might be done calling us to a particular ministry.

When one's image of God is unchangeable, then God becomes little more than an inanimate object. If God is completely immutable, it is most difficult to imagine a future different from the one we've always expected. For this perspective to begin making sense, the transitional pastor must teach and reteach the people we serve about the God of the Bible, who often gets humanity's attention by doing things in utterly unexpected ways. Our job is to remind people that the God we serve is intimately involved with humanity throughout history. The narrative of that relationship includes innumerable endings and beginnings. We are part of God's larger story, which tells us of a God who is fluid, ever moving, ever changing. The God of the Bible does indeed have some incredible unchangeable qualities, such as love, justice, mercy, compassion, wisdom, and an all-encompassing vision for the world. However, ours is not an inflexible, inactive God who is always exactly the same. God continues to move and interact with humanity. There is give and take between the human and the divine. God's responses change as God responds to the suffering and pain in the world. The Holy Spirit is fluid and continually growing and moving within us and around us.

Attachment to the Past

For many church members, individual and family memories are tied to church life. Nearly every significant rite of passage has been observed there. The family photo album is filled with pictures of baptisms, confirmations, weddings, and funerals that took place in this church. For others, the community of faith to which they belong is treasured because of the comfort it offered when the individual was ill or grieving a loss or facing life-altering change. How can one not be attached to the church's past when her or his own most important personal memories still sit in the pews, ring in the belfry, and shine in the stained-glass windows? The idea of moving forward in life without this congregation, this context of cherished memories, is devastating. We grieve because the community's history is intimately connected with our own personal past, and we had assumed it would be intrinsically connected to our future, as well.

Attachment to Roles

In every congregation a core group of individuals have held influential positions in both the formal and informal power structure. For a number of these folks, church life has afforded them leadership roles and power that they have never had in their employment or in their personal lives. Once discussions begin about ending the life of a church, these people begin to see their power and their leadership roles slipping away. They become fearful of giving up the key roles they have played in the community of faith and the respect that they have enjoyed as a result. If transitional pastors and other church leaders make an effort to include these individuals in significant ways as the church's life winds down, the process will often help them come to terms with these personal losses. It should also be added that individuals who have played key roles will sometimes use the power they are afforded to attempt to derail the plans for closing. Pastors can also address these role issues by making sure these individuals get lots of individual pastoral attention and in some cases, helping them find meaningful roles outside the church walls where they could fill the need to feel significant.

Attachment to People and Social Life

Many members are so deeply involved in the life of a church that their social context is the congregation itself. Most, if not all, of their friends, and perhaps family, are members of the same church. Letting the church "die" means those relationships will change, and that is especially frightening to those who fear ending up alone and lonely.

Our church may also be the only place where we feel truly welcome or accepted for who we are. For mentally challenged individuals, for example, the church closing is terrifying. Church is where their friends are. Folks there always used to check on them during the week and drive them to church on Sundays. Will they be forgotten now? For more people than we may even imagine, the closing of their church may bring a profound new loneliness.

Attachment to Place

Although most humans feel a sense of loss when they change homes or places of business, church participants tend to have an even deeper attachment to "the place" they call church. This is not simply because this is the location of so many memories, but because most of us, to one extent or another, tend to think of the sanctuary as the "location" of God. We know in our minds that this is not theologically sound, that God is everywhere, inside and outside of the church building. But in our hearts we have often come to believe that the place where we worship God is the place where God actually lives. Most of the time, we don't even know we believe this until the place is threatened. The result is that when we grieve the loss of the building, we may feel we are losing God as well. It is imperative that the transitional minister working with a congregation that is closing help the people broaden their understanding of who and where God is and empower them to connect with God in new ways. This may be effectively accomplished by teaching the people spiritual practices that can ground them during the transition.

The future is tied up in the church building, as well. Those who sit in the pews every Sunday morning dream of their children being married in this space. They picture their own funeral with the grand pipe organ and the light pouring in through the stained-glass windows. Some even go so far as to picture the memorial plaque or window that will be created to honor them after their death. This church building is often the only place where they might be remembered in concrete ways. To lose the church building can be devastating, because it changes the future they have always pictured. It is the transitional minister's role to help people mourn for the loss of the place and reimagine the future in new ways.

None of these five losses can be addressed as a solitary issue. They will not appear in a linear fashion, but will pop up in mixed order over and over again as the congregation sells the building and disbands. It is crucial for the transitional minister to mine the richness of scripture and tradition to find parallels with these points of grief, as well as to provide theological ways to examine endings and beginnings, healthy good-byes, and the respectful preservation of memories.

THE GRIEVING CONGREGATION

Once the congregation, either by vote or consensus, has discerned a call from God to disband, the response is often akin to receiving a terminal diagnosis. All the aspects of grieving we might expect will come into play in no particular sequence, and each individual, even the transitional pastor, will grieve differently. Grief expert J. William Worden gives us the helpful construct "tasks of mourning," as opposed to stages or phases. He outlines the work of mourning in this way:

> Task 1: Accepting the reality of the loss. Task 2: To work through the pain of grief. Task 3: To adjust to an environment in which the deceased is missing. Task 4: To emotionally relocate the deceased and move on with life. [4]

The tasks of mourning tend to occur all at once, overlapping one another. These tasks will be engaged by different people at different times and can threaten the unity of the congregation. The transitional pastor will be well served by identifying the behaviors that relate to these varied tasks. Ideally, the transitional minister is a nonanxious presence who names what is happening and reminds everyone involved that like any family experiencing loss, each person in the church will mourn in his or her own unique way. The transitional minister needs to teach the congregation to be patient with those who do not grieve the way they do. The pastoral leader must model appropriate respect and consideration for others.

What does it mean that churches that are dying need the same kind of care and support as a person who is facing the end of their earthly life? Hospice nurse Angela Morrow[5] writes that grief can be seen as an opportunity to say five significant things:

- Will you forgive me?
- I forgive you.
- Thank you.
- I love you.
- Good-bye.

The grieving congregation needs numerous opportunities to express forgiveness, mercy, gratitude, love, and farewell.

The challenges of grief will follow the congregation through every aspect of the practical dismantling of its ministry and physical facility. The transitional minister and members of the congregation must work diligently to extend to one another deep compassion, understanding, and respect as they move through the tasks of closing.

THE ROLE OF THE HOSPICE CHAPLAIN

The interim minister makes the most of these opportunities by filling a number of roles in the lives of parishioners, similar to the roles filled by a hospice chaplain. The pastor becomes the one who prays with them and for them, creating meaningful moments of reflection and thanksgiving for individuals, small groups, and the congregation as a whole. The pastor becomes the one who listens. People have all kinds of stories they need to tell, and they need to feel truly heard. The listening clergy draws meaningful parallels between personal and congregational stories and the narratives of scripture. Some people just need a hand to hold so they know they are not alone. By faithfully making pastoral calls on people in their homes, the transitional pastor "holds the hand" of the congregation. She or he helps the church members to know that they are not alone and that God has not abandoned them.

Opportunities for members to share stories with each other should also be plentiful. The pastor becomes the one who provides the contexts in which people share their memories. These opportunities may include after-church gatherings, home meetings, open sharing during worship, or the creation of scrapbooks, photo albums, and written accounts of important events. The pastor's willingness to be open and accepting of the conversations that need to take place is a huge gift to a congregation that is grieving.

The pastor should create a climate in which people are encouraged to share. The result can be deeply meaningful, as it was one afternoon at Grace Church in Framingham, Massachusetts, when a group of church members were sorting through the church belongings and deciding what would be kept and what would be thrown away before a planned move to a new, smaller building. When I walked in, they had stopped sorting and instead were sharing memories of the Boar's Head Holiday Celebration they used to put on for the whole community every year. They were so enjoying themselves as they replayed some of the scenes from the old presentation, complete with their versions of old English accents and props they had found. Then they began recalling how each member of the congregation would react to the unique tradition. Mrs. Peabody was horrified by the bawdy nature of some of the humor, but she still attended every year until she died. Old Mr. Fuller loved the crazy loud singing and could often be heard singing the choruses in the hallway after the play. Children loved watching their parents and Sunday school teachers acting silly. "Oh, and remember Lorna? She sewed the costumes every year. What a great lady she was. I still miss her so much!"

The Pastor Receives Confessions

The transitional pastor also fills a number of other important roles. She or he becomes someone who receives members' fears and confessions. The pastor must inspire confidence and trust. This will be a special challenge in congregations that have been betrayed by previous leaders, but the people need to have someplace they feel secure enough to tell the truth about their fears and hopes. They also need somebody to hear the confessions of what they have done wrong within the congregation in the past, whether it's how they worked to undermine the last two pastors or the money they skimmed off the offering plate when times were hard for their family a decade ago. The pastor, in this context, becomes priest, receiving confessions of sin, suggesting ways to make amends, and granting God's forgiveness to those who earnestly seek it.

The Pastor Creates Opportunities for Forgiveness

As the pastor listens to people's intimate thoughts and experiences, he or she may come across those who are still angry about something that happened long ago. Those individuals should be encouraged to find a way to let go and offer forgiveness to those from whom they have been withholding it. There are also those who need forgiveness for mistakes they have made. This is the time for the giving and receiving of forgiveness so that members can face the end of their beloved church with peace in their hearts. The pastor can even offer to mediate a conversation between two people or plan a ritual that will help them give and receive forgiveness. Corporate services of reconciliation are included in a number of denominational books of worship for use by the whole congregation. Services for such situations can also be found in my book, *Finishing with Grace.*

The Pastor Seeks Care and Support for Him- or Herself

Savvy church members understand that the role of the pastor during the disbanding of a church is a painful one and that the pastor often becomes the conduit for the extreme and varying emotions of the entire congregation. Just as a dying person needs to know that her or his caregivers have support outside the family system, so do the members of a dying church. The pastor caring for this congregation must seek support, wisdom, and care from colleagues, denomination staff, and personal friends and family members. She or he should be sure to let church members and leaders know she or he is doing so. The congregation should take care to give the pastor enough time to seek this kind of support.

The Pastor Helps Plan the Funeral

There are some lovely and creative ways to design the final service for a disbanding congregation. The service itself should reflect the unique personality of the community of faith. Part of the event should celebrate the gifts the disbanding congregation is giving to others. All generations should be included in planning and leading the closing worship. If this means sending church members to bring elder members from their homes or long-term care facilities, then that's what should be done. Children should also have a significant part in the farewell. The service should be scheduled a few months ahead so invitations can be sent to former pastors, college students living away from home, past members, and people in the wider community. This attention to detail is one way that a congregation expresses its love for one another during the good-bye.

As the congregation plans its formal good-bye, people will begin to wonder what happens when it's all over. How do they go about finding a new church home? If they need funeral services or pastoral care or someone to officiate at a wedding before they connect with a new community of faith, what should they do? The transitional pastor can help by providing members with information about local congregations and pastors who are willing to help. She or he may even elicit invitations from other congregations that can be communicated to the members of the closing congregation. Is there another local clergyperson who is willing to be on call for members of the closing congregation in emergency situations? Is the local hospital chaplain aware of the situation so she or he can keep an eye out for members of this congregation? Do the church members know that the chaplain at the hospital knows they are without pastoral care from a church? There needs to be an acknowledgment that everyone involved has spiritual needs that will continue after his or her congregation has ceased to exist.

Most people who know they are dying feel the need to know what will happen when they're gone. They write wills, give gifts, make arrangements for their funeral, and decide what will happen to their body once they have died. Communities of faith are no different. The pastor taking this journey with a congregation needs to help the members determine what will become of their building and its contents after they close. It is safe to say that no one wants to see a fast-food franchise sign on the front of an old cathedral building. We really don't want the place turned into condominiums, but the choices for dealing with a church building that is no longer housing a congregation are extremely limited. In many cases, the church is already renting space to another congregation or nonprofit, and the first and best choice may be to sell the property to the renters (if they can afford it). The church may choose to lower the asking price in order to that the new owner will be someone with whom they are comfortable. Other options for what to do with church property can be explored with an organization called Church Service Realty, a company that specializes in the sale and disposition of religious properties.[6] Another resource is Partners for Sacred Places.[7]

The Pastor Is Creative in the Midst of Grief

The skilled transitional pastor working with a dying church will keep all of these hospice considerations in mind, giving the congregation time to laugh together, cry with each other, and share the deep feelings they are carrying inside them. Giving people opportunities to be creative as they grieve is also important. They can be invited to write about their favorite memories of things that have happened in the church. The written vignettes can be shared during worship or in the newsletter, or collected into a small volume and reproduced for anyone who wants them as a keepsake. Many children and elders will be physically unable to write, but should be encouraged to express themselves in meaningful ways. They can be asked to contribute drawings or photos to the memory book. These remembrances can be videotaped and made into a DVD as well.

Other creative endeavors may include photographing those beautiful old stained-glass windows and framing the pictures for members with specific connections to the images. These photos can also be made into a collection of note cards for church members. Likewise, memorial plaques can be removed and given to the appropriate family members, or charcoal rubbings of memorial plaques can be made, copied, and included in the memory book, adding recollections about those individuals from current church members, or used as part of the note card collection. The skilled transitional minister will find more creative ways to address the grieving process based on local resources and traditions.

PRACTICAL CONSIDERATIONS

As deeply emotional as any dying process may be, there are always practical, logistical matters that must be addressed. In the case of a church, these may include the disposition of the building and its contents and assets, and planning a meaningful farewell.

Most people who know they are dying feel the need to know what will happen when they're gone. They write wills, give gifts, make arrangements for their funeral, and decide what will happen to their body once they have died. Communities of faith are no different. Inevitably, the congregation must deal with the church building and its contents. Along the way, consideration should be given to other churches that could benefit from items used in the closing congregation. Think, for example, how much it would mean to a mission church in Zimbabwe to have a silver communion service or a carved-wood baptismal font, or for a new church start to receive colorful paraments or banners that have been part of the long history of a disbanding church. Each item being gifted to another church or organization should be blessed in worship so the congregation can say good-bye while celebrating the new life these items signify as they are given away.

The timing of a church closing can make a significant difference in how the process goes. In the best case scenario, a congregation makes end-of-life decisions early enough that its decision can benefit others. Thus, the plan may be to close sooner rather than later in order not to waste vital funds and resources but maintain a valuable legacy to leave behind. Congregations that enter into this process before they are down to their last penny will also have more members still around to make final decisions and carry out the necessary functions of disbanding a church. Churches that sell property are left with the question of what to do with the money they receive for the sale of the building. How your church disburses its financial asserts may depend on your own church bylaws or the law of your city and state. For example, in the Commonwealth of Massachusetts, the attorney general's office is very concerned with how assets are distributed. If money is left in restricted endowments, it should, whenever possible, be spent according to the terms of the endowment itself. Again, the bylaws or state/city laws may direct the proper course of action. If money is left in unrestricted endowments, the funds might be gifted to a helping agency, another church, the local denominational body to help other churches, or to the denomination itself. In this way, the church can leave a significant legacy by supporting other ministries. Other creative uses for financial assets may exist in your community or denomination, such as setting up seminary scholarships or endowing a project dear to the heart of your congregation. When making these end-of-church-life decisions, congregational leaders should be certain to consult a competent attorney who specializes in church or nonprofit law. The lawyer should not be anyone in or connected to the congregation (i.e., not good old Bob Withers's brother or Rev. Philby's son) so that your legal counsel does not have a vested interest in the outcome and will give solid and objective advice.

An extreme but miraculous example of the good that can result from a congregation leaving a substantial legacy comes from my home church, United Congregational UCC, Worcester, Massachusetts.[8] It was clear that our dwindling congregation could no longer afford to heat and maintain our thirty-thousand-square-foot building. Our pastor led us through a three-year discernment process[9] to determine what we should do. No options were off the table. We decided to keep going as a church but to give our huge downtown cathedral-like building and four-fifths of our endowment to the Worcester Area Mission Society, an organization that is part of the United Church of Christ and serves those in need in Central Massachusetts. Because we did that before everything was gone, we left a tremendous legacy that will benefit our city and our denomination for years to come. We now rent space from the building's new owners, so we worship and have our offices in a portion of the building we once owned.

SAYING GOOD-BYE

One of the most difficult things any of us ever has to do is to say good-bye to people and things we love, and most of us have never been taught how to do that in a helpful way. The transitional pastor traveling this road with a congregation can teach people how to say good-bye properly. Folks will need words, rituals, remembrances, and the like to make it possible to say their farewells in meaningful ways.

It is clear that caring for a congregation facing death is a profound and multidimensional process. The transitional pastor's role is a key one in helping church members understand and cope with the grief of losing of their church. She or he gives the people companionship and hope as they travel this path together. The wise pastoral leader can faithfully guide and shape the congregational grieving process.

REFLECTION QUESTIONS

1. What skills does a transitional minister bring into a congregation that is facing the end of life as it has known it?
2. What are the five "attachments" that will need to be addressed while giving hospice care to a closing church?
3. What special roles does the transitional minister fill once a congregation has decided to close its doors?
4. When is the best time for a congregation to decide to close the church?
5. How important is it to manage the final business of the church in such a way that it can leave a meaningful legacy behind?

Chapter Twelve

What Next?

Norman B. Bendroth

With keen eyes and wise insights, the authors of this volume have laid out a new vision for transitional ministry built upon the strong foundation of the past thirty-plus years. Many churches have prospered and flourished having used an effective interim minister; others have flagged or failed because the pastor was ineffective or not well trained. Some churches simply do not want to do the work and want a placeholder until the new minister arrives.

There is also a shift in how we use the terms "interim minister" and "transitional minister." In the classic form of interim ministry the interim minister serves a congregation from eighteen to twenty-four months, making observations, raising important questions, and working on the focus points with the congregation. The churches we served were often established, and traditional congregations formed during the time when Christendom was alive and well in America. That concrete ministry has evolved into a subset of transitional ministry. Transitional ministry is a broader, more elastic category than is interim ministry and addresses a host of new issues. In addition to all the skills an interim minister has, practitioners need particular skills in helping churches navigate today's culture and channeling the anxiety those changes raise into a positive force for ministry and mission. Transitional ministers also need a wide variety of ministry skills for the unique ministry settings we enter.[1]

But these shifts raise the question: What next? Themes emerging from these chapters have been born from many years of the practice of ministry by the authors and those who have been part of this conversation. Fresh thinking has emerged about how we might engage the church and culture given a new day, which we will now explore.

KNOW THE NEW LANDSCAPE

Throughout this volume the authors have hammered home the point that the American church is sailing in uncharted waters. We are going through megashifts in culture, media, globalization, gender identity, politics, and technology. Grasping all this new information is like drinking water from the proverbial firehose. Yet, there are signs of life everywhere as churches are recovering their reason for being, taking up spiritual practices, experimenting with new settings for worship and ministry, and investigating new settings for mission. In chapter 3 of this volume, Cameron Trimble has explored the phenomena in "The Changing Landscape of the American Church," as have I in chapter 1, "Whither Transitional Minister?" These chapters would be suitable for key leaders in the congregation to read.

A new task, among the many, for those of us in transitional ministry is to educate ourselves about these megashifts and to teach them to our congregations. People in the pews know something dramatic is happening, but it's hard for them to wrap their heads around it. Appropriate forums for sharing this information include, of course, the pulpit, but also adult forums, after-worship presentations, and workshops. Visiting other churches that are doing creative worship, ministry, or governance or having them make a presentation to your congregation will get the creative juices flowing. Having the leaders or the entire congregation read an accessible book about these new realities will inform the readers of the issues that face the church and help them begin a conversation about the impact on their community.

STUDY THE CONGREGATION

An overriding theme throughout these chapters is that good transitional ministers need to be able to read the environment of their ministry setting and to avoid formulaic solutions. Context, context, context is the watchword. Given the whirlwind of changes in church and society the need to understand the setting, the players, the history, and the culture of each ministry setting is paramount. Transitional ministers need to be like anthropologists, taking borings and soil samples, dusting off artifacts, and digging through the layers of the site. They need to pay attention to the demographics, shifts in the community, the self-perception of the congregation, and their reputation in the community. To use another metaphor, transitional pastors need to be detectives.

To be good detectives, transitional ministers need to have sufficient information and insight into a church's demographic context and modus operandi in order to have a map to lead a congregation toward a new future. A variety of models are available to help congregations and their leaders get a fix on their context. I will share three.

Carolyn Weese and J. Russell Crabtree, experts in the field of church leadership and authors of *The Elephant in the Boardroom: Speaking the Unspoken about Pastoral Transitions*, have developed a useful map for understanding church cultures and strategies to guide churches through transitions.[2] The authors describe four church cultures and how they accordingly behave.

- *The Family Culture Church* is one in which the pastor's role is seen as parent, elder, or brother or sister. This is a pastor centered–style church whose primary purpose is to maintain a way of life rooted in local traditions that give a sense of continuity with the past and predictability for the future. This describes most mainline Protestant churches and smaller community churches.

- *The Archival Culture Church* is one in which the pastor is a curator primarily concerned with maintaining theological tradition and heritage that is deeply grounded in a canon of knowledge and practices, which reach back over the centuries. This is a Tradition-driven (with a capital T, meaning the Great Tradition) church and best describes Roman Catholic and Orthodox churches.

- *The Icon Culture Church* is one in which the pastor functions as a "living logo." This is a personality driven–style or an outcomes-driven church, which is concerned primarily with results measured by the number of people involved in, attending, or committed to the church and its facilities. Many media-driven megachurches and large mainline Protestant churches fit within this culture.

- *The Replication Culture Church* is one in which the pastor is a "multiplier" of ministry, meaning he or she is concerned with duplicating his or her ministry by developing standardized materials to train leaders and to expand the ministry. This is a knowledge-driven, effectiveness church, drawing from the latest in technology, marketing, and psychology. This style describes some megachurches and parachurch organizations.[3]

For each culture the authors give a snapshot of the features, norms, values, and transition tactics. The book is full of strategies, tasks, processes, and practices for each culture, which are transferable and can be adapted to whatever situation transitional pastors encounter.

The *Handbook for Congregational Studies*, by sociologists of religion Jackson Carroll, Carl Dudley, Bill McKinney, and their colleagues, is perhaps the most comprehensive guide for studying congregations. To have a clear reading on the congregation and its context, the authors insist that churches need to explore four areas: program, process, social context, and

identity.[4] The lists give a visual presentation of the four study areas, a definition, and the topics that are useful to observe to get a take on the culture and
practices of a congregation.

Context
(Ecology)
"The social forces and demographic
realities that impact a congregation"
social
neighborhood
community—village, town, city
region
political
economic
religious
judicatory
denomination
ecumenical affiliations and
cooperative networks
interaction of congregation and
context

Culture
(Customs)
"'Ways of being together' that
express the uniqueness of the
congregation"
rituals
customs
norms
values
practices
habits
traditions
stories
symbols
myths
artifacts (worship bulletins,
newsletters, hymnal, liturgy, reports,
mission statement)

Capital
(Resources)
"A congregation's 'capital' for
accomplishing its ministry and
mission"
members, money, building
"relational and spiritual energies"
"connections to community"
history

Conduct
(Process)
"The underlying flow and dynamics
of a congregation that knit together
its common life and shape its morale
and climate"
leadership style
decision making
communication
conflict resolution
problem solving
dynamics of power
patterns and relationship
assumptions about power and
authority

A third essential resource for the study of congregations is *Holy Conversations: Strategic Planning as a Spiritual Practice for Congregations*, by
longtime Alban Institute consultants Gil Rendle and Alice Mann.[5] They
assert that three of the most important questions a congregation can answer
during the transitional time are Who are we? What is God calling us to be

and to do? and Who is my neighbor? These questions helped frame the Interim Ministry Network's curriculum redesign, and the way a congregation answers them informs the five focus areas of heritage, mission, connections, leadership, and future.

Any congregational study needs to be grounded in the Christian story so that it is not just another exercise in organizational development. Many of our congregations have amnesia. In their attempt to keep the institutional church alive, they have forgotten their charter document, the Bible. Pastors need to remind the congregation members that they are not the Rotary Club at prayer, but an outpost of the reign of God in their setting, where the Word is preached and the sacraments are celebrated. They are to be a live expression of the prayer Jesus taught us, "Thy will be done on earth as it is in heaven," proclaiming that we serve a God who has given us the gifts of creation, fiercely loves us, forgives us before we ask, empowers us by the Holy Spirit, and sends us to be healers and prophets in a broken world.

The practice of discernment should be introduced and taught to congregations as well so that the process does not become another series of up and down votes.[6] Learning to listen for the Spirit in the quietness of discerning prayer will be disarming to some folks who may be allergic to more intimate spiritual practices. In my congregational tradition we have an axiom that "God speaks most clearly to a group of people in Covenant with one another."

The scriptural basis for the purpose of the church should be kept in front of the folk in as many ways as possible: from the pulpit, in the newsletter, in small groups, before the beginning of meetings, when gathering to do mission discernment.

WHO ARE WE?

When attempting to "fix" things most congregations begin with their current programs. After all worship, Sunday school, and the annual stewardship dinner are the most visible aspects of church life. Before evaluating programs, churches in transition need clarity about their *identity*. Identity is that "persistent set of beliefs, values, patterns, symbols, stories and style that make a congregation distinctively itself."[7] Program is the "face" with which congregations present themselves, but *identity* is the self-image congregations carry, even when it is unknown or unstated. Identity makes a congregation unique and distinguishes it from its environment. Carroll, Dudley, and McKinney state that church identity has seven elements. These include history, heritage, worldview, symbols, ritual, and character.[8]

- History. Each congregation tells a story about itself. This story includes the day-to-day, Sunday-to-Sunday history of board meetings and worship services. Then there are those revealing "historic" moments: formative events such as the founding of the church, critical turning points, significant events of the past, conflict and splits, and the "heroes" and "heroines" of the congregation.
- Heritage. Heritage includes the broader tradition within which a church sits. Reminding a congregation of its denominational, ethnic, and theological roots helps them recover and affirm a unique part of their identity. A sense of heritage will help the pastor and laypeople understand how their "little tradition" fits in with the "Great Tradition" of the church.
- Worldview. A worldview is an overall belief system, the grid that orders all of life. It is the disposition or posture by which we interpret our world and our lives. Some churches are inherently pessimistic and look at the world through Good Friday lenses, while others take on an optimistic Easter view of life.
- Symbols. A symbol is something that stands for something else and contains powerful emotions. A symbol might be the old sounding board above the pulpit, which conveys a sense of the congregation's history, dignity, and architectural beauty. Symbols usually invoke associations with transcendence, love, power, and justice.
- Ritual. Rituals are those repetitive actions that are ways congregations express themselves through means other than words. They could be how they conduct "rites of passage," such as baptism, confirmation, marriage, and death, as well as how the annual meeting is run.
- Character. Character describes the "personality" of a church. Character, as a specific dimension of a church's identity, refers to the ethical dimensions of congregational life—its values, preferred behavioral tone, ethos, and corporate identity. A worldview reveals what it thinks is going on; character tells what it wishes would go on.

This information ultimately contributes toward a "family story." Just as a nuclear and extended family keeps a photo album or scrapbook, or a matriarch or patriarch of the family might keep genealogies and diaries and write family histories, so each congregation has a story that needs to be recorded so it can be told again and again.

Process

Process continues to answer the question of Who are we? but it focuses on "how" a church functions as opposed to how a congregation perceives itself. Process looks at practices; identity looks at values. Most congregations are not aware of their often unquestioned behaviors until someone like a transitional minister points them out to them. Processes include things like how are decisions made? How does one get new ideas introduced? How does the church deal with conflict? What's the place of children? Process is the underlying current of emotions and interpersonal dynamics between parishioners. When a visitor enters a congregation in conflict, for instance, she or he can "cut the air with a knife" because of the anger and tension. At another time the emotional air might be filled with serenity and joy. A troublesome member may hold a congregation hostage by threatening to leave or withdraw his or her pledge if leadership makes a certain decision. The fact that people tolerate this is part of process. Often processes are unspoken rules, understandings, and folkways that exist among the members of congregation, such as "Mr. Spalding always cooks the Palm Sunday breakfast" or "We never have conflict around here, because we ignore it when it appears."

A key to understanding process is distinguishing between group norms and simple behavior patterns. A norm is a system of "understandings" that every organization has. Norms are not written down anywhere, but become quite apparent when they are broken. The difference between norms and simple behavior patterns is that norms carry sanctions or punishments when they are not observed. Norms are the "ways of being" or "traditions" of every congregation. Norms are normal. Every group has a set of unspoken, governing behaviors that keep its corporate life intact.

Program

Programs are expressions of the values, priorities, and felt needs of the church at a given time. Programs are the "what" of congregations, what do we do? Events, plans, groups, and activities are the mission and ministry to those both within and outside the congregation. Program concerns tend to dominate congregations, even though lethargy in programming may point to real problems in other areas. If a church has lost its sense of identity and purpose, no amount of programming can restore it. Tinkering with dates, times, job assignments, and other details may just be ways to avoid facing the fact that this program has outlived its usefulness. The primary reason for studying programming is that it is one gauge to measure how the church uses its energy and resources.

WHO IS OUR NEIGHBOR?

Before a church can discern its mission it needs to know its social context. Social context is a congregation's setting, local and global. Every congregation lives within and is shaped by its environment. Included in social context are the culture and characteristics of a neighborhood, institutions and civic and social groups, and the various political and economic forces at work in the setting. While questions of context may not necessarily determine the commitments and direction of a congregation, it cannot afford to ignore them.

The best place to begin a study of social context is by gathering demographic and census data. Two excellent resources for demographic data for churches are Mission Insight and Percept.[9] In addition to providing information about population size, educational and income levels, etc., it measures worship preferences, use of social media, lifestyle choices, and what ministries people might look for. Interviews with community leaders, neighborhood walks, and random sample surveys with neighbors are other ways to collect data to help discern "who is my neighbor."

If a church has become insular and missions largely consist of writing checks, answering the question of "Who is my neighbor?" will help parishioners see how much their neighborhood or city has changed, new populations moving in, and needs of which they were not aware. Helping a congregation understand its social realities can be immensely helpful in shaping their mission, in determining the hopes and hurts of their communities, and in designing ministries.

WHAT IS GOD CALLING US TO *B E* AND *D O*?

Struggling with this question aids a congregation in discovering its purpose, mission, and vision. These are bold statements that provide the defining direction of the church, the reason for its being, and its "elevator speech." It answers the question, "If St. Joe's by the 7-11 closed, what would be missing from this town?" Note that the question includes being *and* doing. Churches know how to do things, especially how to keep the institution functioning, as well as how to conduct mission trips, serve at soup kitchens, or bring communion to homebound folks. They are less adept at leaning how "to be" as a people before God and for one another. In her book *Unbinding the Gospel*, Martha Grace Reece tells congregations that before they come up with a mission statement or plan of action, they need to sit in prayer for three months and learn how to tell the story of their walk with God.[10]

Community building beyond coffee hour after worship or at committee meetings helps congregations become the body of Christ instead of a holy club. Beginning board or committee meetings with intentional Bible study, worship, and community building will begin to shape those times into "worshipful work."[11] Small groups, house churches, or *koinonia* groups enable congregants to discover what it means to be vulnerable, open, and caring, Christians together. Many people won't want to be on a board or committee, but they will join a group that feeds their spirit.

Behavioral covenants are also a way to help parishioners learn how "to be" together in healthy ways. It's best not to introduce a behavioral covenant during a conflict when it may be too late but during times of calm and concord. The interim minister may find resistance to such a conversation, since people won't acknowledge that it is necessary. They may play it down or chalk it up to "that's just the way Charlie is. You get used to it." One person told me she didn't need a behavioral covenant to guide her because she always "behaved like a Christian." In spite of this, the process of looking at scriptural expectations for household behavior and learning good tools to use to express oneself, manage anger, and understand what contributes to conflict helps people grow in grace and gives them skills that will build health into a congregation.

"What is God calling us to do?" is the second part of the mission question. The mission is the particular and peculiar task that God has for a congregation to advance the Gospel in its time and place. It should be conceived by letting the answers to "Who are we?" and "Who is our neighbor?" gestate for a while and give birth to a "preferred future," as it is called in Appreciative Inquiry, or to a vision of tomorrow. It should be a bold statement that requires faith and imagination to achieve.

THE ABILITY TO ADAPT

Another consistent theme found in these chapters is the need for the skilled transitional pastor to provide adaptive leadership. In the past, many interim ministers, including me, faithfully followed the five developmental tasks almost in sequential fashion. It didn't take long for me to realize that not every congregation needed to do all that work. Each congregation has its own presenting issues and challenges. It may have a pretty good read on how its history has shaped it or have a grip on how to manage conflict in healthy ways, but its stewardship, governance structure, or use of social media may need attention.

The presenting issue may not be the real issue. For instance, a moderator may complain that he can no longer get a quorum at the monthly council meeting. No one can remember when the council was started, but it has always been an information-sharing body where committee chairs shared minutes and coordinated the calendar. The council decides that the moderator will put a notice in the bulletin and the newsletter and make a stern announcement from the pulpit about the obligation of each committee to send a representative to the council. Most committee chairs feel guilt tripped, and there is a quorum at the next meeting. After that attendance drops off again. While the presenting problem was poor attendance, the adaptive solution asked the questions Why aren't people coming? Has the council outlived its usefulness? Is this the best model to govern a church in today's society? Why does the council exist? The fact is, the meetings are boring and most consider them a waste of time. People said they would be excited about being part of a group that talked about taking the spiritual pulse of the church; reviewing ministries, not minutes; and seeing whether the church was on target with its mission.

Further, as the transitional minister becomes part of the emotional system of the church and becomes part of the daily routine, she or he may find pushback from people who don't want to do the transitional work or folks who are indifferent. She or he seems to have hit a wall that stops forward movement. A transition team that I worked with in one congregation was making great headway proceeding through several interim tasks. The congregation had already worked through conflict over the previous pastor, adopted a behavioral covenant, and ratified a purpose statement. Further, the team members had hosted a history night and gathered and processed the information. They began working on writing a vision statement with the congregation but couldn't get any traction. A host of other issues kept coming up. How are decisions made around here? How is money spent? Should we remain within the denomination? What's our theology? Will we welcome gay people here?

We began brainstorming at one meeting about what was causing the logjam. One by one, we had a dawning recognition that the issues that kept popping up had been underground for the past decade and were emerging during the interim time. There were struggles for power between progressive and conservative folk, old and new members, and those of different theological and political persuasions. These issues needed to be unearthed and looked at in the light.

We came up with a plan called a "Hot Potato Forum," because the underground topics were hot potatoes nobody wanted to touch. We listed ten of the most common complaints or issues that we had been hearing. They were then placed in the bulletin for the next two weeks. Parishioners were asked to rank order which top five issues were most problematic and needed to be addressed. The team then collated them and came up with list of the five items that garnered the most votes.

On a Saturday night the team hosted the "Hot Potato Forum," a buffet of baked potatoes with a host of toppings to choose from. Each person had a colored dot on his or her name tag signifying the number of years he or she had been a member, which assigned them to a table of people they wouldn't normally sit with. After dinner, members of the transition team laid out the issue in as fair and even-handed manner as they could. Each person at every table then had an opportunity to speak to the issue until everyone had a chance to speak. A scribe at each table took careful notes. At the end of the discussion, each person was to complete the statement "This is what I think

God would have us do about this issue." In this way, the focus returned to the presence of God in the midst of their discussions and the need to discern the Spirit's movement. This process broke the logjam. This happened because questions were answered and clarified, false information was corrected, and a sense of the congregation and its preferences became clear. There were those who saw the writing on the wall and decided to move on.

WORSHIP

Another area that the authors and practitioners of transition see as essential is attention to worship during a transitional period. Worship is the primary gathering of any congregation, any given week. It is also the activity that no other organization but churches practice. Not only do preachers have a captive audience, but ideally people come expecting a word from God. During a time of transition, thoughtful worship is a time to provide security and comfort for those grieving or nervous about the future.

In-between times can also be used to experiment with forms and styles of worship if the wine skins have grown rather old. Altering worship can be a tightrope act, balancing the familiar with the new, but the wise interim pastor will discuss the rationale with the leadership and explain to the congregation that this is an opportunity to worship together in new and different ways. The purpose is not change for change's sake, but to introduce new forms and practices that take people deeper in their walk with God or to appreciate new styles. If people do not like them, they can abandon them or evaluate what they like and try it again. The interim time is a time for novelty and experimentation, even as we seek to keep the best from the past that makes the congregation unique.

One ritual I have used, developed by a colleague of mine, is having a display of salt, water, and bread at the front of the worship space on All Saints' Day. The water is ritually poured into the salt as we remember with tears those who have gone before. Salt is also used to make bread. The worship leaders explain that God uses the salty tears of our losses and griefs to make them into goodness, healing, and the restoration of our souls even as bread feeds our bodies. The Bread of Life is present as we ritualize this message of faith and hope. During the pastoral prayer people are encouraged to call out the names of those who have died in the past year or those they wish to remember. This experience can be much more powerful than a sermon on saints or a garden-variety pastoral prayer. Other colleagues have reintroduced Ash Wednesday, Tenebrae, or an Easter vigil.

At the end of the Palm Sunday service at a highly conflicted congregation I served, the deacons brought a large cross made out of birchwood to the front of the sacristy. It remained there during Holy Week. People were free to come into the sanctuary and to pin sticky notes onto the branches. There they wrote how they had contributed to the conflict and shared their anger, resentments, regrets, and hurts. On Good Friday the "tree" was covered with notes. During worship that evening we had a Service of Reconciliation, led by two people on opposite sides of the conflict. There, all shared in and confessed their complicity in the conflict. The last act of the service was to remove all of the notes, carry them to a fire pit outside the church, and burn them. Here was a powerful symbol of the fire of the Spirit purging and purifying the congregation for the hurt they inflicted upon one another. We used it to remind one another that this chapter of conflict was behind them. We symbolically burned it. The congregation made significant strides forward after that event.

Thoughtful, well-crafted worship services that reflect the theme of the lectionary text or the sermon series is a powerful way to touch people's lives. The ultimate goal of discipleship is not information, instruction, or inspiration, but transformation (2 Corinthians 5:17).

TEACHING AND PREACHING

The Sunday morning sermon continues to be the primary teaching platform for most congregations. At times, a congregational transition looms so large in a sermon that it becomes the lens through which scripture is interpreted, the congregation is addressed, the preacher is heard, and God is experienced. If the congregation's worship is lectionary based, the preacher might leave it for a while and explore some different texts and themes that are more pertinent in the life of the congregation. Preaching can also focus on the salient focus themes of the interim time: heritage, mission, connections, leadership, and future as well as grief, conflict, imagining a new future, and the nature of the church to name a few.

The familiar motifs of the Israelites being led by Moses in the wilderness, transferring the prophetic mantle from Elijah to Elisha, or Joshua leading the people into the Promised Land are good texts for interpreting transitions from a biblical perspective and reflecting on how to traverse them. The preacher could also speak of Holy Saturday as a mysterious time of transition between the grief and tragedy of Good Friday and joy and renewal of Easter Sunday. This would be especially good for congregations that have been traumatized. The Ascension and Pentecost stories tell of the transition from Jesus's ministry on earth given to the church as his ambassadors. [12]

Many of our mainline church attendees are biblically illiterate, and it might be appropriate to do a year on "The Bible's Greatest Hits," covering key Bible stories in depth that parishioners likely learned long ago in Sunday school or have never heard. You could also call it "The Bible's Top 40" and do a forty-week preaching series. I have done a series called "It's all Greek to me," focusing on the marks or charisms of the church given in the New Testament: *koinonia* (fellowship), *leitourgia* (worship), *diakonia* (service and mission), *didache* (teaching), and *kerygma* (preaching).[13] The series uses the practices of the early church in Acts 2: 42–48 and reminds the congregation of its charter and purpose.

Be creative. Explore possible themes with leaders and colleagues in light of what you discover at the church. If a church has an "edifice" complex, look at 1 Corinthians 12 about the body of Christ as the church. Transitional ministers have an opportunity to tell the truth and to hold up a mirror in ways that are not always prudent for a settled pastor. Of course, you must smile and be nice as you tell the truth, but trust the Word to do its piercing work (Hebrews 4:12–13).

If the demographers and social scientists are correct, a lot of people in our society have hungry hearts. Twenty percent of those surveyed identify themselves as spiritual but not religious. This includes people within our churches. Offering book studies; Bible studies; courses and workshops on topics such as discerning your spiritual gifts, Theology 101, an Old Testament or New Testament survey; raising compassionate kids; or whatever else you sense are the needs of the church and community would be worth trying out.

Teaching need not be limited to scripture, tradition, or Christian practices. The transitional period can be a time to teach congregations the insights from family systems theory, conflict management, setting boundaries, and Appreciative Inquiry. Often we clergy go to workshops and read books that give us skills and insights that we never share with our congregations. We come back all excited and expect them to share our enthusiasm or to become our guinea pigs as we try out our new techniques. I have developed a PowerPoint slide show called "Understanding How Your Church Family Works," named after Peter Steinke's fine book. The presentation is an overview of how anxiety works in a congregation, how we manage it through triangles, how to break triangles, defining oneself, and staying connected. The scales dropped from the eyes of many as they finally understood the dynamics of their congregation. The same could be done by teaching how to deal with difficult people, effective leadership, running worshipful meetings, and understanding best practices in governance structures. While some may say, "If it ain't broke, don't fix it," others think it's been busted for quite a while and are eager to look at new models.

SPIRITUAL PRACTICES

An important subset of teaching and preaching is to introduce and teach classic spiritual practices. Historically, many of our churches have not done this; they are what I call "neck up" churches that attend to the head, but not as much to the heart. In the past (and still do), attendees wanted to "get something out of the sermon." More often today regular attendees and seekers come to worship or a small group expects to have a transcendent, transformative experience with the Living God. They do not come to church to hear a good movie review, a learned spiritual lecture, or a rant on a social issue. (Don't get me wrong. Intelligent preaching that engages the mind and addresses the issues of the day remains vitally important, but that is not the primary reason people attend worship.)

Spiritual practices are best introduced through small groups. Fine books by Dorothy Bass, Barbara Brown Taylor, and Richard Foster are a great starting place.[14] Read a chapter a week, and assign practicing to the participants as homework until the next gathering. Put together small groups that explore different styles and methods of prayer. Teaching and practicing these can be illuminating. The growing practice of *apophatic* prayer (listening) can be life changing for many as you engage them in centering prayer, meditation, *lectio divina*, praying with scripture, journaling, and walking the labyrinth. In one class I did all of these plus built a wailing wall out of bricks where participants could put slips of paper with their hurts and wounds written on them. We looked at lamentation in Prophets and Psalms even as they mourned their own laments and losses and placed them in God's hands.

One colleague of mine asks that at least one third of the worshiping community commit to participate in twenty-four hours of spiritual practices during the program year. The twenty-four hours could include participating in a book or Bible study, joining a prayer group, starting a practice of daily prayer and scripture reading, going on a retreat or to a conference, or journaling. Practices were interpreted broadly to encourage as much participation as possible. Some found these odd and intimidating, while many found them to be a real boost to their spiritual journey, reminding them that the reason the church gathered was to delight in and glorify God.

NEW MODELS

Part of my research for this book involved gatherings of interim ministers, judicatory executives, Interim Ministry Network faculty and board members, and observers of American church life. Out of those conversations certain patterns, projects, and experiments emerged as we struggled to find common language and define the models more sharply. Others introduced some the pioneering efforts with which they were experimenting.

We first looked at the varying uses of the term interim or transitional minister. This specialized ministry traditionally operated on two primary assumptions: (1) The interim pastor is temporary. This allows a trained transitional specialist who is not part of the church system to accompany the church as it does its work of self-reflection and vision discernment and prepares to call a settled pastor. (2) The temporary pastor cannot be considered as a candidate for the settled position. The rationale for this is that it allows the search committee to be free and unbiased as it discerns God's will with an open and level field of candidates. As you will see below there are special circumstances where this second assumption is negotiable. There are currently five ways in which an interim pastor is used.

Pulpit Supply

Supply pastors often lead worship, preach, and provide essential pastoral care. This is a minimum level of pastoral coverage. This position is almost always part time. Some congregations use this pastor as a bridge until a trained interim pastor arrives or only short term. This model is often used by congregations that can't afford an interim pastor, full or part time, or don't want to do the transitional work. In this case the pastor is largely a "placeholder."

Classic Interim

This is the model of interim ministry that clergy are most familiar with and uses the five focus areas (see chapter 4 in this volume, "Focus Points and the Work of the Congregation") from the Interim Ministry Network training. This is by far the most common form in use in mainline churches and serves a vital and important function during transitional periods.

Sustaining Interim

This is a full-time position focused on maintaining continuity of key ministries while the church undergoes an abbreviated search process. This sometimes is referred as a bridge interim. Interim ministry tasks can be pursued during this time, but they must be focused and strategic.

Two-Tiered Interim Ministry

Some judicatories, such as the Episcopal Diocese of Minnesota, experimented with using an interim priest and an interim consultant. The priest provides pastoral care, preaches and teaches, leads worship, and maintains the ministries of the church. The trained interim consultant, lay as often as clergy, leads the congregation through the work of self-reflection and discerning the purpose, vision, mission, and needs of the congregation. Completing the parish profile is the goal of this process. The priest and the consultant meet regularly to share their discoveries about the congregation and the work they are doing. Another version of this is a long-distance model using a supply pastor plus coaching and consulting from a trained interim pastor. This would be used in regions of the country where hundreds of miles separate pastors, churches, and judicatories.

Designated Short-Term Pastor

This is a pastor brought in to complete a specific task that needs to be accomplished before the church can move toward the search process. Clergy with specialized training or experience are needed in these situations, which usually follows a traumatic incident or severe conflict in the life of the church. The parameters and duration of the ministry must be clear from the outset of the arrangement. Ongoing collaboration between the pastor, the church, and the judicatory is another requisite to ensure success. The designated pastor has a contract with a clear end that would lead into either an open search process or another pastor serving as a classic interim. The types of situations include:

- After misconduct or criminal activity, a traumatic event or natural disaster, a financial crisis, a high level of entrenched conflict, or a move from a full-time pastor to part time.
- A substantial building or governance shift, a move to a new location, or a merger with another church.
- Churches that are reconfiguring their staffing model and need a pastor temporarily while they complete their strategy or are looking to merge with or into another church.

"Crossroads" Pastor

The crossroads pastor works with a congregation that is in survival mode and helps it discern whether it's time to close or to come up with a bold plan toward renewal, and hence are at a crossroads. This model is useful with congregations:

- Facing the financial reality that their funds will likely run out in three to five years.

- Located in geographic or demographic settings where the population has moved or the neighborhood or region has so changed that they have not been able to attract candidates.
- Beginning to explore closing or have already chosen that path. They want to close with intentionality and dignity and leave a positive legacy.
- Making plans to merge with another church or make a bold decision to redefine themselves and essentially start a new church.

The process should end with a congregational vote to approve the direction the church chooses to go. The crossroads pastor may wish to stay on to complete the work if he or she has the skills necessary or hire another pastor with expertise in turning around churches or in closing a congregation.

Repositioning Pastor

The role of the repositioning pastor is to lead a congregation toward revitalization and renewal. The freshest thinking on this has been done by Charlotte Wright and Laura Westby, both interim ministers in the Connecticut Conference in the United Church of Christ. Their proposal, "A New Model for Interim Ministry," was adopted by the Connecticut Conference in September 2013. This model is built upon the life cycle theory of church growth and decline.[15] The name "repositioning" comes from the observation that churches have life cycles just as human beings do. The theory is illustrated by a bell curve as illustrated in the chart on the next page.[16]

The left side of the curve represents the birth of the congregation. As the curve rises it represents the various stages of development, such as infancy, adolescence, and young adult until it reaches a plateau of maturity and stability. Unless a congregation continues to redefine its mission and remind itself of its purpose, it will descend on the right side through various stages of maintenance, decline, and death. The vertical line going through the center of the bell curve is the "line of vitality." On the left side this line signifies growth and vitality, and the right side aging, maintenance, and decline. The horizontal line through the middle of the curve is the "line of sustainability." On the left side this line represents the financial health, energy, and ongoing mission of the church. On the left side, churches are vital and solvent, and on the right, churches are in decline and struggle to meet their budgets. Each of these sections is called a "quadrant," with each of the four representing a different stage in the life cycle of a church.

- **New** (Quad 1) churches are driven by vision, with a strong emphasis on growing the fellowship through outreach and evangelism. The founders have passion and excitement about this new venture. The church is not financially sustainable, but there may be support from the denomination.

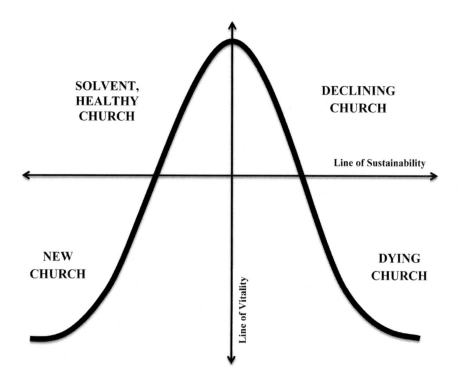

Figure 12.1.

- **Growth** (Quad 2) churches are driven by increased worship attendance, program development, and staffing. Programs are beginning to blossom, and leaders begin to formalize organization to manage ministry. There is a strong sense of mission, purpose, and vision.
- **Decline** (Quad 3) churches focus primarily on maintaining the institution. Relationships, property, programs, and management take priority. The membership has plateaued and is in decline. A sense of purpose or vision no longer motivates ministry. These churches are successful in many areas but lacking a clear focus; much remains status quo. This is the quadrant where a repositioning pastor most likely enters a congregation when it begins asking, "How can we recover what we once had?" or perhaps, "What do we need to do to renew ourselves?"
- **Dying** (Quad 4) churches are in sharp decline. Resources, ministries, programs, and staff are greatly diminished or have disappeared entirely. Because of this decline there is a lot of finger pointing about who is responsible for the decline. These churches often have low self-esteem, high conflict between leaders and staff, and regrets over failure. Feelings of

nostalgia, disappointment, and anger dominate. They also are not financially sustainable without help from endowments, fund-raising efforts. and/or denominational support.[17]

The name "repositioning" describes the work of the interim pastor as he or she leads the congregation that is in the third quadrant or possibly the fourth (a much harder task) back to the second. Most churches want to climb back up the right side of the hill to the peak, the "glory days." Because of the dramatic changes in the culture and the church as described in this book, this can never be. The result will be the same as it was for Sisyphus pushing the proverbial rock up the hill: it will just roll back down. What is necessary is to move across the curve in step-by-step renewal as illustrated below.[18]

An example of the repositioning model at work is from a colleague of mine who was hired by a congregation to help it assess its viability and discern God's next step for it. It could survive on its endowment for another four years and had a mammoth building that was used extensively during the week, but only thirty or so attended worship. It could close, merge with another church, or plan for a turnaround. This congregation decided to make a bold move by selling the building and starting a new church in a storefront. It would then have funds to pay a full-time pastor and concentrate on targeted ministries to the community without the encumbrances of a building and all the trappings of an institution. The pastor may also be considered for the settled position, to maintain the momentum.[19]

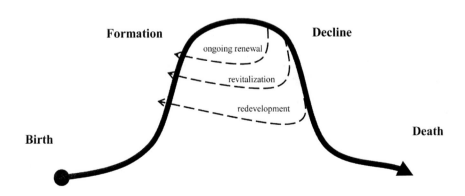

Figure 12.2.

Succession Model

In this model the current pastor and church leadership choose the next pastor while the current pastor is still in place. This has been used most frequently in two settings: a corporate-sized church (worship attendance is consistently from three hundred to five hundred people) and when the founding pastor of a new church leaves. Churches adopting this model still will experience and have to wrestle with the realities of change as described in William Bridges's model of transition.[20] A congregation moves from the past of the previous pastor (ending, losing, letting go) into the transitional time ("the neutral zone"), when the new and old pastor overlap, and the future (new beginnings), when the new pastor is fully engaged and immersed into the congregational system. Many of the focus points (heritage, leadership, mission, connections, and future) of interim ministry will also need to be addressed during this time regardless of whether an intentional interim minister is in place or not. This model was covered in detail in chapter 8 of this volume, "Another Option: Pastoral Succession."[21]

Candidacy

In this model the transitional minister may be considered for the settled position. This is most commonly used in unique situations when there are few qualified candidates, often in rural or urban settings. Another circumstance might be when a spouse is unable to relocate because of health or a job or he or she lives in a region where there are few other opportunities available. This option should be thoroughly vetted with the candidate, the congregation, and the appropriate judicatory before the transition ministry begins. In the Episcopal system there is a position of "Priest-in-Charge" (aka "Rent to Own"), where a priest is assigned to a parish for three years with an option to remain as the settled priest if both the pastor and the congregation feel it is a good match.

With the exception perhaps of the classic interim, all these models are in flux. That is, judicatories and churches have tried and revised them, abandoned them, or used them for impetus to experiment with other models. As I asserted earlier in this chapter, flexibility and adaptability are key components for ministry in our changing religious landscape. Churches, pastors, and judicatories need to be pioneering, willing to risk and to fail, as we rethink how to do transitional ministry.

RESEARCH

All of this, of course, raises the question, How effective is transitional ministry? There is a significant need for serious research for the long-term effectiveness of interim ministry. To date that has not been done on a large scale, but some smaller studies affirm the effectiveness of and need for interim ministry. Susan Nienaber, longtime Alban Institute senior consultant, completed a study of resiliency and recovery among congregations experiencing a high level of conflict or trauma. Of the forty churches she studied across four denominations, twenty-four said they were 80 to 100 percent recovered, and twenty-two attributed that to "excellent and effective interim leadership."[22]

The Center for Congregational Health uses Survey Monkey to evaluate the thirty to forty congregations a year that have used one of its trained interim pastors and have had a new pastor for at least two years. These congregations were asked two questions: Was their church healthier at the end of the interim time than it was at the beginning, and would they would use the same process again? Eighty-seven percent said yes to both questions. To date two hundred congregations have participated in the survey.[23]

In 2007, Research Services of the Presbyterian Church (USA) published a study of the effectiveness of interim pastors in Presbyterian churches, surveying 318 congregations that had interim ministers between 2004 and 2006. When clerks of session and pastors in congregations where an interim pastor had served were queried about the experience, 69 percent of both groups responded, "Yes, it was a very good idea," and another two in ten responded, "Yes, it was a good idea." Responses from Presbytery executives and chairs of committees on ministry were more mixed but still relatively high. The study concluded that support for the use of interim pastors was still strong, but some open questions remained about the usefulness of interim pastors in all situations.[24]

I asked Bill McKinney, president emeritus of the Pacific School of Religion and sociologist of religion, what a study of the effectiveness of transitional ministry might look like. He posed the question to the congregational studies team,[25] an informal collaboration of scholars and researchers who share an interest in the disciplined study of congregations. McKinney, Nancy Ammerman, Ellen Child of Boston University School of Theology, and their first- and second-year research fellows brainstormed about what such a study might look like. Here are their preliminary thoughts.

They would randomly sample from denominational listings congregations that currently have interim ministers and inquire about the process, tasks undertaken, issues that surfaced, and conflicts. The researcher could do some interviews to parse out particular issues surrounding the process of choosing a new pastor and what challenges the interim ministers have had to deal with. In three to five years they would conduct another survey and set of interviews with the same churches to see how the new pastor has settled in and in hindsight how effective the interim time was in preparing the church for the new pastor. Another step in the study would be to randomly sample churches from denominational listings that had an interim eight to ten years before the study and ask about their perceptions of the process (how it went, things they might do differently, benefits gained, resources they used, etc.) and how the pastor is now fitting in with the congregation. "Such a project is very do-able," says McKinney, "and much needed in my view in the discussion of interim ministry and alternative paths to pastoral succession."[26]

WHITHER TRANSITIONAL MINISTRY?

Ministers dedicated to transitional ministry are a rare breed. It is as unique and challenging a ministry as any out there, but in spite of its challenges and headaches, this ministry niche is deeply satisfying when congregations "get it" and begin the work of transformation. Only those with a crystal ball can say what transitional ministry (or all ministry for that matter) might look like in five to ten years. New conversations and practices are gestating in local churches, denominations, and parachurch organizations, and among transitional ministers. We can only guess what might be born.

Given the rapid decline of mainline churches, David Olsen suggests that the best way to recovery is to plant new churches, not to recycle old ones.[27] Planting new churches requires a unique skill set and a temperament that is unique to a church planter, but many transitional ministry skills are transferable, such as understanding systems and family systems theory, spiritual types, conflict management, mission and vision, asset mapping, Appreciative Inquiry, and analyzing the context. Might that be an emerging model for transitional ministry to work with churches that want to close and restart as a new venture, or might transitional ministers be good coaches for church planters?

I also imagine there will be a lot of bivocational interim ministry, because churches that could once afford a full-time pastor can no longer do so. Might we consider circuit-riding ministry by assigning several churches to an interim minister as pastors do in rural settings where they have a two- or three-point charge?

Might there be regional coaching and training for churches in transition that can't afford an interim minister and have part-time pulpit supply or are far apart? Leadership teams could gather monthly or quarterly and receive training to pool resources. With the number of church closings anticipated in the next few decades, might we train specialists to assist churches to close with integrity and leave a faithful legacy?[28]

Another phenomenon worth addressing is that the pool of intentional interim ministers is graying. At most interim ministry gatherings, the attendees are in their fifties or sixties, reflecting not only that this specialized ministry is over thirty years old, but the fact that a person needs ministry experience to do this work. Interim ministry can be financially untenable for younger pastors with families to support, mortgages to pay, and looming college tuition. They can't afford periods of unemployment. Experienced interim ministers would not recommend that someone serve as an interim minister without at least three to five years' experience as a settled pastor. Yet are there ways we might groom young seminary graduates to consider transitional ministry as a career goal? While not necessarily having a "transitional ministry track," might a selection of courses give a student the theory and skills needed for transitional ministry? These are just a few of the questions that have percolated up as I think about the future of transitional ministry. My hope is that this book will raise more for you and your colleagues.

I take great comfort in the fact that none of St. Paul's churches are still in existence, but that the church of Jesus Christ lives on in all its many-splendored colors, quirks, and zaniness. It has faithfully adjusted and adapted to new circumstances as the Holy Spirit has renewed the church. I'm sure our forebears in Christ would not recognize the struggles and concerns and the theological and ethical issues with which we wrestle or the structures and practices of our churches today. But they might be pleasantly surprised by what we have become. My hope is that as we look back upon how transitional ministry has evolved that we will be equally and pleasantly surprised.

REFLECTION QUESTIONS

1. In addition to the skills and practices suggested in this chapter, what others do you think are necessary for effective transitional ministry today?
2. What models of transitional ministry, other than those named in this chapter, have you seen used? How effective were they? What models have you thought about and wanted to test?
3. Where do you think transitional ministry will be in ten years?

Notes

1. WHITHER TRANSITIONAL MINISTRY?

1. Anthony Robinson, "The Decline of Interim Pastorates, *Call & Response Blog*, Faith and Leadership, January 25, 2011, http://www.faithandleadership.com/blog/01-25-2011/anthony-b-robinson-the-decline-interim-pastoratesJim Keck, "Reflections," First Plymouth Congregational Church, UCC, http://macucc.s3.amazonaws.com/A32C77D907BD4F69B2BB463D3492776D_Jim Keck%27s Reflections.pdf

Richard Floyd, "Ten Theses about Interim Ministry," *When I Survey . . .*, August 9, 2010, http://richardlfloyd.com/2010/08/09/ten-theses-about-interim-ministry/

2. See Molly Dale Smith, *Transitional Ministry: A Time of Opportunity* (New York: Church Publishing, 2009), iv–ix, where Loren Mead gives a more complete history.

3. Roger S. Nicholson, ed. *Temporary Shepherds: A Congregational Handbook for Interim Ministry* (Herndon, VA: Alban Institute, 1998). This has been the bible of interim ministry for fifteen years and is organized around the developmental tasks. While dated, it still has much useful material.

4. Erik H. Erickson, *Childhood and Society* (New York: W. W. Norton & Company, 1993), 72–91, 247 ff.

5. Robert J. Havighurst, *Developmental Tasks and Education* (New York: McKay Publisher, 1972).

6. B. Leslie Robinson, Jr., "Reframing the Tasks: A Report to the Board of the Center for Congregational Health" (July 2007), also published in *The Intentional Interim Ministry Training and Resource Notebook*, rev. ed., B. Leslie Robinson, Jr., ed. (Winston Salem, NC: Center for Congregational Health, 2008).

7. Anthony Robinson, "Rethinking Interim Ministry," *Congregations* 4 (2012): 15–16.

8. A host of new books explore this new reality, including *The Great Emergence* (Grand Rapids, MI: Baker Books, 2008) and *Emerging Christianity* (Grand Rapids, MI: Baker Books, 2012) by Phyllis Tickle; and *Christianity for the Rest of Us* (New York: HarperOne, 2007) and *Christianity after Religion: The End of Church and the Birth of a New Spiritual Awakening* (New York: HarperCollins, 2012) by Diana Butler Bass.

9. Robert Bellah, "Civil Religion in America," *Dædalus* 96, no. 1 (Winter 1967): 1–21.

10. Daniel L. Marsh, *Unto the Generation: The Roots of True Americanism* (Buena Park, CA: Arc Incorporated, 1970).

11. See my "Civil Religion: The 500-Pound Gorilla," *ESA* (*Evangelicals for Social Action*), May 17, 2005, http://www.evangelicalsforsocialaction.org/holistic-ministry/civil-religion-the-500-pound-gorilla/

12. Will Herberg, *Protestant – Catholic – Jew* (Garden City: NY: Doubleday Anchor, 1960), 39.

13. Diana Eck, *A New Religious America: How a "Christian Country" Has Become the World's Most Religiously Diverse Nation* (New York: HarperCollins, 2001).

14. Phyllis Tickle, *The Great Emergence* (Grand Rapids, MI: Baker Books, 2008), 98–101; *Emergence Christianity* (Grand Rapids, MI: Baker Books, 2012), 191–99.

15. See Diana Butler Bass, *Christianity after Religion: The End of Church and the Birth of a New Spiritual Awakening* (New York: HarperCollins, 2012), 41–52, for a thorough review of the data on shifts of religious belief from 1960 to 2013.

16. Pew Forum, *U.S. Religious Landscape Survey,* June 2008, http://religions.pewforum.org/pdf/report2-religious-landscape-study-full.pdf, 26. In 2011, Public Religion Research found that number to be 20 percent, http://publicreligion.org/site/wp-content/uploads/2011/11/PRRI-2011-American-Values-Survey-Web.pdf

17. Pew Research Religion and Public Life Project, "'Nones' on the Rise," October 9, 2012, http://www.pewforum.org/2012/10/09/nones-on-the-rise/http://www.pewforum.org/2012/10/09/nones-on-the-rise/

18. Ibid.

19. Robert Putnam and David Campbell, *American Grace* (New York: Simon & Shuster, 2010), 91–133.

20. Diana Butler Bass and Phyllis Tickle both write about mainline churches that are doing pioneering work in reclaiming the Great Tradition for twenty-first-century believers and seekers. Diana Butler Bass, *Christianity for the Rest of Us: How the Neighborhood Church Is Transforming the Faith* (New York: HarperCollins, 2006), and Phyllis Tickle, *Emergence Christianity: What It Is, Where It Is Going, and Why It Matters* (Grand Rapids, MI: Baker Books, 2012). See also the work of Elizabeth Drescher, who teaches religion and pastoral ministries at Santa Clara University, "Quitting Religion but Not the Practice of Prayer," Religion Dispatches, USC Annenberg, March 28, 2013, http://religiondispatches.org/quitting-religion-but-not-the-practice-of-prayer/

21. The term is best known for its use by Jean-François Lyotard in the following quotation: "Simplifying to the extreme, I define postmodern as incredulity towards metanarratives." By this, Lyotard meant that the postmodern condition is characterized by an increasingly widespread skepticism toward universal overarching narratives, such as the unique status of the individual and the march of progress, which gave order and meaning to Western thought during modernity. Lyotard, Jean-François, *The Postmodern Condition: A Report on Knowledge,* trans. Geoff Bennington and Brian Massumi (Minneapolis: University of Minnesota Press, 1984).

22. See Stanley J. Grenz, *A Primer on Postmodernism* (Grand Rapids, MI: Wm. B. Eerdman's Publishing, 1996), and James K. A. Smith, *Who's Afraid of Postmodernism? Taking Derrida, Lyotard, and Foucault to Church,* The Church and Postmodern Culture Series (Grand Rapids, MI: Baker Publishing Group, 2006).

23. Peter L. Berger and Thomas Luckmann, *The Social Construction of Reality: A Treatise in the Sociology of Knowledge* (Garden City, NY: Anchor Books, 1966), 6.

24. David T. Olson, "Turning the Church Crisis Into a Spiritual Revolution: Is the American Church Really in Crisis?" *Enrichment Journal,* http://enrichmentjournal.ag.org/201001/201001_030_Turning_crisis.cfm

25. "Church Closing Rate Only One Percent," John Dart, *The Christian Century* 125, no. 9, May 6, 2008, 14, http://www.christiancentury.org/article/2008-05/church-closing-rate-only-one-percent

26. Ibid.

27. Bill McKinney, a sociologist of religion and recently retired president of Pacific School of Religion, has said, "Counting members of religious groups remains problematic as there is no common understanding of 'member' across religious groups." (From a personal e-mail, November 13, 2013.)

28. "U.S. Membership Report," *The Association of Religion Data Archives,* http://www.thearda.com/rcms2010/r/u/rcms2010_99_us_name_1980_ON.asp. See also Association of Statisticians of American Religious Bodies (http://www.asarb.org) and The Pew Research Religion and Public Life Project U.S. Religious Landscape Survey (http://religions.pewforum.org).

29. Dean M. Kelley, *Why Conservative Churches Are Growing* (New York: Harper & Row, 1972), 1–2. Similarly Benton Johnson, Dean R. Hoge, and Donald A. Luidens, "Mainline Churches: The Real Reason for Decline," *First Things* 31 (March 1993): 13–18, argued that baby boomers that had dropped out of Presbyterian churches after confirmation and later returned to church often went to conservative churches. The best predictor of those who returned adhered to orthodox Christian doctrine, especially the teaching that Jesus Christ was the only road to salvation and that hell was the consequence of disbelief.

30. Michael Hotit, Andrew Greeley, and Melissa Wilde, "Demographics of Mainline Decline: Birth Dearth," *The Christian Century* 122, no. 20 (October 4, 2005): 24–27.

31. Roger Finke and Rodney Stark, *The Churching of America 1776–1990: Winners and Losers in Our Religious Economy* (New Brunswick, NJ: Rutgers University Press, 1992), 246.

32. José Casanova, "Rethinking Secularization: A Global Comparative Perspective," *The Hedgehog Review* 8, nos.1–2 (Spring/Summer 2006): 7–22.

33. Peter Berger, ed. *The Desecularization of the World: Resurgent Religion and World Politics* (Grand Rapids, MI: Wm. B. Eerdmans Publishing, 1999). Mark Chaves, "Secularization as Declining Religious Authority," *Social Forces* 72, no. 3 (March 1994): 750–72.

34. David A. Hollinger, "After Cloven Tongues of Fire: Ecumenical Protestantism and the Modern American Encounter with Diversity," *The Journal of American Religious History* (June 2011): 21–48.

35. Amy Frykholm, "Culture Changers: David Hollinger on What the Mainline Achieved," *The Christian Century*, July 2, 2012 , http://www.christiancentury.org/article/2012-06/culture-changers

36. Hollinger, "After Cloven Tongues of Fire," 23.

37. Ibid., 39.

38. Hollinger likens the choices ecumenical leaders made to the choices President Lyndon Johnson had to make around Civil Rights legislation. After the passage of the Voting Rights Act of 1964 Johnson is reported to have said, "We [Democrats] have lost the South for a generation." Similarly, by standing firmly against racism and imperialism and supporting abortion and same-gender rights, ecumenical leaders lost people in the pews. Ibid., 42.

39. N. J. Demerath III, "Cultural Victory and Organizational Defeat in the Paradoxical Decline of Liberal Protestantism," *Journal for the Scientific Study of Religion* 34 (March 1995): 458–69. Cited in Hollinger, 46.

40. Ibid., 38. Historian Warren Goldstein (himself a Jew) exhorts mainline Christians to remember "that the gospel of love and justice, preached openly and inclusively (and with media savvy) rather than doctrinally and punitively will draw people in and help them sustain and nourish ideas that are temporarily out of political favor." He further counsels that ecumenicals "ought not to forget their past or give in to the dominant narrative of their own demise." Warren Goldstein, "A Liberal Dose of Religious Fervor," *The Chronicle of Higher Education* 51, no. 44 (July 8, 2005): B8.

41. See also, Jill K. Gill, *Embattled Ecumenism: The National Council of Churches, the Vietnam War, and the Trials of the Protestant Left* (DeKalb, IL: Northern Illinois University Press, 2011).

42. Ron Heifetz, *Leadership without Easy Answers* (Cambridge, MA: Harvard University Press, 1994), 87.

43. Russ Douthat, "Can Liberal Christianity Be Saved?" *The New York Times Sunday Review*, July 14, 2012 http://www.nytimes.com/2012/07/15/opinion/sunday/douthat-can-liberal-christianity-be-saved.html?_r=0http://www.nytimes.com/2012/07/15/opinion/sunday/douthat-can-liberal-christianity-be-saved.html?

44. Gary Dorrien, "American Liberal Theology: Crisis, Irony, Decline, Renewal, Ambiguity," *Cross Currents* 55, no. 4 (Winter 2005–2006), http://www.crosscurrents.org/dorrien200506.htm

2. RETHINKING THEOLOGICAL REFLECTION ON TRANSITIONAL MINISTRY

1. Johanna van Wijk-Bos, *Making Wise the Simple: The Torah in Christian Faith and Practice* (Grand Rapids, MI: Eerdmans, 2005), xvi.

2. Walter Brueggemann, *Theology of the Old Testament: Testimony, Dispute, Advocacy* (Minneapolis: Fortress Press, 1997), 685.

3. John Cobb, "Alfred North Whitehead," in *Twelve Makers of Modern Protestant Thought*, George L. Hunt, editor (New York: Association Press, 1971), 130, 133.

4. All quotes from James are from Peterson's paraphrase, *The Message*.

5. Catherine Keller, *On the Mystery: Discerning Divinity in Process* (Minneapolis: Fortress Press, 2005), 33–47.

6. J. Philip Newell, *The Book of Creation: An Introduction to Celtic Spirituality* (New York: Paulist Press, 1999).

7. van Wijk-Bos, *Making Wise the Simple*.

8. Eric Liu and Nick Hanauer, *The Gardens of Democracy: A New American Story of Citizenship, the Economy, and the Role of Government* (Seattle: Sasquatch Books, 2011).

9. Ibid., 11.

10. Wendell Berry, *Jayber Crow: The Life Story of Jayber Crow, Barber, of the Port William Membership, as Written by Himself: A Novel* (Washington, DC: Counterpoint, 2000), 185.

11. Allan Gripe, *The Interim Pastor's Manual* (Louisville: Geneva Press, 1997).

12. James Hopewell, *Congregation: Stories and Structures* (Minneapolis: Fortress Press, 1987).

3. THE CHANGING LANDSCAPE OF THE AMERICAN CHURCH

1. For more information about this, read Phyllis Tickle's new book, *Emergence Christianity: What It Is, Where It Is Going, and Why It Matters* (Grand Rapids, MI: Baker Books, 2012).

2. Thomas Brackett, "Midwifing the Movement of the Spirit," Presentation at the National Church Leadership Institute, West Coast Event, Pasadena, CA, November 1–12, 2011, http://www.diovermont.org/PDFs/stirrings-of-the-spirit/MidwifingtheMovementoftheSpirit.pdf

3. Nancy Gibbs, "Looking Back to the Future," TimeFrames, *Time*, November 24, 2010, http://content.time.com/time/specials/packages/article/0,28804,2032304_2032746_2032955,00.html

4. Fresh Expressions, "About Us: Changing Church for a Changing World," https://www.freshexpressions.org.uk/about

5. Fresh Expressions: "What Is a Fresh Expression of Church? Definition," https://www.freshexpressions.org.uk/guide/about/whatis

6. Stuart Murray, *Church after Christendom* (London: Paternoster Press, 2004), 73, as noted on http://en.wikipedia.org/wiki/Emerging_church

7. "Taizé Community," *Wikipedia*, http://en.wikipedia.org/wiki/Taizé_Community

8. "Iona Community," *Wikipedia*, http://en.wikipedia.org/wiki/Iona_Community (March 27, 2014).

9. Jean Houston, *The Possible Human: A Course in Enhancing Your Physical, Mental, and Creative Abilities* (New York: Penguin Putnam, Inc., 1982).

10. Video Shredhead, "Did You Know 2012 (Officially Updated for 2012) HD," February 28, 2012, http://www.youtube.com/watch?v=YmwwrGV_aiE

11. Bureau of Labor Statistics, United States Department of Labor, "Number of Jobs Held, Labor Market Activity, and Earnings Growth Among the Youngest Baby Boomers: Results from a Longitudinal Study," July 25, 2012, https://www.google.com/url?q=http://www.bls.

gov/news.release/pdf/nlsoy.pdf&sa=U&ei=wak0U8_rEenO2wWduYGoAQ&ved=
0CAYQFjAA&client=internal-uds-cse&usg=AFQjCNEFNRy_rF_fduMrgKQscsaO67i4ew

12. Susan Schept, "Church collection plates may go empty as electronic giving rises," *Reuters*, January 23, 2011, http://www.reuters.com/article/2011/01/23/us-churches-donations-idUSTRE70M10C20110123

13. Robert Wuthnow, *After the Baby Boomers: How Twenty- and Thirty-Somethings Are Shaping the Future of American Religion* (Boston: Princeton University Press, 2007), chapter 1.

14. Ibid.

15. Edwin I. Hernández, Milagros Peña, Rev. Kenneth Davis, CSC, and Elizabeth Station, *Strengthening Hispanic Ministry across Denominations: A Call to Action*, Pulpit and Pew Research on Pastoral Leadership (Durham, NC: Duke Divinity School, 2005).

16. United States Department of Labor, Office of the Secretary, "The US Population Is Becoming Larger and More Diverse," http://www.dol.gov/oasam/programs/history/herman/reports/futurework/report/chapter1/main.htm

17. Pew Research Religion and Public Life Project, "Religious Landscape Survey," http://religions.pewforum.org/comparisons

18. Pew Research Religion and Public Life Project, "Asian Americans: A Mosaic of Faiths," July 19, 2012, http://www.pewforum.org/Asian-Americans-A-Mosaic-of-Faiths-overview

19. Joel Kotkin, "Where Americans Are Moving," *Forbes*, November 27, 2012, http://www.forbes.com/sites/joelkotkin/2012/11/27/where-americans-are-moving/

20. W. Edwards Deming, *The New Economics for Industry, Government, Education*, 2nd ed. (Cambridge, MA: MIT Press, 1993).

21. William Easum, *Gourmet Cows Make Sacred Burgers: Ministry Anytime, Anywhere, by Anybody* (Nashville: Abingdon Press, 1995).

5. TRANSITIONAL MINISTRY AS AN OPPORTUNITY TO LEAD

1. See our article "The Three 'Rs' and Your Congregation's Future," in *Congregations*, 3–4 (2011) 13–16, for a discussion of the distinctions that we note between resisting, reacting, and responding.

2. On this point, we think of Edgar Schein's comment: "The learning leader and the learning culture must therefore be built on the assumption that the world is intrinsically complex, nonlinear, and overdetermined." *Organizational Culture and Leadership*, 2nd ed. (San Francisco: Jossey-Bass), 372.

3. The concept of cultural capital is developed and applied to the pastor–congregational relationship in George's books, *How to Get Along with Your Church: Creating Cultural Capital for Doing Ministry* (Cleveland: The Pilgrim Press, 2001; reprinted by Wipf and Stock, Eugene, OR, 2012), and *How to Get Along with Your Pastor: Creating Partnership for Doing Ministry* (Cleveland: The Pilgrim Press, 2006).

4. A discussion of the history and varied approaches of organizational theory is found in W. Richard Scott, *Organizations: Rational, Natural, and Open Systems*, 4th ed. (Upper Saddle River, NJ: Prentice Hall, 1998). Chapter 2 introduces the rational system perspective and chapter 4, the open systems perspective that forms the theoretical basis of this chapter.

5. For a discussion of this concept, which is an open systems definition, see Leonard Greenhalgh, "Organizational Decline," in Samuel B. Bacharach, ed., *Research in the Sociology of Organizations: A Research Annual*, vol. 2 (Greenwich, CT: JAI Press, 1982), 232. George first used this definition in his book *Treasures in Clay Jars: New Ways to Understand Your Church* (Cleveland: The Pilgrim Press, 2003), 152–53.

6. This concise definition also appears in *How to Get Along with Your Church*, 6.

7. See *How to Get Along with Your Pastor*, Part One, especially chapter 1, "Cultural Depths: Your Church's Swamp."

8. Beverly A. Thompson and George B. Thompson, Jr., *Grace for the Journey: Practices and Possibilities for In-Between Times* (Herndon, VA: The Alban Institute, 2011).

9. Lovett H. Weems, Jr., *Church Leadership: Vision, Team, Culture, Integrity*, rev. ed. (Nashville: Abingdon Press, 2010), 23.

10. John Heider, *The Tao of Leadership: Lao Tzu's Tao Te Ching Adapted for a New Age* (New York: Bantam Books, 1986), no. 78.

11. Ibid.

12. Slightly adapted from Gil Rendle and Alice Mann, *Holy Conversations: Strategic Planning as a Spiritual Practice for Congregations* (Herndon, VA: The Alban Institute, 2003), 3–6.

13. See our book *Grace for the Journey*.

14. Plenty of literature in psychology and pastoral care makes these points, but they also are framed in organizational literature as well. Within the kind of cultural perspective that this chapter advances, see Edgar Schein's discussion of accounting for psychological issues in *Organizational Culture and Leadership*, 4th ed. (San Francisco: Jossey-Bass, 2010), chapter 17, "A Conceptual Model for Managed Culture Change."

15. Beverly uses these terms in seminary courses in her discussion of vision. John Kotter implies this distinction in his book *Leading Change* (Boston: Harvard Business School Press, 1996), when he emphasizes that "Vision creation is almost always a messy, difficult, and sometimes emotionally charged exercise" (79). Kotter also argues that first drafts get worked over, usually requiring a period of months or so to complete (81).

16. As recorded by Lucien Price, *The Dialogues of Alfred North Whitehead* (New York: Mentor Books, 1954), 205.

17. Heider, *The Tao of Leadership*, no. 17.

18. Beverly and George Thompson, *Grace for the Journey: Practices and Possibilities for In-Between Times.*

19. Edgar Schein's notes on "exercising learning leadership" seem very fitting in this context. He persuasively argues for five qualities: perception and insight, motivation, emotional strength, ability to change the cultural assumptions, and ability to create involvement and participation. See the discussion in his groundbreaking work, *Organizational Culture and Leadership*, 4th ed. (San Francisco: Jossey-Bass, 2010), 380–83.

6. LEADERSHIP TRANSITION WITHIN IMMIGRANT AND AFRICAN AMERICAN CHURCHES

1. I intentionally choose the term "immigrant church" and not "ethnic church" to describe churches consisting of members of non-European descent with a recent migration history because we all have a distinct ethnic background; hence, all are ethnic.

2. The terms "African American church" and "Black church" are used interchangeably in literature. I will use the "African American church," but quotations may contain the term "Black church," depending on the author's preference.

3. Other important acts have been the U.S. Refugee Act of 1980, which opened the door for more African refugees, and the Immigration Act of 1990, which created the congressionally mandated the Diversity Immigrant Visa Program. *New England's Book of Acts* is a good reference to explore the growth of churches of the different ethnic groups in New England. *New England's Book of Acts*, http://neba.egc.org/

4. R. Stephen Warner, "Coming to America: Immigrants and the Faith They Bring," *The Christian Century*, February 10, 2004, 20.

5. Carolyn Chen, *Getting Saved in America: Taiwanese Immigration and Religious Experience* (Princeton: Princeton University Press, 2008).

6. Warner, "Coming to America," 20.

7. More information about the churches in Boston can be found in the Emmanuel Gospel Center Church Directory 2013, egcbcd.com

8. Hofstede's research has been expanded and further developed by others, for example, in the Globe Study: Robert J. House et al., eds., *Culture, Leadership, and Organizations: The GLOBE Study of 62 Societies* (Thousand Oaks, CA: Sage, 2004). Despite the danger of gener-

alization and oversimplification inherent to such studies, Hofstede's framework helps to understand the complexity of culture and leadership.

9. The Hofstede Centre, "Dimensions," http://geert-hofstede.com/dimensions.html

10. Chen, *Getting Saved in America*, 193.

11. Helen R. Ebaugh and Janet S. Chafetz, *Religion and the New Immigrants : Continuities and Adaptations in Immigrant Congregations* (Walnut Creek, CA: AltaMira Press, 2000), 385.

12. Raymond Brady Williams, *Christian Pluralism in the United States: The Indian Immigrant Experience* (Cambridge, MA: Cambridge University Press, 1996), 186; and Mark Mullins, "The Life-Cycle of Ethnic Churches in Sociological Perspective," *Japanese Journal of Religious Studies* 14, no. 4 (1987): 323.

13. Helen Lee, "Can the East Asian church in America reverse the flight of its next generation?" *Christianity Today*, August 12, 1996, http://www.christianitytoday.com/ct/1996/august12/6t9050.html

14. Mullin, "The Life-Cycle of Ethnic Churches," 323–28.

15. Depending on the denomination or church structure, the lay leadership group can also be called elders, parish council, or leadership team. In this chapter, "board" includes all these entities.

16. Ebaugh and Chafetz, *Religion and the New Immigrants*, 352. See also Williams, *Christian Pluralism*, 222.

17. John Butosi, "The Calvin Synod: 500 Years of Tradition Lead to the UCC," *God Is Still Speaking, United Church of Christ*, http://www.ucc.org/about-us/hidden-histories/the-calvin-synod-500-years.html

18. Williams, *Christian Pluralism*, 222.

19. Boston Chinese Evangelical Church, "Who We Are," http://www.bcec.net/about/

20. Daniel A. Rodriguez, *A Future for the Latino Church* (Downers Grove, IL: InterVarsity Press, 2011), 127f.

21. Ralph C. Watkins, *Leading Your African American Church through Pastoral Transition* (Valley Forge, PA: Judson Press, 2010), 2.

22. James Henry Harris, *The Courage to Lead: Leadership in the African American Urban Church* (New York: Rowman & Littlefield), 70.

23. Stacey Floyd-Thomas et al., *Black Church Studies: An Introduction* (Nashville: Abingdon Press, 2007), 6.

24. Anne H. Pinn and Anthony B. Pinn, *Fortress Introduction to Black Church History* (Minneapolis: Augsburg Fortress, 2002), 8.

25. Floyd-Thomas et al., *Black Church Studies*, 8f.

26. C. Eric Lincoln and Lawrence H. Mamiya, *The Black Church in the African American Experience* (Durham, NC: Duke University Press, 1990), 3. This book is also a good resource for further information about these denominations.

27. Floyd-Thomas et al., *Black Church Studies*, 3.

28. Anson Shupe and Janelle M. Eliasson-Nannini, *Pastoral Misconduct* (Piscataway, NJ: Transaction Publishers, 2012), 33.

29. Pinn and Pinn, *Fortress Introduction to Black Church History*, 133.

30. Shupe and Eliasson-Nannini, *Pastoral Misconduct*, 39.

31. Peoples Baptist Church of Boston, "Our History," http://www.pbcboston.org/about-us/our-history/

32. Twelfth Baptist Church, "Pastoral History," tbcboston.org/tbc/pastoral-history/

33. Read more about pastoral misconduct in Shupe and Eliasson-Nannini, *Pastoral Misconduct*.

34. James H. Burnett III. "Embracing fear, rather than running from it," *The Boston Globe*, May 7, 2013, http://www.bostonglobe.com/lifestyle/2013/05/06/rev-liz-walker-asks-boston-embrace-fear-rather-than-run-from/uxtppGXSulELA0OxWWYiyM/story.html

35. This chapter is written not to offer practical advice on how to transition well and which steps are helpful, but to explore the context, approaches, and challenges. However, Ralph C. Watkins has written a helpful resource, *Leading Your African American Church through Pastoral Transition* (Valley Forge, VA: Judson Press, 2010).

9. AN APPRECIATIVE INQUIRY PARADIGM FOR
TRANSITIONAL MINISTRY

1. I do not know the text from which this quote is taken. A parishioner gave me a poster of it, with the Martin Buber attribution, as a going-away present many years ago, and it has hung on my office wall ever since. An Internet search suggests it is from Buber's *Tales of the Hasidim.*

2. This story was told in a college class in the mid-1980s. The details are now somewhat hazy, but I think the therapist was Jay Haley, who was one of the founders of strategic family therapy.

3. See Jane Watkins and Bernhard Mohr, *Change at the Speed of Imagination* (San Francisco: Jossey-Bass, 2001). The authors provide a more detailed description of the origins of Appreciative Inquiry and its use in organizational development.

4. See Barbara Frederickson's research on the impact of positive emotion on creativity (http://www.positivityratio.com).

5. Milton Erickson (not to be confused with Erik Erickson, the developmental theorist) used an approach that was unique and a major break with the psychological approaches of the mid-1900s. He viewed his clients' history and their unconscious as a wonderful treasure trove of resources, rather than a repository of darkness, that they could use to create their preferred future. He developed and used a variety of trance strategies not to uncover dark secrets, but to associate and re-associate experiences in ways that left the client equipped to meet her challenges and achieve her goals. For an introduction to Erickson's approach I recommend Jay Haley's *Uncommon Therapy: The Psychiatric Techniques of Milton H. Erickson, M.D.* (New York: W. W. Norton, 1973). See also www.erickson-foundation.org.

6. In more recent years, Steve Andreas has been my major teacher in helping me create replicable change processes. Together with his wife, Connirae, Steve has studied people who rapidly resolved problems such as grief, resentment, and trauma, and then organized the results as patterns of healing that others can use to resolve their problems. Much of the Andreas's body of work can be found at Real People Press (www.realpeoplepress.com).

7. I do not know the specific origins of this assumption, but I have been taught it in a variety of contexts and found it very useful in creating an attitude of acceptance and compassion toward congregations and the people I work with.

8. See Sue Annis Hammond, *The Thin Book of Appreciative Inquiry* (Bend, OR: Thin Book Publishing, 1998), 20–21.

9. See Barbara Fredrickson and Marcial Losada, "Positive Affect and the Complex Dynamics of Human Flourishing," *American Psychologist* 60 (2005): 678–86. Frederickson's work on the impact of positive emotion can also be reviewed at the Positive Emotion and Psychophysiology website: http://www.unc.edu/peplab/home.html. The research on intuition was conducted by Nalini Ambady and reported by Lea Winerman, "What We Know without Knowing How," *Monitor on Psychology* 36, no. 3 (March 2005): 50.

10. Stephen Gilligan was a student of Milton Erickson and made this comment during a class at an International Congress on Ericksonian Approaches to Psychotherapy. Gilligan's body of work can be found at http://www.stephengilligan.com.

10. A TRAUMA TREATMENT MODEL FOR INTERIM WORK WITH
CHRONICALLY DYSFUNCTIONAL CONGREGATIONS

1. Peter L. Steinke, *Healthy Congregations: A Systems Approach* (Herndon, VA: The Alban Institute, 1996), 91.

2. Nancy Myer Hopkins and Mark Laaser, *Restoring the Soul of a Church: Healing Congregations Wounded by Clergy Sexual Misconduct* (Collegeville, MN: The Liturgical Press, 1995), 155f.

3. Beth Ann Gaede, ed., *When a Congregation Is Betrayed: Responding to Clergy Misconduct* (Herndon, VA: The Alban Institute, 2005), 46–50.

4. See Jill M. Hudson, *Congregational Trauma: Caring, Coping, and Learning* (Herndon, VA: The Alban Institute, 1998).

5. Loren B. Mead, *The Once and Future Church* (Herndon, VA: The Alban Institute, 2001), 33f; Edwin H. Friedman, *Generation to Generation: Family Process in Church and Synagogue* (New York: The Guilford Press, 1987), 31f.

6. Roger S. Nicholson, *Temporary Shepherds: A Congregational Handbook for Interim Ministry* (Herndon, VA: The Alban Institute, 1998), 3–13.

7. Judith L. Herman, *Trauma and Recovery: The Aftermath of Violence—from Domestic Abuse to Political Terror* (New York: Basic Books, 1992), 236f.

8. Amy Banks, *Post-traumatic Stress Disorder: Relationships and Brain Chemistry—A Manual for Lay People* (Wellesley MA: Stone Center, Wellesley College), 2006.

9. Sandra L. Bloom, "An Elephant in the Room: The Impact of Traumatic Stress on Individuals and Groups," in *The Trauma Controversy: Philosophical and Interdisciplinary Dialogues*, ed. Kristen Brown and Bettina G. Bergo (Albany: SUNY, 2009), 160–66.

10. Herman, *Trauma and Recovery*, 133f.

11. Ibid., 70 and 176f.

12. Elisabeth Kübler-Ross, *On Death and Dying* (New York: Routledge, 1969).

11. HOSPICE CARE FOR STRUGGLING CONGREGATIONS

1. Edwin H. Freidman, *A Failure of Nerve: Leadership in the Age of the Quick Fix* (New York: Church Publishing Inc., 2007).

2. Linda M. Hilliard and Gretchen Switzer, *Finishing with Grace: A Guide to Selling, Merging or Closing Your Church* (Bangor, ME: Booklocker.com, 2010).

3. Crossroads Massachusetts, a program of the Massachusetts Conference of the United Church of Christ, 2012, http://www.macucc.org/crossroads

4. Worden, J. William, *Grief Counseling and Grief Therapy: A Handbook for the Mental Health Practitioner*, 4th ed. (New York: Springer, 2009).

5. Angela Morrow, "The Five Tasks of Dying: Finding Closure and Peace at the End of Life," Dying, Funerals and Grief, About.com, May 16, 2014, http://dying.about.com/od/thedyingprocess/a/5_tasks_dying.html

6. Church Service Realty, www.churchrealty.com

7. Partners for Sacred Places, www.sacredplaces.org

8. United Congregational Church, www.ucc-worcester.org.

9. Three excellent discernment resources for congregations: Suzanne G. Farnham, Joseph P. Gill, Taylor McLean, and Susan M. Ward, *Listening Hearts: Discerning Call in Community* (Harrisburg, PA: Morehouse Publishing, 2011); Lon Fendall, Jan Wood, and Bruce Bishop, *Practicing Discernment Together: Finding God's Way Forward in Decision Making* (Newberg, OR: Barclay Press, 2007); and Elizabeth Liebert, *The Way of Discernment: Spiritual Practices for Decision Making* (Louisville: Westminster John Know Press, 2008).

12. WHAT NEXT?

1. In my conversations with colleagues in small groups this is a list of what an effective transitional minister should be familiar with: family systems theory; theories and research and analysis of the changing landscape of ministry; conflict mediation/resolution skills; legacy or church closings; redevelopment/revitalization theory and best practices; theories of change in systems and organizations; leadership theory; impact of a long-term pastorate; impact of clergy misconduct (including sexual misconduct particularities); grief theory; boundary awareness

208 *Notes*

theory and best practice; church size theory (particularly size transition, for example, pastoral to program, full to part time); Appreciative Inquiry methodology; staff evaluation and human resources protocols (e.g., protocol to dismiss staff); church assessment; strategic planning and visioning with appropriate evaluation/monitoring; capital campaign; and church governance and restructuring. In its training manual, the Interim Ministry Network has identified the following personal characteristics as being important for transitional pastors to possess (Fundamentals of Transitional Ministry—Work of the Leader, Appendix 26): clear sense of calling to the practice of transitional ministry; a life of prayer; good ego strength: secure, mature, and emotionally stable; clear personal boundaries; action/goal oriented; flexible and adaptable; patient, empathetic, and understanding; effective level of physical and emotional vitality; sound, positive, and growing faith; ability to maintain an optimistic attitude; good sense of humor; and commitment to continuing education in the field of professional transitional ministry.

2. Carolyn Weese and J. Russell Crabtree, *Elephant in the Boardroom: Speaking the Unspoken about Pastoral Transitions* (San Francisco: Jossey-Bass, 2004).

3. Ibid., 62–68.

4. Jackson W. Carroll, Carl S. Dudley, and William McKinney, eds. *Handbook for Congregational Studies* (Nashville: Abingdon Press, 1986), 11–15. You can download the book at http://hirr.hartsem.edu/bookshelf/out_of_print_congstudhndbk.html. For an accessible, comprehensive, and practical tool that explains these categories and how to conduct a congregational study, go to http://studyingcongregations.org/

5. Gil Rendle and Alice Mann, *Holy Conversations: Strategic Planning as a Spiritual Practice for Congregations* (Alban Institute, 2003). Another helpful resource is *Discerning Your Congregation's Future: A Strategic and Spiritual Approach*, by Roy Oswald and Robert E. Friedrich Jr. (Alban, 1998).

6. Two good resources, both by Rose Mary Dougherty, are *Discernment: A Path to Spiritual Awakening* (Mahwah, NJ: Paulist Press, 2009) and *Group Spiritual Direction: Community for Discernment* (Mahwah, NJ: Paulist Press, 1995).

7. Carroll et al., *Handbook*, 12.

8. Ibid.

9. The two best resources for finding demographics tailored for local churches are http://www.missioninsight.com and www.perceptgroup.com.

10. Martha Grace Reece, *Unbinding the Gospel: Real Life Evangelism* (Chalice Press, 2004), 43.

11. See http://www.worshipfulwork.org/

12. See Craig A. Satterlee, *When God Speaks through Change: Preaching in Times of Congrega tional Transition* (Alban 2005) for strategies and texts.

13. Hans Hoekendijk, World Council of Churches theologian, came up with this shorthand for articulating the biblical key concepts in communicating the gospel when he addressed the World Council of Churches in 1970. See *Horizons of Hope* (Nashville: Tidings, 1970), 26–35. Gabriel Fackre, emeritus professor of theology at Andover Newton Theological School, also sees marks of the church corresponding to the gifts of the Spirit. For a thorough discussion on these themes see *The Christian Story* (Grand Rapids: Eerdmans, 1996), 159–71. See also Avery Dulles, *Models of the Church* (New York: Doubleday Image Books, 1987).

14. Dorothy Bass, *Practicing Our Faith: A Way of Life for a Searching People* (Jossey-Bass 2010); Richard Foster, *Celebration of Discipline: The Path to Spiritual Growth* (HarperCollins, 1984); and Barbara Brown Taylor, *An Altar in the World: A Geography of Faith* (HarperCollins, 2009).

15. The authors draw particularly upon the work of Tim Rogers-Martin, "Life Cycles and Church Health," prepared for the website of the Congregational Transformation Team of the Presbytery of Greater Atlanta and published July 12, 2007. Much of his work draws upon George Bullard (http://sed-efca.org/wp-content/uploads/2008/08/stages_of_church_life_bullard.pdf), Alice Mann (http://s3.amazonaws.com/storage.nm-storage.com/columbiafumc/downloads/resourcee_understanding_your_church_s_life_cycle.pdf), and Martin Saarinen in *The Life Cycle of a Congregation* (Alban Institute, 2001 revised edition). See also Alice Mann,

Can Our Church Live ? : Redeveloping Congregations in Decline (Alban, 1999), and George Bullard, *The Congregational Life Cycle Assessment* (Atlanta: Chalice Press, 2013).

16. Michael Piazza and Cameron Trimble, *Liberating Hope!* (Pilgrim Press, 2011), 29. Used with permission.

17. Michael Piazza and Cameron Trimble, *Liberating Hope!* (Pilgrim Press, 2011), 29–40. See also the work of John E. Piper, *Breakthrough to Creative Change* (iUniverse, 2002).

18. Michael Piazza and Cameron Trimble, *Liberating Hope!* (Pilgrim Press, 2011), 39. Used with permission.

19. There are scores of books on how to do "repositioning" or "turnaround" ministry. Simply search for "church renewal" or "turnaround churches." To name a few: Molly Phinney Baskette, *Real Good Church: How Our Church Came Back from the Dead, and Yours Can, Too* (Cleveland, Pilgrim Press 2014); Ed Stetzer and Mike Dodson, *Comeback Churches: How 300 Churches Turned Around and Yours Can Too* (Nashville: B&H Publishing Group 2007); and Mary Louise Gifford, *The Turnaround Church: Inspiration and Tools for Life-Sustaining Change* (Alban Institute, 2009).

20. William Bridges, *Managing Transitions: Making the Most of Change*, 3rd edition (Philadelphia: DaCapo Press, 2009), 3–6.

21. See the recent study by sociologist of religion William McKinney on successful transitions in large United Church of Christ congregations: http://www.psr.edu/files_psr/Pastoral-TransitionReport_booklet_2-1.pdf

22. See her article in *Faith & Leadership*, the newsletter of leadership development at Duke Divinity School: http://www.faithandleadership.com/content/susan-nienaber-leading-through-conflict

23. B. Leslie Robinson, Jr., "Reframing the Tasks." A report to the board of the Center for Congregational Health®, July 2007. Material later published in the *Intentional Interim Ministry Training and Resource Notebook*, copyright 2008, revised 2014, Center for Congregational Health®, B. Leslie Robinson, Jr., editor, writer. https://www.healthychurch.org/

24. http://www.pcusa.org/resource/study-effectiveness-interim-pastors/

25. See its website at http://studyingcongregations.org/

26. Personal e-mail from the author, November 2014.

27. David T. Olson, *Turning the Church Crisis Into a Spiritual Revolution: Is the American Church Really in Crisis?* http://enrichmentjournal.ag.org/201001/201001_030_Turning_crisis.cfm

28. See the recent research of Dr. Gail Cafferata on church closings and their pastors: http://www.bu.edu/cpt/2014/02/13/new-research-on-church-closings/

Bibliography

APPRECIATIVE INQUIRY

Branson, Mark Lau. *Memories, Hopes and Conversations: Appreciative Inquiry and Congregational Change.* Herndon, VA: Alban Institute, 2004.

Cooperrider, David L., and Diana Whitney. *Appreciative Inquiry: A Positive Revolution in Change.* San Francisco: Berrett-Koehler Publishers, Inc., 2005.

Whitney, Diana, and Amanda Trosten-Bloom. *The Power of Appreciative Inquiry: A Practical Guide to Positive Change.* San Francisco: Berrett-Koehler Publishers, 2003.

CHANGE AND TRANSITION

Bridges, William. *Managing Transitions: Making the Most of Change*, 3rd ed. Philadelphia: DeCapo Press, 2009.

———. *Transitions: Making Sense of Life's Changes.* Cambridge, MA: Da Capo Press, 2004.

Herrington, Jim, Mike Bonem, and James H. Furr. *Leading Congregational Change: A Practical Guide for the Transformational Journey.* San Francisco: Jossey-Bass, 2000.

McFayden, Kenneth J. *Strategic Leadership for a Change: Facing Our Losses, Finding Our Future.* Herndon, VA: Alban Institute, 2009.

Olsen, Charles M. *Transforming Church Boards into Communities of Spiritual Leaders.* Herndon, VA: Alban, 1995.

CHANGING CULTURE

Bass, Diana Butler. *Christianity after Religion: The End of Church and the Birth of a New Spiritual Awakening.* New York: HarperCollins, 2012.

———. *Christianity for the Rest of Us: How the Neighborhood Church Is Transforming the Faith.* New York: HarperCollins, 2007.

———. *The Practicing Congregation: Imagining a New Old Church.* Herndon, VA: Alban Institute, 2004.

Clark, Kelly James. *Return to Reason: A Critique of Enlightenment Evidentialism, and a Defense of Reason and Belief in God.* Grand Rapids, MI: Eerdmans, 1990.

Grenz, Stanley. *A Primer on Postmodernism.* Grand Rapids, MI: Eerdmans, 1996.

Law, Eric. *The Wolf Shall Dwell with the Lamb: A Spirituality for Leadership in a Multicultu-ral Community*. Atlanta: Chalice Press, 1993.

Habermas, Jurgen. *An Awareness of What Is Missing: Faith and Reason in a Post-secular Age*. Molden, MA: Polity Press, 2010.

Healy, Anthony E. *The Post Industrial Promise: Vital Religious Community in the 21 st Century*. Herndon, VA: Alban, 2005.

Law, Eric. *The Wolf Shall Dwell with the Lamb: A Spirituality for Leadership in a Multicultu-ral Community*. Atlanta: Chalice Press, 1993.

Smith, James K. A. *Who 's Afraid of Postmodernism? Taking Derrida, Lyotard, and Foucault to Church*. Grand Rapids, MI: Baker Academic Books, 2006.

Taylor, Charles. *A Secular Age*. New York: Random House, 2007.

Tickle, Phyllis. *Emergence Christianity: What It Is, Where It Is Going, and Why It Matters*. Grand Rapids, MI: Baker Books, 2012.

———. *The Great Emergence: How Christianity Is Changing and Why*. Grand Rapids, MI: Baker Books, 2008.

CONGREGATIONAL STUDIES, ANALYSIS, AND ASSESSMENT

Ammerman, Nancy T., Jackson Carroll, Carl Dudley, and William McKinney. *Studying Con-gregations: A New Handbook*. Nashville: Abingdon Press, 1998.

Ammerman, Nancy Tatom. *Congregation and Community*. New Brunswick, NJ: Rutgers, 1997.

Brown, Juanita, with David Isaacs and the World Café Community. *The World Café: Shaping Our Futures Through Conversation s That Matter*. San Francisco: Berret-Koehler Publish-ers, 2005.

Ammerman, Nancy Tatom. *Congregation and Community*. New Brunswick, NJ: Rutgers, 1997.

Bullard, George. "The Life Cycle and Stages of Congregational Development." http://bullardjournal.blogs.com/bullardjournal/2004/01/the_life_cycle_.html

Brown, Juanita, with David Isaacs and the World Café Community. *The World Café: Shaping Our Futures Through Conversation That Matter*. San Francisco: Berret-Koehler Publishers, 2005.

Dudley, Carl S., and Nancy T. Ammerman. *Congregations in Transition: A Guide for Analyz-ing, Assessing, and Adapting in Changing Communities*. San Francisco: Jossey-Bass, 2002.

Galindo, Israel. *The Hidden Lives of Congregations: Discerning Church Dynamics*. Herndon, VA: The Alban Institute, 2004.

Mann, Alice. *The In-Between Church: Navigating Size Transitions in Congregations*. Herndon, VA: The Alban Institute, 1998.

Oswald, Roy M., and Robert E. Friedrich, Jr. *Discerning Your Congregation's Future: A Strategic and Spiritual Approach*. Herndon, VA: Alban, 1996.

Rendle, Gil, and Alice Mann. *Holy Conversations: Strategic Planning as a Spiritual Practice for Congregations*. Herndon, VA: The Alban Institute, 2003.

Robinson, Anthony B. *Transforming Congregational Culture*. Grand Rapids, MI: Eerdmans, 2003.

———. *Changing the Conversation: A Third Way for Congregations*. Grand Rapids, MI: Eerdmans, 2008.

Snow, Luther K. *The Power of Asset Mapping: How Your Congregation Can Act on Its Gifts*. Herndon, VA: Alban, 2004.

FAMILY SYSTEMS THEORY

Blessing, Kamila. *Families of the Bible: A New Perspective*. Santa Barbara, CA: Praeger, 2010.

Bowen, Murray, and Michael Kerr. *Family Evaluation: An Approach Based on Bowen Theory.* New York: W. W. Norton & Co., 1988.
Kerr, Michael E. *One Family's Story: A Primer on Bowen Theory.* Washington, D.C.: Georgetown Family Center, 2003.
Friedman, Edwin H. *Generation t o Generation.* New York: The Guildford Press, 1985.
Galindo, Israel. *Perspectives on Congregational Leadership: Applying S ystems Thinking for Effective Leadership.* Richmond, VA: Educational Consultants, 2009.
Johnson, Spencer. *Who Moved My Cheese? An A-Mazing Way to Deal with Change in Your Work and in Your Life.* New York: G. P. Putnam's Sons, 1998.
Kerr, Michael E. *One Family's Story: A Primer on Bowen Theory.* Washington, DC: Georgetown Family Center, 2003.
Parsons, George, and Speed Leas. *Understanding Your Congregation as a System.* Herndon, VA: Alban Institute, 1993.
Senge, Peter M. *The Fifth Discipline.* New York: Doubleday, 1990.
Steinke, Peter L. *How Your Church Family Works: Understanding Congregations As Emotional Systems.* Herndon, VA: The Alban Institute, 2006.
———. *Healthy Congregations: A Systems Approach.* Herndon, VA: Alban Institute, 1996.

GENERAL SYSTEMS THEORY

Meadows, Donella H. *Thinking in Systems: A Primer.* White River Junction, VT: Chelsea Green, 2008.
Rendle, Gil. *Leading Change in the Congregation: Spiritual and Organizational Tools for Leaders.* Herndon, VA: Alban Institute, 1998.
Wheatley, Margaret. *Leadership and the New Science: Discovering Order in the Chaotic World.* San Francisco: Berett-Koehler, 2006.

LEADERSHIP

Friedman, Edwin, and Edward W. Beal and Margaret M. Treadwell, eds. *A Failure of Nerve: Leadership in the Age of the Quick Fix.* New York: Seabury Books, 2007.
Goleman, D., R. Boyatzis, and A. McKee. *Primal Leadership: Learning to Lead with Emotional Intelligence.* Boston: Harvard Business School Press, 2002.
Hahn, Celia. *Growing in Authorit y , Relinquishing Control: A New Approach to Faithful Leadership.* Herndon, VA: Alban Institute, 1994.
Heifetz, Ronald A. *Leadership without Easy Answers.* Boston: Belknap/Harvard University Press, 1994.
Heifetz, Ronald, Marty Linsky, and Alexander Grashow. *The Practice of Adaptive Leadership: Tools and Tactics for Changing Your Organization and the World.* Cambridge, MA: Cambridge Leadership Associates, 2009.
Hotchkiss, Dan. *Governance and Ministry: Rethinking Board Leadership.* Herndon, VA: Alban Institute, 2009.
Kotter, John P. *Leading Change.* Boston: Harvard Business School Press, 1996.
———. *A Force of Change: How Leadership Differs from Management.* New York: The Free Press, 1990.
Marcuson, Margaret. *Leaders Who Last: Sustaining Yourself and Your Ministry.* New York: Seabury Books, 2009.
Rendle, Gil. *Behavioral Covenants in Congregations: A Handbook for Honoring Differences.* Herndon, VA: Alban Institute, 1999.
———. *Leading Change in the Congregation: Spiritual and Organizational Tools for Leaders.* Herndon, VA: Alban Institute, 1998.
Robinson, Anthony B. *Leadership for Vital Congregations.* Cleveland: Pilgrim Press, 2007.

Steinke, Peter. *Congregational Leadership in Anxious Times: Being Calm and Courageous No Matter What.* Herndon, VA: Alban Institute, 2006.
Stevens, R. Paul, and Phil Collins. *The Equipping Pastor: A Systems Approach to Congregational Leadership.* Herndon, VA: Alban Institute, 1993.

TRANSITIONAL MINISTRY

Child, Barbara, and Keith Kron, eds. *In the Interim: Strategies for Interim Ministers and Congregations.* Boston: Skinner House Books, 2013.
Gripe, Allan. *The Interim Pastor's Manual.* Louisville: Westminster/John Knox Press, 1997.
Mead, Loren. *A Change of Pastors . . . and How It Affects Change in the Congregation.* Herndon, VA: The Alban Institute, 2005.
Nicholson, Roger S., ed. *Temporary Shepherds: A Congregational Handbook for Interim Ministry.* Herndon, VA: The Alban Institute, 1998.
Oswald, Roy M., James M. Heath, and Ann W. Heath. *Beginning Ministry Together: The Alban Institute Handbook for Clergy Transitions.* Herndon, VA: Alban Institute, 2003.
Smith, Molly Dale, ed. *Transitional Ministry: A Time of Opportunity.* New York: Church Publishing, 2009.

TRAUMA

Banks, Amy. *Post-traumatic Stress Disorder: Relationships and Brain Chemistry—A Manual for Lay People.* Wellesley, MA: Stone Center, Wellesley College, 2006.
Bloom, Sandra L. "An Elephant in the Room: The Impact of Traumatic Stress on Individuals and Groups." In Brown, K. and Bergo, B. (eds.). *The Trauma Controversy: Philosophical and Interdisciplinary Dialogues.* Albany: SUNY, 2009, 143–69.
Child, Barbara, and Keith Kron (eds). *In the Interim: Strategies for Interim Ministers and Congregations.* Boston: Skinner House Books, 2013.
Friedman, Edwin H. *Generation to Generation: Family Process in Church and Synagogue.* New York, The Guilford Press, 1987.
Gaede, Beth Ann, ed. *When a Congregation Is Betrayed: Responding to Clergy Misconduct.* Herndon, VA: The Alban Institute, 2005.
Herman, J. L. *Trauma and Recovery.* New York: Basic Books, 1992.
Herman, Judith L. *Trauma and Recovery: The Aftermath of Violence—from Domestic Abuse to Political Terror.* New York: Basic Books, 1992.
Hopkins, Nancy Myer, and Mark Laaser. *Restoring the Soul of a Church: Healing Congregations Wounded by Clergy Sexual Misconduct.* Collegeville, MN: The Liturgical Press, 1995.
Hudson, Jill M. *Congregational Trauma: Caring, Coping, and Learning.* Herndon, VA: The Alban Institute, 1998.
Kübler-Ross, Elisabeth. *On Death and Dying.* New York: Routledge, 1969.
Mead, Loren. *The Once and Future Church Collection.* Herndon, VA: The Alban Institute, 2001.
Nicholson, Roger S. *Temporary Shepherds: A Congregational Handbook for Interim Ministry.* Herndon, VA: The Alban Institute, 1998.
Steinke, Peter L. *Healthy Congregations: A Systems Approach.* Herndon, VA: The Alban Institute, 1996.

Index

acceptance: in Appreciative Way, 125–127; aspects of, 127; in transitional ministry, 126–127

adaptation, 16, 183–185

administration, 49

African American churches: denominations, 90; generational drift in, 94; Great Awakening, 90; history of, 89–91; interim pastors and transitional ministry, 94–95; leadership within, 89–95; Methodism and, 90; pastors in, 91, 94, 94–95; reflection questions regarding, 96; resources for, 94; senior pastor-centered church, 93

After the Baby Boomers (Wuthnow), 46

age: African American churches and generational drift, 94; generational challenges, to immigrant churches, 80; generational demographics, 46–47

A.M.E. Church, 92

American civil religion: Christianity compared to, 8; diversity relating to, 8–9; rituals of, 7–8; transitional ministry relating to, 7–8; values of, 14

appreciation, 136

Appreciative Inquiry: asking questions, 135–138; background on, 123–124; characteristics of, 124; finding what works, 129–130; focus creating reality, 131–133; interim ministry and assumptions of, 129–143; language and

reality, 141–143; multiple realities, 133–135; past relating to, 138–140; reflection questions, 144–145; *The Thin Book of Appreciative Inquiry*, 129; uses for, 124; valuing differences, 140–141

Appreciative Way: acceptance in, 125–127; assumptions, 124–129; of interim ministry, 123–129; love in, 124–125; positive intention in, 127–129; reflection questions, 144

archival culture church, 177

ARDA. *See* Association of Religion Data Archives

Asbury, Francis, 90

asking questions, 135–138

Association of Religion Data Archives (ARDA), 12

attachment: congregations' five attachments, 165–167; to past, 166; to place, 167; to roles, 166; to social life and people, 166–167; to static God, 165

attendance, 72

Augustine, 27

authority: leadership relating to, 65; in transitional ministry, 9

Barna, George, 12

BCEC. *See* Boston Chinese Evangelical Church

behavioral covenants, 183

beliefs, 9–10

215

Yo, Bill, 4

About the Contributors

Norman Bendroth, MDiv, DMin, is the coordinator for clergy and church resources for the New England Pastoral Institute (http://www.nepastoral.org) and is a Professional Transitional Specialist certified by the Interim Ministry Network and serves on its faculty. He has served as a settled pastor in two United Church of Christ congregations and as a senior interim minister in nine other UCC congregations. He has also worked in the nonprofit world for ten years as an executive director, development associate, and director of communications. Dr. Bendroth has additional training in mediation skills for church leaders from the Lombard Mennonite Peace Center, Appreciative Inquiry from the Clergy Leadership Institute, coaching from Coaching4Clergy and the Center for Congregational Health, and consulting and facilitator training from the Center for Congregational Health. Dr. Bendroth has published articles in the *Christian Century*, *Reformed Worship*, *Perspectives*, and *Sojourners.*

Bianca Duemling is the director of intercultural ministries "Together for Berlin," an interdenominational urban ministry organization in Berlin, Germany. Her ministry largely involves applied research, training, consulting, networking, and collaboration. Prior to this position, Bianca was assistant director of intercultural ministries at Emmanuel Gospel Center in Boston, Massachusetts. She is also a founding member of Foundation Himmelsfels, for which she served two years as the project coordinator for an intercultural reconciliation project. She completed her PhD at the University of Heidelberg, studying emerging immigrant churches in Germany and their relationship with mainline churches. Raised in the southern part of Germany, close to the Black Forest, Bianca earned her degree in European Community Education Studies as a licensed social worker in Koblenz and a master of arts in Intercultural Work and Conflict Management in Berlin.

The Rev erend John F. Keydel, Jr., is an Episcopal priest working in his fourth engagement as an intentional interim minister, currently in the Cincinnati area. Prior to his work as an intentional interim, Keydel spent nine years on the staff of the Episcopal Diocese of Michigan, with responsibility for congregational development, clergy and congregational transitions (including oversight of interim processes in congregations), ministry development, and "other duties as may be required from time to time." A lifelong Episcopalian, Keydel worked for approximately fifteen years as a retail banker in Southern Connecticut before being called to ordained ministry in 1991. Keydel is a convicted education addict, and in addition to several master's degrees and a broad range of continuing education, he is ABT (All But Thesis) in both congregational development and organizational transformation.

Michael Piazza currently serves as the director for congregational vitality for the Center for Progressive Renewal. Rev. Piazza served as the senior pastor of the Cathedral of Hope during a time of unprecedented growth. When he arrived in Dallas in 1987, the church had 280 members and a budget of $280,000. When he retired to become dean of the cathedral, the church's membership was more than 3,500, with a consolidated budget of more than three million dollars. This growth took place in a setting that was hostile to the church's constituency and during a time in which the church performed more than 1,500 funerals for persons with HIV/AIDS. Rev. Piazza is an adjunct professor teaching church planting and renewal with the Pacific School of Religion and Chicago Theological Seminary. He coauthored the book *Liberating Hope* with Cameron Trimble in 2011. He is also the author of a number of other books including *Gay by God* and *Prophetic Renewal*. He also serves as the senior pastor of the Virginia Highland Church.

The Reverend Dr . Deborah J. Pope-Lance is a Unitarian Universalist minister, a licensed psychotherapist, and a clinical member of the American Association of Marriage and Family Therapists. She serves nationwide as a consultant with clergy, congregations, and denominations and maintains a psychotherapy practice in Natick, Massachusetts, for individuals and relationships. She has served extensively, over four decades, in parish, transitional, and community ministries. She taught thematic preaching for twenty years at Andover Newton Theological School in Newton, Massachusetts, and on behalf of the Interim Ministry Network, the Alban Institute, and a variety of faith traditions, has provided programming on the ethics of ministerial practice and congregational life and on the unique challenges of after-pastor ministries. Dr. Pope-Lance was a principal contributor to a previous Alban

Institute book, *When a Congregation I s Betrayed: Responding to Clergy Misconduct*. As a strategic coach for after-pastors, she has helped hundreds of clergy do their best work in the traumatic aftermath of a predecessor's misconduct.

Anthony Robinson is an ordained minister of the United Church of Christ who has served four congregations, the most recent of which was Plymouth Congregational/UCC in Seattle (1990–2004). In 2004 he established The Robinson Practice LLC. Today his ministry is as a speaker and teacher, consultant and coach, and author and blogger whose mission is to "Strengthen Congregations and Their Leaders." Tony is the author of twelve books. His most recent book, coauthored with Robert W. Wall, is *Called to Lead: Paul ' s Letters to Timothy for a New Day* (2012). He is also a frequent contributor to magazines and journals, including *The Christian Century*, *Journal for Preachers*, and *Congregations*. He contributes regularly to several online sites, including Faith and Leadership (Duke) and Day One: Key Voices.

David R. Sawyer, PhD, is a writer and consultant with Flourishing Church Consultations, specializing in conflict utilization, leadership development, and organizational transformation. In 2012 he retired as professor of leadership and administration and director of lifelong learning and advanced degrees at Louisville Presbyterian Theological Seminary. His experience in transitional ministry includes serving as an interim pastor in two congregations, advocating for transitional ministers as a judicatory staff member, and teaching in interim ministry educational programs with the Presbyterian Church and the Interim Ministry Network. Besides his chapter in Temporary Shepherds, he is the author of *Hope in Conflict: Discovering Wisdom in Congregational Turmoil* and *Work of the Church: Getting It Done in Boards and Committees*. He lives in Louisville, Kentucky, with his wife, the Rev. Dr. Deborah Fortel, and their wheaten terrier and tuxedo cat. Besides regular visits to their four children and four amazing grandchildren, they enjoy theater, music, baseball, and wilderness hiking.

Gretchen J. Switzer has been an ordained minister in the United Church of Christ for twenty-six years. Over a period of eighteen years, she specialized in intentional interim ministry in churches at risk, following clergy sexual misconduct, dwindling finances, and uncontrolled conflict. In a number of those situations, Gretchen has experienced firsthand the frustration and grief that accompany end-of-life decisions in our beloved congregations. Gretchen has retired from parish ministry and now spends her time writing and tending to her home life, husband, and two teenage children.

Beverly and George Thompson serve as pastors and missional transformation coaches in the Presbytery of Coastal Carolina. Previously, George was professor of leadership and ministry practice at the Interdenominational Theological Center, Atlanta. Beverly was an adjunct professor at ITC and served several congregations in metro Atlanta. They are working on a book about leadership readiness.

Cameron Trimble is the executive director of the Center for Progressive Renewal. She most recently served as an adviser to the congregational vitality and discipleship team of local church ministries for the United Church of Christ and as associate conference minister of church development in the Southeast Conference of the UCC. In her ministry in the national setting, Rev. Trimble was responsible for the development of national strategy for birthing new churches. In her conference setting, she directly oversaw the birthing of churches throughout the Southeast Conference. Each setting has given her a unique perspective on the challenges of cultivating leaders equipped to meet the needs of the future of mainline Protestantism. Rev. Trimble is an adjunct professor teaching church planting and renewal with the Pacific School of Religion and Chicago Theological Seminary. She has coauthored the book *Liberating Hope* with Michael Piazza in 2011.

Rob Voyle is the cofounder of the Appreciative Way and director of the Clergy Leadership Institute. His personal mission in life is to be "helpful, humorous and healing," which is manifested in his teaching and coaching. He created and teaches a certificate in transitional ministry program that is based in the Appreciative Way. Rob is also the author of the books *Restoring Hope: Appreciative Strategies to Resolve Grief and Resentment*, and along with his wife, Kim, *Assessing Skills and Discerning Calls: A Comprehensive Guide for the Clergy Search Process*. Rob's training schedule and books can be found at http://www.clergyleadership.com.